a practical guide to mooting

a practical guide to mooting

jeffrey hill
LLB Barrister
Senior Lecturer in Law
Manchester Metropolitan University

Series editor: Marise Cremona
Professor of European Law
European University Institute
Florence, Italy

This edition first published 2009 by
PALGRAVE MACMILLAN
Houndmills, Basingstoke, Hampshire RG21 6XS and 175 Fifth Avenue, New York, N.Y. 10010
Companies and representatives throughout the world

PALGRAVE MACMILLAN is the global academic imprint of the Palgrave Macmillan division of St. Martin's Press LLC and of Palgrave Macmillan Ltd. Macmillan® is a registered trademark in the United States, United Kingdom and other countries. Palgrave is a registered trademark in the European Union and other countries.

ISBN 13: 9780230220683

This book is printed on paper suitable for recycling and made from fully managed and sustained forest sources.

A catalogue record for this book is available from the British Library.

Printed and bound in Great Britain by CPI Antony Rowe, Chippenham and Eastbourne

Contents

Preface

Mooting is an upwardly mobile subject. Luckily for the modern law student who is keen on improving their advocacy skills, there are now more opportunities to become involved in mooting than ever before. More and more universities, in particular, are including mooting as an optional "subject" on their law degree programmes. Some institutions are even including an element of mooting in their compulsory units on legal skills. There are now more national and international mooting competitions than there were previously, giving students the chance to pit their wits against students of other institutions from all over the world. As well as growing in importance in universities and law schools, mooting also still takes place and flourishes in the four Inns of Court, where it originated centuries ago.

As a result of the above, it could be argued that mooting is regaining its place at the heart of legal education, after years spent in the wilderness as a mere extra-curricular activity. This development bodes well for the future of the legal profession, as more and more law students are now gaining some experience of advocacy at the academic and vocational stages of legal education. Because of this, more students have a realistic idea of where their talents lie and, consequently, the direction in which their careers should go. If a law student decides to pursue a career as an advocate, it should be on the basis of some experience of being on their feet. Being involved in activities such as mooting allows these important choices to be made on a properly informed basis.

The need for guidance on the essential elements of mooting has, therefore, grown. The aim of this book is to provide all students involved in mooting, or thinking about becoming involved, with a readable and comprehensive guide to what mooting is all about, and to enable them to avoid the many pitfalls that can assail the mooter. Much of the book is aimed at moots taking place in the setting of the English appellate courts, but it is hoped that the book will be of equal use to those mooting at law schools and in competitions outside England and Wales. Many of the skills involved in mooting are not specific to a particular country. As a result, it is hoped that this book will be of value to mooters wherever they may be, and whether they are at the academic or the vocational stage of legal education.

Notwithstanding the above, chapter 12 of the book is dedicated specifically to those who are involved in, or are thinking of becoming involved in, international mooting competitions.

A note on the sample moot problem: *R v Owen Owens*

This criminal law moot problem is referred to throughout this book to provide specific guidance and examples, to illustrate some of the points being made. This moot is also used as the basis for the electronic resource which accompanies this book and which you can watch by going to www.palgrave.com/law/hill. Chapter 8 is dedicated to analysing the moot footage which you can watch on the web, and to providing practical examples and commentary on matters discussed in a more abstract way earlier in the book.

The structure of the book

The book is divided into **three** parts.

Part one consists of two chapters, covering first the basic issues of what mooting actually is, and then the background knowledge of the legal system that is required if you are going to moot successfully.

Part two of the book consists of six chapters, and looks at the main points that judges are looking for when they score a moot. As a result, the main areas where you will pick up marks or impress the judges are dealt with. There are, therefore, chapters dedicated to style and presentation of argument, structure and content of argument, responding to your opponents, dealing with the judges, and use of legal authorities. The final chapter in this part of the book is dedicated to an analysis of the recorded moot that you can access by visiting www.palgrave.com/law/hill.

Finally, **part three** looks at a number of miscellaneous issues. It includes chapters on dealing with feedback, skeleton arguments, mooting opportunities in England and Wales, international moots and further reading.

The appendices, at the end of the book, include more examples of moot problems, as well as a sample mooting feedback sheet, with sample weightings of assessment criteria, to help give you further insight into how your mooting will be judged or assessed.

Dedication

This book is dedicated to my partner, Nino Loladze. Without her love and encouragement, it would never have been written.

Much of the book was written at the excellent Heaton Chapel Reform Club.

Acknowledgments

The original version of *R v Owen Owens* was written by Peter Rayburn, formerly of Manchester Metropolitan University. Amendments to *R v Owen Owens* were made by Richard Lee, Senior Lecturer in Law at Manchester Metropolitan University. I thank them for allowing me to use this moot problem.

I would like to thank the English-Speaking Union for allowing me to reproduce some of the materials from the Essex Court National Mooting Competition in the appendices to this book. Thanks also go to Vandana Rajwani of Hong Kong University for her help, particularly in respect of aspects of international mooting.

My thanks also go to Rebecca Fairclough and Mark Cooper for their help in filming the accompanying performances of *R v Owen Owens* and to Jasmin Naim and Rob Gibson of Palgrave Macmillan.

Table of statutes

Table of cases

Part 1

Introductory issues

Chapter 1

An introduction to mooting

1.1 Structure of chapter 1

This chapter will essentially deal with **three** main issues.

First, the bulk of this chapter will consider what mooting actually is and what is involved for the participants in a moot. This will include a sample moot problem, the criminal case of *R v Owen Owens*, and some explanation of what it contains. This will enable you to get started on mooting in a practical way in the context of a real moot. **The pages dedicated to this moot problem are edged with grey for ease of reference.**

Secondly, there will be a brief look at the history and origins of mooting.

Finally, the chapter will deal with how mooting is useful and relevant to law students and practitioners today.

1.2 What does mooting involve?

In very simple terms, a moot is a simulation or mock version of a hypothetical case in one of the appellate courts. In England and Wales, this would therefore mean either the High Court (sitting in its appellate capacity), the Court of Appeal (Civil and Criminal Divisions), or the House of Lords. Even though a moot is a fictitious case, without real parties and without (in most cases) fully qualified lawyers, it can still be a fairly realistic reflection of what goes on in the appellate courts if it is done well.

A moot is different from a mock trial in that, as with real life appeals in the appellate courts, the hearing is not normally a complete rehearing of the case, with all the evidence and witnesses being heard. Mooting does not involve the cross-examination of witnesses and arguing about the facts. Instead, the hearing in a moot usually consists of the following.

1.2.1 Legal submissions on behalf of the appellant

This is the party appealing against the decision(s) of a lower court, and therefore submitting that the appeal should be allowed.

1.2.2   Legal submissions on behalf of the respondent

This is the party who will be arguing that the decision(s) of the lower court should be upheld, and that the appeal should therefore be dismissed.

1.2.3   A reply by counsel for the appellant

Because counsel for the appellant will not have heard the submissions from the respondent until after they have spoken, some extra time is normally allowed for them to respond to the submissions made.

Note that the appellant is the party who is bringing the case and who is asserting that the decision(s) of the lower court should be reversed. The respondent is the other party in the case who is, presumably, happy to let the decision(s) of the lower court stand. The respondent will, as the name suggests, respond to or contest the submissions made by the appellant and argue that, on the contrary, the appeal should be dismissed.

At the end of the submissions, the judge(s) will then announce the winner of the moot. This will not necessarily be the side with the winning legal argument, but will be the side that has demonstrated the best mooting and advocacy skills. Winning the case is not, therefore, the same thing as winning the moot.

The law may often, unless the moot is brilliantly written, favour one side more than the other. For example, the appellant may have a stronger case than the respondent, but this does not mean that the appellant is bound to win the moot. On the contrary, counsel for the respondent may demonstrate far greater mooting and advocacy skills than counsel for the appellant. As a result, counsel for the appellant will receive lower marks from the judges, and counsel for the respondent will win the moot. Thus, even a mooter who has a very difficult argument in legal terms can still emerge victorious in a moot. The judges will generally be aware that one side may have an easier argument than the other and will normally take this into account when judging or assessing the moot. As well as mastering the relevant law, much of the skill in mooting is to adopt a style that is persuasive and appropriate to a court setting. For some, this comes naturally; for others, this requires much thought and practice.

1.3 Mooting, mock trials and debating compared and distinguished

Whilst there is a degree of overlap between these three activities, there are also some very important differences.

As has been stated above, a moot is not the same thing as a mock trial. The moot hearing is never a trial of the factual issues in a case, as one would see in a court of first instance. Mooting never involves the calling of witnesses and their subsequent examination in chief and cross-examination. It does not involve making speeches to juries on which version of the facts to accept. As a result, the style expected in moots is a rather less impassioned style than might be expected from an advocate in a trial or mock trial. In the English and Welsh context, you are trying to simulate the type of advocacy that you would see in the Court of Appeal or the House of Lords. There is more on this in chapter **3**, but you should visit a range of courts in order to get a flavour of the differences between trial and appellate advocacy.

Nevertheless, there are some similarities between mock trials and moots. The most obvious is that both involve simulating a real-life case in a court of law. The mock trial simulates the trial at a first instance court, and the moot simulates a hearing in one of the appeal courts, as stated above; and both involve the participants demonstrating the important skill of adopting the mannerisms and speech that are appropriate to appearing in court as a lawyer.

The reality is that the legal practitioner may have a mixture of cases, both trials and appeals. It is therefore recommended that, time permitting, students attempt to involve themselves in both activities. Finally, both mooting and mock trials will involve students demonstrating some ability to understand and argue the law. A general understanding will rarely be enough with either of these activities, particularly in mooting. Instead, it is necessary to engage with the law in a more detailed way than most law students do in preparation for tutorials etc.

Perhaps more obviously, a moot is different from a debate, in that a debate can be on any issue, not necessarily a legal one. Like mooting, debating involves public speaking in the form of speech making and responding to points made by the other side. Unlike mooting, debating does not involve a highly stylised form of speech. As will be discussed later, mooters do have some freedom in terms of their own personal style. However, debaters undoubtedly have more freedom than mooters in terms of adopting a style which suits their own personality and way of speaking. The obvious reason for this is that the debater is not confined by the conventions and traditions of courtroom speaking.

1.4   The moot problem

When you first take part in a moot, the organiser (either the organiser of the competition or, if you are doing mooting as part of a course of study, a lecturer) will give you the moot problem, along with other guidance.

This will usually consist of:
1) The **facts of the case**, including which court(s) the case has already been heard in.
2) The **decision(s) of the lower court** on those facts.
3) The **legal reasons** for the decision(s) of the lower court.
4) The **legal authorities** relied on by the judge(s).
5) Details of **the court** in which the appeal (and therefore the moot) will be heard.
6) What **your role** in the moot will be (moots normally have four participants, excluding the judge(s)).
7) What the **grounds of the appeal** are. The moot problem should normally make clear which grounds of appeal should be dealt with by each of the participants.

For example, in a criminal case, such as *R v Owen Owens*, the original trial could have been heard by a Crown Court judge sitting with a jury. The appeal for such a case (and therefore the moot) would normally be heard in the Court of Appeal (Criminal Division). You might be given the role of senior counsel for the appellant. In the case of appeals to the Court of Appeal (Criminal Division), the appellant is, more often than not, the original defendant from the trial. If you are senior counsel for the appellant in the above example, it would therefore be your role to argue/submit that the trial judge at the crown court had made a mistake in terms of point 2, 3 or 4 listed above. An example in the criminal law context above might be that the judge misdirected the jury on the law in his or her summing up, and that the conviction is therefore unsafe. Counsel for the respondents would be representing the Crown, and therefore submitting that the appeal should be dismissed and that the conviction is safe.

Points 1 to 7 listed above will now be considered in more detail.

1) The general rule is that you are stuck with the facts of the moot problem that you are given. The skill of mooting is not disputing the basic facts. It is not a good argument to say that the facts are wrong, or to dispute facts that appear to be concrete in the moot problem. If there is some evidence that is unclear, or if a dispute on some facts is specifically disclosed by the moot problem, then it is fine to raise these issues in your submissions. If not, please do not waste your own time, or that of the judges, by getting involved in this sort of dispute.

An important difference between a moot case and a real case is that, in the latter, the advocate is attempting to win the case, or get the best result possible for the client. In a moot, the motives of the advocate are completely selfish. The mooter's aim is to win the moot and get through to the next round, in the context of a mooting competition, or to get a high mark in the context of an assessed moot which is part of a student's course of study. The problem is fictitious and the client does not exist, so the mooter has no reason to care about the actual outcome and whether the appeal would be allowed or dismissed. Being declared the winner in the moot, or getting a good mark, is everything. It is of little consolation to the client in a real case to be told, after he or she has been sent to prison or ordered to pay damages, that their lawyer would have won the moot.

2) This information will tell you how the decision of the judge(s) in the lower court affects the parties to the moot, that is the appellant and the respondent. The appellant is, it follows, going to be the party who was, for some reason, unhappy with the decision of the lower court, and is therefore appealing to have that decision reversed. The respondent, on the other hand, will be keen for the status quo to be maintained.

3) The key to mooting is the ability to use the law to argue either that the lower court got things wrong (counsel for the appellant), or that the lower court got it right (counsel for the respondents). As stated above, the moot problem will not simply tell you the decision of the lower court, but it will also give you the legal basis for the decision, and the authorities upon which the decision was based.

Mooting is not about saying what one believes or thinks; it is about making submissions based on legal argument. As a mooter, once you know why the judges(s) at the lower court arrived at their decision, you immediately have the basis of your case. If you are counsel for the appellant, your job will be to use the law (primarily cases, statutes and delegated legislation, in England and Wales) to submit that the decisions or pronouncements of the lower court were wrong in law. The respondent's job is to use the law to submit that the lower court was correct in its application of the law to the facts. Whichever side you are representing in the moot, one of your first tasks will be to look carefully at the legal reasons for the decision of the lower court, as provided by the moot problem.

4)   The authorities relied on by the judge are vital to the mooter. Counsel for the appellant will want to read the authorities referred to, in order to ascertain whether the judge(s) of the lower court made a mistake in applying them in the way they did. For example, counsel for the appellant may try to argue that cases which seemed to be treated as binding by the judge in the lower court can actually be distinguished from the present case. As a result of such submissions, they will ask that the appeal be allowed. Counsel for the respondent will be looking at the same authorities to find the passages on which the judge(s) may have relied, in order to argue that the appeal should be dismissed. It is in using these authorities, and any others that are relevant, that the mooter will build the arguments that suit the case being made.

Indeed, it should be stressed that mooters are not confined to referring to the cases and other authorities mentioned by the judge(s) of the lower court. On the contrary, the basis of a mooter's submissions may be that the judge(s) did not refer to the authorities that they should have. From the above, it hopefully goes without saying that mooting involves a great amount of engagement with primary sources of law, such as case law. A superficial engagement with a source, such as a case or a treaty, will usually not be enough. The mooter will normally be required to read the full judgment or text, and to be able to refer to passages therefrom in order to support his or her submissions.

5)   Your knowledge of the court hierarchy and the doctrine of judicial precedent will tell you that point 5 above is important, because the level of court in which you are mooting will determine what arguments can be employed.

For example, if you are mooting in the Court of Appeal, as in the example above, you will be bound by any relevant House of Lords' decisions and, possibly, by decisions of the Court of Appeal in previous cases. If your moot is in the House of Lords, then you have more freedom, as the House of Lords is, of course, free to depart from its own previous decisions since the Practice Statement [1966] 3 All ER 77.

Some law students, quite wrongly, seem to regard these basic principles as somewhat beneath their radar. The reason for this is that these issues are normally studied at the very beginning of most law courses. By the time that most students start mooting, they will already be immersed in the detail of substantive legal subjects, such as contract and tort. As a result, these vital principles can sometimes be forgotten, or relegated in the mind of the law student, to a lower level of importance than should be the case. This applies especially to less meticulous students, who rely solely on secondary sources of law, such as the recommended texts for their course of study. For more on knowledge of aspects of the legal system, and their relevance to the mooter, see chapter **2**.

6)   Clearly this is vital as, without this information, the mooter would have no basis for his or her preparations and submissions. This will also tell you who your opponent is and who, if applicable, are your teammates.

7)   As with the facts, as stated above, you are pretty much stuck with the grounds of appeal. If you are counsel for the appellant, these will tell you the legal basis on which you should argue that the decision(s) of the lower court were wrong. If you are counsel for the respondent, these are the grounds that you will be opposing in your submissions.

The golden rule here is not to argue outside the grounds of appeal. The reason why you should not do this is simple: in a real-life case, a party wishing to appeal against a decision of a lower court, whether in a criminal or civil case, is required to state precisely the grounds on which they are seeking to challenge the decision. This is so that the other side has notice of the arguments they will face, and can prepare accordingly. If the appellants were to draft their grounds of appeal, and then decide to change them at the hearing, this would mean that the respondents would probably not be in a position to continue, as they would be unprepared. If the respondents tried to argue outside the grounds of appeal, the appellant would have the simple retort that the arguments are irrelevant, because they do not address the reasons why the decision of the lower court is being challenged.

The same is the case in a moot. Both sides must stick to the grounds of appeal, as laid down in the moot problem; otherwise, the moot simply will not work.

There may, however, be some room for disagreement as to what matters fall within the grounds of appeal. Wherever language is involved, there is always room for argument about interpretation of that language. As a result, if you are raising a matter that may be of borderline relevance, you must ensure that you can justify its inclusion in your submissions. If a judge deems a matter to be irrelevant to the grounds before the court, he or she will probably not wish to hear submissions on it.

1.5 A sample moot problem

The sample moot problem below is to help you to identify points 1 to 7 in the previous section, and to get you started with preparing a moot. You will see that points 1 to 7 are covered again after the problem, so that they can be understood in the context of this specific moot problem.

This moot problem is referred to throughout the following chapters of the book to illustrate a number of the points made. It is also the basis for the recorded moot, which can be accessed by visiting www.palgrave.com/law/hill, and the accompanying analysis in chapter **8**.

IN THE COURT OF APPEAL (Criminal Division)
R v Owen Owens

In January 2008, Megan Morgan, aged 18 and unmarried, gives birth to conjoined twins, Glen and Glenys, in a small hospital in a remote country district in Mid-Wales. The twins are joined at the waist but are otherwise perfectly formed, although Glen, the weaker of the two, has substantial and serious breathing difficulties and is diagnosed as requiring major heart surgery in the near future if he is to have any long-term hope of survival.

A week after the birth, Dr Owens, the senior consultant at the hospital, who has the reputation of being a brilliant but unorthodox surgeon, informs his junior colleagues that he intends to operate in order to separate the twins. His colleagues are uncertain whether the hospital has adequate facilities for such an operation, either in the form of equipment or surgical and nursing staff with the necessary expertise, and that, irrespective of where it takes place, the operation should be delayed until the twins have grown stronger, particularly Glen who would have little chance of surviving such an operation at this time.

However, Dr Owens insists on performing the operation, asserting that, if Glen were to die before the twins are separated, Glenys would die also, and that a successful operation of this

---

nature would be of enormous benefit financially to the hospital and to the medical careers of all concerned. Megan refuses to give her consent to the operation and applies for a court order restraining the hospital from carrying it out, but before any judicial hearing can be arranged the operation is performed by Dr Owens with the unwilling assistance of his colleagues. Glenys survives the operation, but Glen dies as a result. Dr Owens is subsequently charged with murder in respect of Glen's death.

At the trial at Llareggyb Crown Court before Evans HHJ, expert medical evidence is given for the prosecution to the effect that it was extremely inadvisable to undertake such an operation in such circumstances so soon after the birth of the twins. On the other hand, the defence was able to call evidence that there was an immediate danger to both their lives at the time, as Glen was so ill and could have died at any time. It was accepted by both experts that, had Glen died at any time before the separation, that would have been fatal to Glenys.

Dr Owens pleads that he had no intention to cause any physical harm to Glen, but he believed that it was necessary for the operation to be performed so soon after the birth because there was a serious risk that both the twins would die if they were not separated.

Evans HHJ held that:

1. Following *R v MOLONEY* (1985), HL, the jury must convict of murder if they conclude that Dr Owens intended the operation to result in Glen's death or to cause him really serious physical harm.

2. Alternatively, following *R v HANCOCK & SHANKLAND* (1986), HL, and *R v WOOLLIN* (1998), HL, if the jury conclude that it was a highly probable consequence that Glen would die or suffer really serious harm as a result of the operation, and that Dr Owens must have been aware that there was such a risk, they may infer that he must have intended that the operation would have such an outcome and convict him of murder on that basis.

3. Following *R v DUDLEY & STEPHENS* (1884), DC, and *R v HOWE* (1987), HL, the defence of necessity is not available on a charge of murder, nor is the common law plea of self-defence or private defence admissible in the absence of any

present immediate threat to the life of either the accused himself or any third party at the time of the act which results in death.

Dr Owens appeals to the Court of Appeal, asserting that:

1.   Evans HHJ was incorrect in his direction as to the basis of liability for murder where there is no evidence of any intention to cause death or really serious bodily harm.

2.   Even assuming the existence of a legally acceptable basis of liability for murder, Evans HHJ misdirected the jury as to the non-availability of a defence of necessity since, in the light of *RE A (CHILDREN)* (2001), CA, the situation in *R v DUDLEY & STEPHENS* is distinguishable from the circumstances of the present case.

3.   There was equally a misdirection as to the inadmissibility of a plea of self- or private defence.

Leading counsel for each side should argue point 1 of the appeal; junior counsel should argue points 2 and 3.

1.5.1   Guidance on R v Owen Owens

From the case of *R v Owen Owens*, you will hopefully be able to spot the things mentioned in points 1 to 7 above. Here, however, is some basic guidance on how those points apply to this specific moot problem:

1)   The **facts of the case** are provided in a reasonable amount of detail. As was stated earlier, you are pretty much stuck with the facts of the moot. However, you may have spotted that, on these facts, there is some room for argument on the medical evidence, which is contradictory.

2)   The **decision** of the lower court, in this case Llareggyb Crown Court, was to convict Dr Owens of murder. Evans HHJ was the judge who will have directed the jury on the relevant law.

3)   As this is a decision of the Crown Court, we do not know the jury's precise **legal reason(s)** for convicting Dr Owens. However, we do know the pronouncements that Evans HHJ made on the law, presumably in his summing up to the jury, and at other points during the trial.

The basis of an appeal in this type of case will normally be the appellant alleging that the jury made their decision with the wrong law ringing in their ears. Because the wrong law was given to them it would, no doubt, be argued by an appellant that the jury were unable to direct their minds to the correct legal issues. As a result of this, they reached the wrong verdict. Alternatively, it might have been that the judge made rulings on the applicable law in the absence of the jury, which the appellant now wishes to contest in the Court of Appeal. Evans HHJ gives his legal reasoning in points 1 to 3 of the part of the moot problem that starts with the words "Evans HHJ held that". Here, the judge gives his views on the applicability of the law on intention in murder, and the defences of private defence and necessity, to the facts of the case. The appellant will presumably be submitting that this application of the law was incorrect.

Note that, as the case is now an appeal, Dr Owens transforms from being the defendant at the original trial to the appellant. The party contesting the decision of the lower court is always the appellant, and the party defending it is always the respondent.

4)   As well as providing his views on the application of the law to the facts, Evans HHJ also provides **legal authorities,** in the form of cases, to support the pronouncements that he makes. It goes without saying that a mooter would wish to read the judgments in these cases to ascertain whether they really do say what Evans HHJ thinks they do. The basis of mooting is not simply to ramble on about your opinions, but to back up the submissions you make with relevant law. The cases used by the judge(s) are the obvious starting point for building your case.

5)   In criminal law terms, this is a straightforward appeal, against conviction from a decision of the Crown Court, to the Court of Appeal (Criminal Division). As noted previously, knowledge of the **court** hierarchy will be relevant to you to help you decide which precedents are binding on the Court of Appeal (Criminal Division) and, therefore, the moot court.

6)   The moot problem concludes by dealing with the **roles of the participants** in the moot, stating which grounds leading and junior counsel should deal with. You will be allocated a role by the organiser of your moot. You must stick to these roles and the grounds of appeal that go with them, and you must not divide things up in your own way with your partner.

7)   The precise **grounds of appeal,** which the mooters should stick to, are set out in the part of the problem that starts with the words "Dr Owens appeals to the Court of Appeal asserting that". These grounds of appeal relate clearly to the pronouncements made

by Evans HHJ at the trial, as mentioned at point 3 above. Whilst the grounds of appeal are based on the judge's legal rulings at the trial, they should not be confused with them.

1.6   Before the moot takes place

There are two things that, depending on the rules of the competition or institution, may be required of you before the actual moot hearing.

1.6.1   Exchange of authorities

A) What is exchange of authorities?

Exchange of authorities is the requirement that all participants in the moot send a list of all the authorities they intend to use in the moot to both their opponents and the judges. Some competitions and institutions do not require this, but many do. The organisers of your moot will inform you as to whether this is a requirement that you have to comply with.

B) What is the reason for exchange of authorities?

A general principle that is often followed in the real courts is that, if a party is intending to use legal arguments and authorities, they must notify the other side and the judges of them in advance. The idea behind this is that none of the above will be unduly surprised at points raised and that, as a result, cases will not have to be adjourned to give the parties, or the judges, time to prepare. Exchange of authorities in moots imitates this, and provides mooters with a valuable insight into what the other side might say. Clearly, exchange of authorities is something you will be avidly waiting for if you are involved in a moot where it is a requirement. For more on using exchange of authorities as a valuable source for your preparation, see chapter 5.

C) Limits on numbers of authorities

The rules of the institution you are mooting with may have restrictions on how many authorities you can use in a moot. You should check this with the organisers if they have not told you. Numbers may well differ between institutions, but it is common for mooting rules to allow about 10 authorities per mooter. This number should normally be more than enough, bearing in mind the fact that most moots will normally put a time limit on your submissions. If you propose to refer to an authority, such as a case, more than once during your submissions, it will only count once on your list of authorities. The same applies with statutes, where you intend to refer to more than one section. If the institution where you are mooting has a stricter approach in this respect, you should be informed of this by the organisers.

D) Do not use authorities that are not on your list

It hopefully goes without saying that you should only refer in your submissions to authorities that are on the list that you have exchanged with the other side and given to the judge. If you attempt to use other sources, you will not only be acting unethically as a mooter, but you will also leave yourself open to reprimand from the judges and comments from your opponents when they are responding to you. The authorities you wish to rely on are there in black and white for all to see. The judges will not be amused if you try to shift the goal posts by referring to hitherto unmentioned authorities during the moot. Even if you are only using an authority very briefly, and only to make what you think is an uncontroversial point, you must include it on your list of authorities.

E) When does exchange take place?

This will vary depending on the rules of the institution you are mooting with, but it is usual for exchange to take place long enough before the moot to allow you to do some extra research on the authorities mentioned on your opponents' list. Obviously, there is little point in being given a long list of authorities as you are going through the door of the courtroom, as you will have little chance to consider them.

F) Deciding not to use an authority that is on your list

It may be the case that, in the latter stages of your preparation, you will decide not to use an authority that you have already included on your list. If so, whilst you are not bound to use such authorities in your submissions, you should still exercise a degree of good manners in the way that you deal with the issue. If you do not, you risk creating a poor impression, not just with your opponent but with the judges as well.

The first thing that you can do in this situation is to let your opponent know, as soon as possible, which authorities you will no longer be referring to. A quiet word just before the moot hearing will probably suffice, although it is arguable that, with communication methods such as email, you should probably make contact with your opponent as soon as you decide not to use an authority.

Secondly, you should also make it clear to the judges that there are authorities on your list that you will now not be using. A simple announcement to the judges along the following lines will normally be appropriate:

> "I would be grateful if your Lordships would briefly refer to my submitted list of authorities. There are two cases on that list upon which I no longer intend to rely. They are the Crown and Smith and the Crown and Roberts. I have already informed my learned friend of this, my Lords, and apologised for any inconvenience caused."

Note that, if you do make an announcement of this sort, you should be prepared for the fact that the judges may ask for further explanation as to why you are no longer using the authority.

G) Listing cases that you do not intend to refer to

It has been known for mooters to include some authorities in their list when they have no intention of referring to them in the actual moot. As a result, their opponents waste much time researching issues that are not part of their case. Needless to say, this is not an ethical way to go about mooting. The legal profession only operates effectively on the basis of the integrity of its members. If you intend to join the legal profession, you must develop a good sense of what is ethical.

Additionally, most judges will take a very dim view if they suspect that such sharp practices are being employed. Some judges may also deduct marks if you do not refer to authorities you have listed, without adequate explanation. The basic rule is, therefore, that you should only include authorities in your list if you really do intend to refer to them.

1.6.2   Submission of skeleton arguments

There are some moots that require all participants to submit a skeleton argument at some point before the actual moot hearing takes place. The idea behind this is that the judges will know in advance what the nature of the submissions for both sides will be, as well as what authorities they will rely on to back up those submissions. For more on skeleton arguments and how to go about writing them, see chapter 12.

1.7   The format of a moot

> Most moots have four participants, who could make their submissions in the following order:
>
> 1) Senior counsel for the appellant
> 2) Junior counsel for the appellant
> 3) Senior counsel for the respondent
> 4) Junior counsel for the respondent.

After the main submissions from the four participants, counsel for the appellants are normally given a brief **right to reply** to the submissions raised by the respondents. The reason for this is that one of the skills of mooting, and advocacy generally, is the ability to respond to submissions made by the other side. When the appellants make their submissions (if done in the order above), they will not have heard the respondents' submissions. As a result, they are given a brief amount of time to do this at the end of the moot. Counsel for the respondent are expected to deal with points raised by the appellants in the course of their submissions as, by the time they speak, they will already have heard the appellants' submissions.

Note: some institutions or competitions may deviate from the running order of speakers suggested above.

> An alternative running order may be as follows:
>
> 1) Senior counsel for the appellant
> 2) Senior counsel for the respondent
> 3) Junior counsel for the appellant
> 4) Junior counsel for the respondent.

In the above running order, the **rights of reply** for both counsel for the appellants could either be at the end of the moot, or after each of the respondents' submissions.

The running order of speakers is usually given to you in advance but, if in doubt about this, double check with the organisers of the moot you are involved in.

Also, whilst most moots will have four participants, as in the example above, this does not have to be the case. A moot could consist of **any even number**, so that every participant will have an opponent, who will be dealing with the same ground(s) of appeal. As a result, each participant will have some submissions to respond to. As will be discussed in chapter 5, the ability to respond well to your opponent is an important skill that the judges will be looking for you to demonstrate evidence of.

After submissions have been made by the participants, the judge(s) will decide what marks to give each participant, if the moot is a formally assessed part of a course of study. If the moot is part of a mooting competition, the judge(s) will decide which team or which advocate is the winner of the moot, and therefore will progress in the competition.

The judge(s) may also give a **judgment on the legal aspects of the case**, which will consist of their legal reasons for either allowing or dismissing the appeal. Sometimes, particularly if a moot is part of a formal assessment process, the judge(s) may refrain from giving a judgment on the legal issues. This is because other students, who have yet to be assessed on the same moot problem, may find out about the judge's reasons for either allowing or dismissing the appeal. These students would then clearly have an unfair advantage. In assessed moots, the most important issue for the participants is the marks that they receive. This differs from competition moots, where the main concern will be progression to the next round.

1.8   The timing of mooting submissions

It is normal practice for moot organisers to put a time limit on submissions. There are two reasons for this. The most obvious is to prevent counsel from rambling on for too long, and the moot thereby becoming a marathon. Perhaps another reason is that having a time limit imposes a certain discipline on mooters, in that it forces them to complete the main submissions they wish to make within the allotted time. This requires some skill and planning ability.

Having a time limit also obliges the mooter to distinguish between the relevant and the irrelevant, and to prioritise the points they wish to make in the order of their importance to the case being put.

The time limits for moots will vary according to institutions and competition organisers, so you must check the rules of the moots you are participating in on this. In most cases, however, the time limit for submissions will be somewhere between 10 and 20 minutes. The extra time given to appellants for their right of reply will normally be around five minutes.

It is highly desirable that you use as much of this time as possible. If the time limit is, for example, 15 minutes, and you only speak for six minutes, the likelihood is that this will make a poor impression on the judges. It will probably mean that you are poorly prepared and short of material. Good preparation should ensure that you fill the allotted time with useful submissions that are relevant to the ground(s) of appeal.

Whilst it is difficult to be precise, it is advised that you should aim to conclude your submissions close to, but still within, the time limit. If you run over your allotted time, and the judge has to stop you in your tracks, this is not a very impressive way for your case to end. It is much better if you can conclude strongly and on your own terms. For more on concluding your submissions, see chapter **3**.

Usually, one of the judges, or the clerk of the court if there is one, will be responsible for time keeping. They will normally have a **stop-watch** of some sort for this purpose, and may stop the clock at the times when the judges are asking questions and the mooters are answering them. You should check with the organisers of your moot whether the clock will be stopped for this reason.

The person in charge of time keeping may also hold up **reminder cards**, telling the advocates how long they have left, for example "Five minutes remaining". Be prepared for this, as some mooters can be distracted by these cards. Others, such as those who are reading their submissions with their head down, do not even notice these reminders. This generally creates a bad impression on the judges, for reasons already mentioned above.

1.9 The chronology of a moot

The following diagram gives you the chronology of a whole moot from beginning to end. As discussed in chapter **10**, parts of this chronology may vary between institutions.

A) Receive moot problem
See section **1.4** above for more on what this includes.

B) Preparation for the moot

C) Exchange of authorities
If required, according to the rules of the institution where you are mooting. See section **1.6** above for more on this.

D) Submit skeleton argument

If required, according to the rules of the institution where you are mooting. See chapter **12**.

E) Final preparation after exchange of lists of authorities

F) The moot hearing

Submissions and replies to submissions given by the participants. See sections **1.7** and **1.8** above. For more on what specifically the judges will be looking for in your submissions, see chapters **3** to **8**.

G) Announcement of who has won the moot, possibly including the legal reasons for why the appeal has been allowed or dismissed

If the moot is an assessed part of a course of study, the judges may refrain from this until all assessments are complete.

H) Provision of feedback

If the moot is part of a competition, the feedback will probably be oral. If the moot is assessed, feedback can be verbal, written or in the form of a recording of the moot. For more on the importance of feedback, see chapter **9**.

1.10 The origins of mooting

A detailed history of mooting as an aspect of legal education and training is beyond the scope of this book. However, it will certainly do no harm to the prospective mooter to know a little bit about the long tradition of mooting in English legal education.

In the English and Welsh legal education context, mooting originates in the four Inns of Court (the institutions that still enjoy a monopoly over calling law students to the bar). Moots still take place in all four inns, namely Lincoln's Inn, Gray's Inn, Middle Temple and Inner Temple, on a purely voluntary basis. In the past, however, mooting played a much more pivotal role in legal education.

The Inns of Court are ancient institutions, thought by most legal historians to date back at least more than 600 years. In the past, the inns bore something of a resemblance to a kind of legal finishing school, where student barristers would live, eat and study. The aim of all this was, of course, call to the bar. It was only in the twentieth century that the path to becoming a barrister became highly formalised, culminating in the current Bar Vocational Course. Prior to the more formal approach to vocational legal education that students experience today, call to the bar, by one of the four Inns of Court, was arguably, on a more ad hoc basis.

The principal forms of legal education on offer by the inns were readings, which were similar to the modern-day lecture, and participation in moots. The format of the moots was somewhat different to moots done by students today, in that mooters would also be tested on their knowledge of the many different forms of writs and summonses which were used to begin different types of case. Moots would take place before the "benchers" or senior members of the inn and, on the basis of a student's performance in these moots, the student may eventually be called to the bar. He or she would then be eligible to join a set of barristers' chambers as a pupil.

Today, mooting is not required as a compulsory element of training for either barristers or solicitors, although advocacy assessments do have to be undertaken on the Bar Vocational Course and the Legal Practice Course. Nevertheless, mooting obviously provides excellent background and practice for those intending to practise as either a barrister or a solicitor.

For students interested in the history of the Inns of Court and the history of mooting, there is a wealth of material available. For more information on this, see chapter **13**.

1.11 The benefits of mooting

In spite of what some students think, involvement in mooting is not compulsory for those wishing to practise as lawyers. Some students wrongly believe that mooting is a formal requirement for those wishing to embark on the vocational stage of training. It is quite possible to do no mooting, gain a place on either the Bar Vocational Course or the Legal Practice Course, and be a successful practitioner thereafter. However, whilst it is certainly not the end of the world to do no mooting as a law student, there are many good reasons for engaging with mooting during your student years, or when you are a junior practitioner.

Some of the main reasons why the modern law student should give serious thought to mooting are considered below.

1.11.1　Useful practice

The most obvious reason is that, for those intending a career in the law, mooting provides an excellent way of practising one's advocacy, and familiarising oneself with the mannerisms and etiquette of the courtroom. Some take to this highly stylised form of speech like ducks to water, whilst others find it incredibly difficult to adopt an appropriate style and to actually sound like a lawyer. For such students, mooting is a chance to make mistakes at an early stage, where the consequences of a mistake are not nearly as grave as they would be in practice.

When I read for the bar, I was astonished in my first term at the poor standard of some students' public speaking skills, and the fact that many of them had never been on their feet before. This is why mooting is such a good idea at the academic stage of legal education, and why more and more law students are becoming involved in it. Any student who is really serious about a career as an advocate should ideally have had some public speaking experience before embarking on either of the legal vocational courses. The reasoning behind this is obvious. Some experience of advocacy or public speaking will give you a good indication of whether advocacy really is for you, in the sense that it will indicate (a) whether you have much ability as an advocate, and (b) whether you derive, or could derive, any pleasure from the activity. If a student feels that he or she has little ability as a speaker, and does not enjoy advocacy, then it may be better to consider practising in an area where advocacy is not commonly resorted to, or possibly a career outside the law.

It is important, however, despite the above, not to draw negative conclusions about mooting and advocacy too early. Many students find their feet only after a few attempts at mooting, and only after some humbling experiences. Mooting is a new and difficult skill to most students, and requires perseverance and hard work. Be realistic about yourself, but do not give up too easily. For most students who are prepared to put in the hard work, the rewards are usually there to be had.

1.11.2　Confidence

Mooting can sometimes be a humbling experience, but it can also be a great confidence builder, for those who work hard and do well. The confidence gained from participation in activities like mooting, mock trials and debating, it goes without saying, can be highly beneficial to those beginning a legal career. Even for those students who do not go on to a legal career, the benefits of these activities can still be considerable.

The Bar Vocational Course and the Legal Practice Course both require a degree of confidence. The same obviously applies, to an even greater extent, when you go into practice. If you are experienced at being on your feet and speaking in public, you are much more likely to thrive in these environments.

1.11.3   Pleasure

For many law students, the reason for wanting to be a lawyer in the first place is the desire to be an advocate. Prior to being involved in mooting, the closest that most students will get to lawyer-like activities is the writing of essays and answers to problem questions. Whilst there is certainly a lot to be said for these activities, they can seem somewhat remote from the business of practice as a lawyer.

Mooting is, therefore, the first opportunity for many law students to do something which really feels similar to the practice of law. It goes without saying that, for those students who engage with mooting properly, and who put in the necessary hard work, it can be a highly pleasurable and rewarding experience. Perhaps for the first time, students experience the pleasure of using legal sources to construct an argument from the point of view of one side in a case. Because of this, mooters have to approach the law in the same creative way that lawyers do, in that they have to make the best of the available legal authorities to suit the argument of their fictitious client.

Additionally, the mooter experiences the tension of being an advocate and presenting an argument in a court environment, along with the difficulties and pleasures associated with responding to their opponents' submissions and answering judicial questions. In short, students learn to take pride in their advocacy and legal skills. As a result, irrespective of how successful they are, most students enjoy mooting, at least to some extent. For those who really master the art of advocacy, mooting can be the beginning of something that will be with them for the rest of their lives.

1.11.4   Career enhancement

As noted above, mooting is in no sense a compulsory pre-requisite to a successful legal career. However, there is little doubt that engagement with activities like mooting is the sort of thing that law firms and barristers' chambers are looking for when they look at applications for training contracts and pupillages. Students who have been very successful as mooters, either in competitions or in assessments, therefore have a great advantage over students who have no such experience.

It is also recommended that students engage in mooting as an extra-curricular activity, whether or not they are involved in mooting as an assessed part of their studies. The reason for this is that it demonstrates to prospective employers a willingness to do more than the bare minimum to get through a course of study. The legal jobs market is highly competitive, and employers can therefore pick and choose. The law student who comes across as a student who has only done the bare minimum is therefore less likely to impress, especially bearing in mind the fact that most employers do expect their successful candidates to have a high capacity for hard work. For more on extra-curricular mooting opportunities, see chapter **10**.

Students who wish to go on to practise as lawyers are well advised to get into the habit of hard work during their student days. If you are in the habit of hard work from an early stage, you are much less likely to resent it when it is forced upon you in later life.

1.11.5 Teamwork

It should be noted that some of the best advocates have been anything but good team players. Advocacy, at the end of the day, is a highly solitary activity. When you are on your feet, speaking in court, the help that can be given to you by others is highly limited. If an advocate is going to make a hash of their submissions, then there is very little that their friends or team members can do to save them. Having said all of this, it is certainly true that teamwork can play a big part in the way that a mooter prepares.

Normally, in a moot there will be a senior and a junior counsel for both the appellant and the respondent. It is advisable that you should use your partner or team member during preparation as somebody to "bounce" your ideas off. Two heads are normally better than one, and it is likely that some submissions or ideas, which strike you as a good at first, will not seem as good after some discussion with a team member. Many students, of course, do not avail themselves of this potential advantage, perhaps because they do not know, or trust, their partner. This is unfortunate as, in practice, it is often the case that more than one lawyer will be involved in a case. For example, in many cases, a client will instruct both a solicitor and a barrister, who will have to try to work together effectively as a team, whether they like it or not. As a result, even the greatest of advocates do sometimes suffer from a lack of ability to work as an effective part of a team. Try to develop this ability early in your career through moot-ing, if possible.

1.11.6   Engaging with primary sources of law

One excellent aspect of mooting is that it obliges you to really engage with primary sources of law such as cases and statutes. Many law students, and some practitioners, are far too reliant on secondary sources of law, such as textbooks and practitioner texts. As a result, they seldom actually consult a primary source without the help of a middleman, in the form of an author. One of the big benefits of mooting is that it obliges you to use primary sources, and use them in a creative way to actually construct submissions for your fictitious client.

All of this is essential if you are to practise as a lawyer. It simply will not do to stand up in court and refer to a case simply by reference to what a textbook says on it. The judges will expect you to have read the case and be able to refer them to passages in the judgments that support your submissions. Additionally, it may be that, if you are dealing with a new aspect of the law, there will be no available text-books to help you.

The best lawyers are not afraid to consult primary sources to find and interpret the law themselves. Instead, they relish the opportunity to do so. Weaker lawyers always require guidance from secondary sources like textbooks, and are often uncomfortable without this safety net. Mooting allows you to become one of the former, by developing good habits early on.

Chapter 2

Knowledge of key aspects of the legal system

2.1 Introduction

Understandably, many mooters, when they first start to prepare for a moot, concentrate their attentions on the area(s) of substantive law (for example tort or criminal law) that the moot directly engages with. In their haste to master the area of law involved, they often forget the importance of knowledge of the relevant legal system. A good knowledge of the legal system is essential to mooting, as it constitutes the knowledge behind the knowledge of substantive law areas. If you do not have a good knowledge of the legal system, it is unlikely that you will have a good knowledge of areas like criminal law and tort in isolation from the general principles.

Perhaps surprisingly, many law students, especially those who are well into a law degree, often tend to regard the basic principles of the legal system as somewhat beneath their radar. Since the study of the legal system is, rightly, at the beginning of a course of study, it is as though students feel that they are done with the "Janet and John" material, and have moved on to bigger and better things. In mooting, this is a cardinal error. All good practitioners, and therefore mooters, have a sound understanding of the principles underpinning the legal system in which they practise. This knowledge provides a solid base and context for the detailed knowledge they will have in their own specialist areas. Time and time again, moot judges are surprised at mooters who let themselves down because of poor knowledge of issues that they should have mastered at the beginning of their studies. They often find that their approach to the substantive area of law they are dealing with is flawed, due to an imperfect understanding of fairly basic concepts.

A couple of common examples are students reading from the headnote of a law report, or reading from a dissenting judgment, thinking that it is binding. Such problems with lack of knowledge of the legal system come across particularly prominently when mooters are obliged to answer questions from the bench. In this situation, the mooter is dragged away from the security of their notes or script, and has to rely solely on their understanding and knowledge of the law. It is at this point that mooters often realise that what they always thought of as background knowledge is actually highly relevant knowledge, and that the lack of it is highly prejudicial to their performance.

2.1.1   The aims of this chapter

The aim of this chapter is to urge students to re-engage with the basic principles of their legal system, to avoid such elementary errors. Like the rest of the book, the chapter is written in the context of the English legal system. The chapter considers how certain key aspects of the legal system can be relevant, and even crucial, in a mooting context. The chapter is not intended as a comprehensive text on the English legal system, and students are therefore advised to consult one of the many books available, or their old notes, on this subject.

The aim of this chapter is simply to look at the legal system from the mooter's point of view, and to help you to understand how certain key elements of the system may affect you.

2.2   Sources of English law

When you make submissions in a moot court, you are not expressing your own personal opinions, but making submissions on behalf of your fictitious client backed up by legal authority. If what you submit is not backed up by some sort of legal authority, then there is little reason why the court should regard themselves as bound or persuaded by it. It is, therefore, essential that you know what the sources of English law are, and how much weight should be attached to them.

2.2.1   Principal or primary sources of law

A) Statute law and case law

The most significant source of law in England is undoubtedly statute law. The doctrine of parliamentary supremacy states that Parliament can make or unmake any law it wishes, on any subject and for anywhere in the world. Parliament cannot bind its successors, and existing legislation can be repealed or amended. Legislation can also be passed to amend or abolish any common law (ie case law) principles. Normally, if it is felt that a major change to the law is needed, the courts will be happy for this to be left to Parliament to legislate on.

It is also essential that you understand the status and extent of the various types of secondary or delegated legislation, such as by-laws and statutory instruments. Vast amounts of this type of legislation are created every year. In many areas of law where there is a statute, or where there is a statutory power being exercised, it is very difficult to know the law well without reference to such sources.

Despite the above, case law is also a very significant source of English law, due to our system of binding precedent. The courts can set precedents on areas of law not covered by legislation, and can set precedents on the correct interpretation of legislation, hence the various rules on statutory interpretation. A good knowledge of these basic concepts provides you with the confidence to know what you can and cannot argue in a moot court. For example, if you had a good understanding of the doctrine of parliamentary supremacy, you would know how unrealistic it would be to argue that a court should ignore a piece of legislation or set a precedent that was contrary to the provisions of a piece of legislation. Similarly, you might be reluctant to submit that the court adopts a line of argument which would result in a major change to the law, as the court may think such major changes are more properly left to Parliament.

B) Equity

If your moot concerns a civil law issue – for example, trusts, contract law or land law – it is possible that the distinction between common law and equity will be an issue that you may need to make submissions on, or may be asked about by the judge(s). Equity refers to the set of rules that originated from the Court of Chancery. The basic idea was that equity was supposed to be a fairer system than the common law, with the Court of Chancery initially priding itself on providing remedies to those who could not get justice in the common law courts, due to excessive rigidity. In time, though, as depicted in Charles Dickens' "Bleak House", the experience of a litigant in the Court of Chancery became even more hellish than in the common law courts. The Judicature Acts 1873–5 fused the common law courts and the Court of Chancery. However, it is still correct to refer to "common law rules" and "equitable rules", the former originating in the common law courts, and the latter in the Court of Chancery.

C) European Union law and The European Convention on Human Rights

For better or for worse, the face of English law has been changed dramatically by EU law and the Convention. As a result, it is now highly likely that, whatever the topic of your moot, some knowledge of at least one of the above will be required. Your study of the English legal system should have prepared you so that you can deal with these European angles. If you have allowed yourself to forget this material, or did not understand it in the first place, then this could be highly damaging to your prospects of being a successful mooter.

Make sure that, to begin with, you are at least acquainted with the basics, so that you are aware of how, and to what extent, these two sources are incorporated into English law. In the EU context, this means the provisions of the European Communities Act 1972 and landmark judgments such as *Factortame v Secretary of State for Transport (No 2)* [1991]. As far as the Convention is concerned, it goes without saying that a good knowledge of the main articles of the Convention is highly desirable. The Human Rights Act 1998 is also a vital source, as it provides guidance on the status of the Convention in English law, namely how the Convention binds public authorities, how domestic legislation should be interpreted in light of the Convention, and how claimants arguing a breach of a Convention right, by a public authority, can seek remedies in the domestic courts.

Even if you do not take human rights as an optional subject, you will have studied the basic concepts mentioned above in the context of constitutional or public law, or when you studied the English legal system at the start of your course.

You cannot get away from these two sources, so make sure that you do not overlook them. If a European point does arise in a mooting context, ignorance of this now vital aspect of English law will look very bad. On the other hand, a sound knowledge may create a very favourable impression on the judges. Try to see these two areas as an opportunity to develop your arguments, rather than as an obstacle.

2.2.2   Secondary sources of law

It is in their dealings with secondary sources of law that some mooters come unstuck. By secondary sources, I am referring to sources such as textbooks and articles in learned journals. By all means, sources like this should be used by the mooter, as it is always a good idea to read around the subject. However, whilst the use of secondary sources should be welcomed and is pretty much inevitable, it is worth sounding a note of caution. Your knowledge of basic principles should tell you that such sources have no binding effect on a court. This is the case no matter how eminent the author of the textbook or article may be. Some textbooks and practitioner texts have been around for many years, and are often written or edited by some of the most well regarded academics or practitioners of the day. This may tempt you to think that these texts should be read out as authoritative statements of the law during a moot. However, the contents of such works are not "the law". They are merely a version of the law seen through the lens of a middle-man. The actual legal rules are only to be found in primary sources such as statutes and cases. As a result, the opinions of academics and practitioners as to what those legal rules mean are not binding on anyone, least of all the appellate courts which form the setting for a moot.

On the other hand, the above is not intended to put you off using such sources, as long as you make it clear to the court that you know that the opinions being offered by the academic or practitioner in question have no binding effect on the court. You also have to be careful in the secondary sources that you choose. Some sources are far more respectable than others. If your moot is set in the House of Lords, to stand and ask the Lords of Appeal to follow the recommen-dations of a "Nutshell" book runs the risk of seeming a bit amateur-ish. Such books certainly have their place, but they are not, to my knowledge, routinely used by advocates in the higher courts. The same really goes for the use of most student textbooks, although there are some exceptions: for example, Smith and Hogan on crimi-nal law is regarded as a pretty authoritative source in the criminal courts on matters of substantive criminal law.

It is far better to quote from the case or the statute in question than to quote from the commentary on them in a textbook. I will return to this point in chapter 7.

Another source that is often referred to by mooters is reports by law reform agencies such as the Law Commission. These will nor-mally be in the form of a report detailing the current law and its defects and suggesting possible reforms. These reports can offer the mooter, who is looking for arguments, something of a lifeline. However, a note of caution should also be sounded here. If the report is suggesting wholesale change to the law, the court may take the view that major changes in the law are a matter for Parliament and not the courts. Nevertheless it is submitted that you should be courageous in using such arguments, provided that they are not wholly unrealistic.

A Use of secondary sources in moots set in the House of Lords

If your moot is in the House of Lords, the opinions of leading aca-demics may be more relevant. This is because the House of Lords is not bound by the decisions of lower courts, or by its own previous decisions since the issuing of the *Practice Statement (House of Lords: Judicial Precedent)* [1966]. It is rare for the Lords to use the Practice Statement to overrule one of their own previous decisions, and an advocate or mooter urging this course of action needs to provide good reasons for the court to do so. If a previous House of Lords decision has attracted strong criticism from leading academics and practitioners in the field, then their arguments may provide the reasons that a mooter can use to argue that it should happen in the case in hand. For a recent example of this, see *R v G* [2004] where the House of Lords overruled its own previous judgment in *R v Caldwell* [1982] on the issue of the definition of recklessness in criminal damage. One of the reasons for this use of the Practice Statement was that the decision in *R v Caldwell* had been heavily criticised by leading academics.

Reports from law reform agencies, as mentioned above, can be used with a bit more freedom and confidence in the House of Lords because of the Practice Statement. However, you may still hit a brick wall with this type of argument if the change to the law you are arguing for is a major one that calls for detailed and extensive legislation.

In short, secondary sources should be used to help you research your moot. In the moot itself, they should only be cited with caution, and you should be careful to demonstrate that you understand the nature of the source you are using and the fact that it is not strictly binding. For heaven's sake, do not stand up and start quoting from Wikipedia!

2.3   The court hierarchy and appeals structure

This is another area where mooting students can demonstrate a surprising lack of knowledge. It goes without saying that a thorough knowledge of the court structure, and the various routes for appeals, is very important for the successful mooter. The ways in which this knowledge can be relevant are briefly dealt with in this section.

2.3.1   Knowledge of the types of judge who heard the case in the lower court(s) and the types of judge that will preside over the moot

The tendency of some mooters is to focus entirely on their moot hearing in isolation from the other hearings that may have already taken place in the moot case. It is as though the moot is a one-off hearing with no case history. Of course, a moot is a fictitious case. However, to moot successfully, you need to think of the matter as though it were a real-life case. As was mentioned in chapter **1**, most moots will be an appeal case set in one of the appellate courts. This means that there will be a previous decision by a judge in a lower court. The judge(s) in the moot may well ask you about the lower court's decision, which means you will have to refer to the judge(s) correctly; this, in turn, will require a knowledge of the type of judges that were involved. For more on this, see section 3.14 on modes of address in chapter **3** and section 7.5.11 on referring to judges other than the moot judges in chapter **7**.

It goes without saying that you need to know the correct modes of address applicable to the types of judge you are dealing with in your moot.

Knowledge of the routes of appeal and bases upon which appeals can be allowed

It will be taken for granted by most moot judges that you have a good knowledge of the courts involved in the moot problem. This knowledge should include their jurisdiction, the routes of appeal from them, which precedents are binding on them, and the types of judges who sit in them. Moot judges will often be pretty fed up with students who have not troubled to learn such basic matters. It is also a big blow to your confidence if you are constantly being picked up on basic issues, and are, therefore, not getting your point across on the substantive legal issues that you are there to argue.

You will also need to be aware of which court the judge on whose decision the appeal is based was sitting in, and on what bases an appeal can be made to the court in which the moot is being held. For example, in the sample moot *R v Owen Owens*, the case involves an appeal against a murder conviction. Murder is an indictable only offence, which means that the trial must have been held at the Crown Court (that the trial was in the Crown Court is, in fact, stated clearly in the moot problem). If you consult the "Appeals from the Crown Court" section of any criminal procedure textbook, you will come across section 2 of the Criminal Appeal Act 1968, as amended by the Criminal Appeal Act 1995. Here it states that the only ground for appeal against conviction by the defence is that the conviction is "unsafe".

The purpose of this book is not to provide a detailed analysis of criminal or civil procedure, but it would clearly be a good idea for a mooter doing a criminal moot, such as *R v Owen Owens*, to engage in some research as to what "unsafe" means. Similar research would also be fruitful on the nature of appeals in civil cases. Again, this is the sort of point that is often missed by many mooters. Understandably perhaps, many get bogged down in the substantive law issues. Another problem is that the student at undergraduate or graduate diploma in law level will probably not have studied criminal or civil procedure yet. However, for the mooter who wants to do well, this sort of knowledge can provide you with many highly relevant and persuasive arguments. If you are asking for an appeal to be allowed or dismissed, you need to know the grounds upon which the judges in the moot can come to their decision, so that you can be persuasive in putting forward your submissions. If you appear to be in the dark on these issues, the impression that the judges get of you will often be a poor one.

2.3.3 Knowing who the appellants and respondents are, and what they were at the earlier hearing(s)

In a civil case heard at first instance, the party bringing the case is known as the claimant. The person being sued or defending the case is known as the defendant. In criminal cases, the party bringing the case is the prosecutor, and the person facing the criminal charge is the defendant. In the vast majority of criminal cases, the prosecution is brought in the name of the monarch, so the case will always read as *R v Smith* etc, with the "R" standing for Rex (King) or Regina (Queen), as appropriate. In some cases, the prosecution will be brought by other bodies that are empowered to bring cases, such as the Environment Agency or Her Majesty's Revenue and Customs.

A point that is sometimes missed by mooters is that, on appeal and therefore in a moot case, the titles of the parties will change, so that the party bringing the appeal to the appeal court will become the appellant. The other party, who will presumably be resisting the appeal and arguing that the decision of the lower court was correct, will become the respondent. Try to avoid referring to the parties by their original titles from when the case started. In the *R v Owen Owens* context, it is easy to keep referring to Dr Owens as the defendant when, in fact, on appeal, he will be the appellant in the case, as he is arguing that the conviction from the Crown Court should be quashed. This is an especially easy mistake to make where the moot problem refers to the parties according to the titles at the original hearing.

2.3.4 The jurisdictions of lower courts

When referring to authorities, it is important that you understand the context and status of the cases which you introduce to the court in your submissions. The reason for this is that you could encounter embarrassing difficulties when questioned by the judge. To give an example, in a purely criminal context, make sure you know whether a case you are referring to was a simple appeal from the Crown Court to the Court of Appeal, or whether it was a different kind of appeal, such as an appeal by way of case stated on a point of law. This is important, because it will prevent you from making errors, such as muddling up who the appellants and respondents were. If you refer the moot judges to cases, you want them to form the impression that you have a mastery of those cases. Judges will sometimes test your knowledge with little questions such as "Were there any dissenting judgments in this case?", or "Isn't this an appeal by way of case stated from the magistrates' court?". A good knowledge of the various courts and their jurisdictions will help you to make a positive impression when you are referring to authorities such as case law.

2.4   When is a precedent binding?

This section looks at the major courts which set precedents in England and Wales, and considers the status of their judgments and the extent to which they are bound by the decisions of higher courts. Once you begin constructing your legal arguments in preparation for a moot, this will become crucial to you, as you will be looking for cases which not only suit the submissions that you will make but also are from a court of sufficient seniority for you to argue that the moot court should follow them.

2.4.1   The courts and the court hierarchy

A) European Court of Justice

This is the supreme court on all matters of European law. This includes the interpretation of all aspects of European law and assessing the validity of actions taken by the institutions of the European Community. As a result, the decisions of the European Court of Justice on such matters are binding on all domestic courts. This sentiment finds its statutory reflection in section 3(1) of the European Communities Act 1972. The European Court does not operate a system of binding precedent, and so does not regard *itself* as bound by its own previous decisions. However, previous decisions are treated as persuasive.

As a result, if you are mooting on an area of law that is affected by EU law, you may need to become acquainted with decisions of the European Court of Justice. Ignorance of this important extra tier in the English legal system could spell disaster for you in a moot.

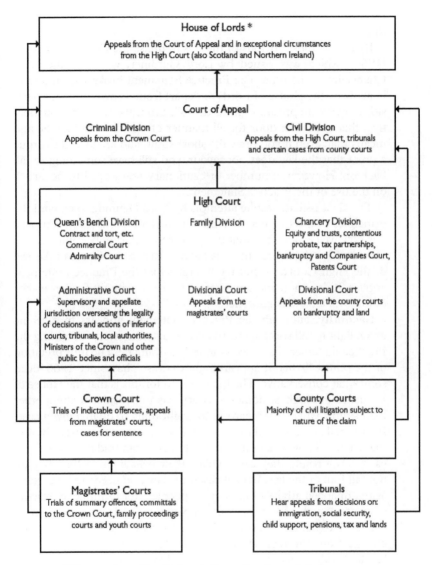

(Diagram from Her Majesty's Court Service website)

B) House of Lords

The House of Lords is the highest domestic court and its decisions bind all domestic courts lower down in the court hierarchy. If you find yourself in a moot set in the House of Lords and faced with an unfavourable House of Lords judgment, then this is clearly highly problematic. There are, however, a number of possible ways round this.

By far the most obvious of these is to utilise the *Practice Statement* [1966], which was issued by Lord Gardiner, who was the Lord Chancellor at the time. The Practice Statement broke with tradition in allowing the House of Lords to depart from its own previous decisions "when it appears right to do so". From the mooter's perspective, this opens the door for all manner of possible arguments, and means that, even if you draw the short straw, and are forced to argue a point that the law does not favour, you still have something to fall back on. However, a number of cautionary notes need to be struck on the use of the Practice Statement.

The **first** is that, despite attempts by Lord Denning to expand the principles of the Practice Statement to include the Court of Appeal, it is now well established that this power to depart only applies to the House of Lords. If your moot is taking place in the Court of Appeal or the High Court, do not try to argue that the Practice Statement applies. It does not, and any attempt to use it, without further elaboration, will look like ignorance.

Secondly, although the Practice Statement appears to give the green light for all sorts of creativity, in reality the effects of issuing the Practice Statement have been rather less dramatic. The interpretation of the phrase "when it appears right to do so" has, since 1966, been somewhat conservative. The main reason for this is that the House of Lords, as the highest domestic court, has to consider matters other than simply what they regard as the right thing to do in a given case. In criminal law, it is vital that the law does not change constantly, and that citizens know what the criminal law is or can find it out relatively easily. As a result, they can regulate their behaviour so that they do not fall foul of the law. In civil cases, the law also needs to be certain, as the financial affairs of millions of people – for example, in respect of matters such as contracts of employment and property rights – will be based on the current law. If the law is subject to regular change from the highest court in the land, it not only makes the law look ridiculous but can cause absolute turmoil in the affairs of man.

As a result of the above, the Practice Statement has been used sparingly since 1966. It has even been known for the House of Lords to refuse to use the Practice Statement, notwithstanding the fact that it has accepted that the ratio of an earlier decision was wrong (see *Jones v Secretary of State for Social Services* [1972]). As a result of this conservative approach, the Practice Statement was not used at all until 1972, in the landmark occupiers' liability case of *British Railways Board v Herrington* [1972].

Lord Scarman in *R v Secretary of State for the Home Department, ex parte Khawaja* [1984] AC 74 at 106 said that the Practice Statement will only be used if a two-stage test can be satisfied. He said:

> "The House must be satisfied not only that the adherence to the precedent would involve the risk of injustice and obstruct the proper development of the law, but also that a judicial departure by the House from the precedent is the safe and appropriate way of remedying the injustice and developing the law. The possibility that legislation may be the better course is one which, though not mentioned in the Practice Statement, the House will not overlook."

Even though the Practice Statement was used in the above case, it seems that Lord Scarman was intending that the bar be set fairly high for its use. The overriding concern seems to be for the preservation of certainty in the law. The Practice Statement should only be used if it is the safe and appropriate way of changing the law. If the change would be a major one, the best option may well be for Parliament to pass remedial legislation and for the House not to act.

In spite of the above, the Practice Statement has been used a number of times since 1966, and for a number of different reasons. To give just two examples, in *Arthur JS Hall and Co v Simons* [2000], the case of *Rondell v Worsley* [1969] was departed from, on the basis that the immunity of advocates from actions in tort, though a sound principle when it was established, could no longer be justified in modern times. In short, the House of Lords was changing the law to move with the times, where a legal rule had become outdated.

In *R v G* [2003], a case on the meaning of recklessness in criminal damage cases, the House of Lords overruled its earlier decision in *R v Caldwell* [1982] for a number of reasons, including strong academic criticism of the rule from *R v Caldwell*, and the fact that the *Caldwell* (or objective) type of recklessness was contrary to fundamental principles of criminal law, and unjust.

Many mooters, who could make use of such arguments, seem to miss the opportunity to use the Practice Statement. In some cases, this is through a lack of knowledge, and in others it is due to a lack of confidence. Perhaps some students feel that it is too audacious an argument to ask the moot court to depart from a well known, established House of Lords precedent. This is a shame, because the Practice Statement can provide such a rich source of argument in moots based in the House of Lords. Try to avoid such shyness. Courage is one of the characteristics of the good advocate and, as long as you use arguments on the Practice Statement realistically, there is no reason why the judges should not give you credit for it.

On the other hand, a few students in my experience have tried to use the Practice Statement too lightly, and have argued that a well-established and perfectly sound precedent should be departed from, for no good reason, apart from the fact that it suits their case. Whenever you are arguing that the Practice Statement should be used, or opposing such a submission, it will be of benefit to you to look carefully at the cases where use of the Practice Statement has been an issue, and make the best of the principles espoused in those cases to suit your arguments.

Thirdly, a House of Lords authority does not have to be followed if it has been overruled by statute or by a decision of the European Court. Clearly, in these circumstances the authority is no longer binding.

Fourthly, a decision of the House of Lords could also be argued to be *per incuriam*, meaning that the House came to the decision on an erroneous basis, in that it did not take into account other authorities that it should have been bound by. The chances of this being applicable to a decision of the House are remote as, in order to get to the House of Lords, the case would have gone through the full court system first. It is, therefore, unlikely that all of the courts involved would have completely missed a binding authority. Nevertheless, this is still a line of argument that is worth considering.

The **fifth** way of avoiding an inconvenient House of Lords authority is by arguing that the case can be distinguished from the moot case. For more on distinguishing, see section.

The **final** avenue for avoiding a House of Lords authority that does not suit you is to argue that the Practice Statement could be used, bearing in mind the fact that the Human Rights Act 1998 obliges the courts to act in a manner which is compatible with the European Convention on Human Rights, and to interpret legislation in a manner which is consistent with the articles of the Convention wherever possible. If you have a House of Lords authority which was decided before the implementation of the Convention, and which, for example, involves the interpretation of a statute, you may be able to argue that the interpretation of that legislation should now be different in order to be compatible with the Convention. Indeed, this way of avoiding a precedent can now be applied to all of the courts that are involved in the setting of precedents.

It is hopefully clear that an unfavourable House of Lords authority does not necessarily mean the end of your arguments. As was mentioned in chapter 1, sometimes the moot problem will favour one of the parties. This simply means that the mooters affected should make the best of a bad situation. If anything, this should be treated as an opportunity to impress, rather than as a signal that you will not win.

C) Court of Appeal (Civil Division)

As one would expect, decisions of the Court of Appeal (Civil Division) are binding on all courts lower down the court hierarchy. The Civil Division is also bound by the House of Lords and by the European Court of Justice on matters to do with European law. It is common for moots to be set in the Court of Appeal, so a more commonly recurring issue for mooters is the extent to which the court is bound to follow its own previous decisions. The **general rule** here is that the Court of Appeal (Civil Division) is bound by its own previous decisions, as laid down in *Young v Bristol Aeroplane Co Ltd* [1944].

However, as with the House of Lords, that is not necessarily all that there is to say on this issue. Of course, as with any other court, there is the possibility for advocates and judges to be creative with case law, and to put forward reasons why precedents can be distinguished from the case in hand.

The **major exceptions to the general rule** from *Young* in respect of the Civil Division were laid down by Lord Greene MR in the same case. Here, it was held that the Court of Appeal (Civil Division) could decline to follow one of its own previous decisions if one of three exceptional circumstances existed. These are:

1) If there are two conflicting Civil Division decisions, the court may choose which one should be followed. If this is done, and nothing is indicated to the contrary, the decision not followed will be regarded as overruled. It is, therefore, good advice to the mooter faced with an unfavourable Civil Division decision to do a trawl to see whether there are any conflicting decisions of the same court. As the court generally follows its own previous decisions, this should not happen very often as a matter of logic, but you never know what you may find.

2)   The second exception to the general rule arises when the Civil Division is faced with one of its own previous decisions, which has not been expressly overruled by the House of Lords, but is nevertheless inconsistent with a more recent House of Lords decision. Here, the Civil Division should follow the more recent House of Lords decision. Hopefully, this will not arise too often, as the House of Lords would normally be aware of Court of Appeal cases that were highly relevant to the issue before it. However, these lapses will sometimes happen. In the rare event of a Civil Division decision being inconsistent with an earlier House of Lords decision, there are two conflicting lines of authority as to what the Court of Appeal should do: see *Turton v Turton* [1988] and *Miliangos v George Frank (Textiles) Ltd* [1976] for more on this.

3)   The Civil Division can decline to follow one of its previous decisions if that decision was given *per incuriam*. This basically means that the court came to its decision without regard to, or in ignorance of, a relevant case or statute. As a result, the reasoning is that the chain of authority has been broken and that the law, as stated by that case, is not as it should be. In modern times, with electronic help to find the right authorities, it is arguably less likely that courts will erroneously make decisions on this basis. If, in a moot context, you wish to run this type of argument, it is safest to do so only when there was no mention of the cases that you are submitting should have been binding in the case in question. If the court refers to these authorities, but decides they can be distinguished, for example, then it is much more difficult, if not impossible, to argue that the decision was given *per incuriam*.

As will hopefully be clear, mooting in the Court of Appeal affords nearly as much room for manoeuvre and creativity as in moots held in the House of Lords. However, the fact that the Practice Direction does not apply in this court inevitably cuts down the options for the mooter who is looking for an argument.

D) Court of Appeal (Criminal Division)

The decisions of the Criminal Division are binding on all courts lower down the court hierarchy. The Criminal Division is also bound by all courts above it, most notably the House of Lords. However, as many moots are held in the Court of Appeal, the more frequently pressing issue is the extent to which the Criminal Division is bound by its own previous decisions. As with the Civil Division, the general rule is that the court is bound by its previous decisions and by decisions of the Civil Division where relevant, subject to the exceptions laid down in *Young v Bristol Aeroplane Co Ltd* [1944]. Despite this, there is one important exception to this rule, which is that the court may decline to follow one of its own previous decisions where to do so would result in injustice to an appellant. Because the liberty of the subject is often at stake in criminal cases, this exception represents something of a more relaxed approach to the strict rules of precedent, compared to the more rigid way that things are dealt with in the Civil Division. A statement on the nature of this exception was given by the court in *R v Spencer* [1985]:

> "As a matter of principle we respectfully find it difficult to see why there should in general be any difference in the application of the principle *stare decisis* between the Civil and Criminal Divisions of the court, save that we must remember that in the latter we may be dealing with the liberty of the subject and if a departure from authority is necessary in the interests of justice to an appellant, then this court should not shrink from so acting."

This exception to the general rule provides an opportunity for the mooter who is involved in a Criminal Division-based moot and who wishes to argue that an unfavourable authority should not apply. For example, in *R v Owen Owens*, a moot set in the Court of Appeal, it might be possible for the appellant to argue the point from *Spencer*, above, since following *R v Dudley and Stephens* [1884] rigidly and applying *Re A (Children)* [2001] narrowly may result in injustice.

Much of your success will depend on your ability to put the time and effort into researching your lines of argument. If you give your submissions plenty of thought, and are prepared to read around the subject, then these more subtle avenues of argument become a realistic possibility. With good research of aspects of the legal system such as the above, you will find that all manner of ideas are opened up for you. As a result, even having a role in the moot that is not favoured by the law will not seem so bad.

E) High Court

The Divisional Courts are, in civil cases, bound by the European Court of Justice, the House of Lords and by the Court of Appeal (Civil Division). The Divisional Courts are also bound by their own decisions, but are subject to the same exceptions to the general rule as is the Court of Appeal (Civil Division). The decisions of the

Divisional Courts are also binding on judges of the same division of the High Court sitting in their first instance capacity.

When the Administrative Division of the Queen's Bench Division sits in criminal cases, the situation is that these decisions will bind all lower courts, but that the court is bound by its own decisions in precisely the same way as the Court of Appeal (Criminal Division).

High Court judges sitting as first instance judges make decisions that bind all lower courts, and are bound by all higher courts, but are not bound by previous decisions at the same level. This means that moots in the High Court can be an enjoyable experience, as the moot judges will not be bound to follow any previous decisions at High Court first instance level, no matter how well reasoned they may be. As a result, the case history of the High Court is littered with examples of conflicting authorities. Whilst previous decisions are not binding, however, they are certainly of some persuasive force. It is certainly not the case that the High Court declines to follow its own previous decisions willy-nilly. As a result, if you are arguing that a previous decision should not be followed, then you need to back this up with some sound reasoning.

F) Crown Court, Magistrates' Courts and County Courts

Because the decisions of these courts rarely appear in the law reports, their decisions have no binding effect on other courts. As a result, if you are aware of a decision of one of these courts, you must exercise extreme caution before using it. Nevertheless, as mentioned earlier, a knowledge of the jurisdiction and constitution of these courts is essential to the mooter as, unless the moot has an international flavour, it is likely that your moot problem will involve an initial decision by either one of these courts or the High Court. You cannot understand why the appeal, and therefore the moot, is taking place unless you understand the nature of the work of the relevant lower court.

It will hopefully be apparent from the preceding passages that a good working knowledge of the court hierarchy is an absolutely essential aspect of the armoury of the successful mooter. You should give some serious consideration to these issues before you start your main research for a moot.

G) Judicial Committee of the Privy Council

The Judicial Committee of the Privy Council is not a domestic court, and its decisions are not binding on the courts dealt with above. However, it should still be remembered that the Privy Council is actually made up of the Lords of Appeal in Ordinary who make up the Judicial Committee of the House of Lords. As a result, whilst not technically binding, decisions of the Privy Council are hugely persuasive in the domestic courts. If there are no relevant domestic authorities on a point covered by a Privy Council decision, it is highly likely that the domestic court would follow it.

Furthermore, there was a surprising development in the criminal law when the Court of Appeal in *R v James and Karimi* [2006] followed the Privy Council decision of *Attorney General for Jersey v Holley* [2005] in spite of the technically binding House of Lords decision in *R v Smith (Morgan)* [2000]. The reasoning was that the Privy Council had intended a full review of the relevant law (on provocation as a defence to murder), and that any appeal to the House of Lords, where substantially the same judges would hear the case, would therefore be a foregone conclusion.

There are a number of objections to this reasoning, for example, that the majority in the Privy Council in *Holley* may have become the minority in any subsequent appeal to the House of Lords on the same issue. This decision, therefore, clearly offends the normal rules on the operation of the doctrine of precedent and the domestic court hierarchy.

Such confusion, however, is an opportunity for the mooter, and these developments in the law on provocation are arguably a green light to be more courageous in the use of Privy Council judgments. In any event, Privy Council judgments can offer a valuable route of argument for the mooter who, for example, is arguing that the *Practice Statement* [1966] should be used. The reasoning in a Privy Council judgment may well provide the ammunition you need for persuading the moot court not to follow a previous House of Lords judgment. For example, in *Holley* the majority in the Privy Council gave a pretty damning verdict on the reasoning in *R v Smith*. If a case ever did go to the House of Lords on the same issue, there is every possibility that the House of Lords would use the Practice Statement on the basis of some or all of the reasons mentioned in *Holley*.

In conclusion, the law is seldom as certain as some parties would wish for it to be. This lack of certainty is something that you should seize upon as a mooter, as long as your arguments are within realistic parameters.

2.5 Which part of a precedent is binding?

Once you have narrowed your moot research down and found some cases that are relevant to your submissions, you then need to consider the extent to which the precedents you have found really can be used to further your submissions. It is therefore crucial that you appreciate the difference between the parts of a judgment that are binding and the parts that are not. If there is a doubt about the status of a precedent that you are referring to, then you need to be aware of it. There is a saying that "one man's *ratio* is another man's *obiter*", meaning that it is no easy feat to decide whether part of a judgment is the *ratio decidendi* or a statement made *obiter dicta*. Again, the uncertainty can be seen as an opportunity for the mooter. However, I would not wish readers to run away with the impression that, just because there is uncertainty, anything goes. There will be some parts of a precedent that definitely will, or will not, be binding. The courage in putting forward arguments that I have previously alluded to can only be exercised within certain parameters of accepted principle. I will now deal briefly with the concepts of *ratio decidendi* and *obiter dicta*, and explain their significance for those taking part in moots.

2.5.1 Ratio decidendi

As students will be aware, this is the part of a judgment that will be regarded as binding, subject to the rules already mentioned on the court hierarchy. The *ratio* is the reason (or reasons, if the case was concerned with more than one ground) why the court came to the verdict that it did, either in convicting or acquitting in a criminal case or in finding for one party or another in a civil case. The *ratio* is therefore the rule of law contained within the decision that can survive from a case long after the original parties are dead and buried. The verdict that the court comes to on the facts is not binding on anyone, except, of course, the parties to that specific case. This holds true even if a case arises with identical facts to those of an earlier case. The court in the later case will only be bound by statements of law made in the earlier case, and not by the inferences drawn by the judge or jury on those facts. One of the tasks of the mooter or the lawyer is to locate the parts of the judgment that form the *ratio decidendi*.

In a judgment, the judge(s) will make findings on what are the material facts in the case. They will also highlight the law that is deemed to be applicable to those facts; and, finally, they will apply the law to those facts, stating their reasons for doing so in that way. It is this last element that comprises the *ratio* of a case. It is the judge's reason for applying the law to the material facts in a certain way.

If a judge deals with facts other than the material facts, those comments will not form part of the *ratio*. This is because, when a judge sits on a case, he or she is only obliged to deal with the legal issues which the facts of that case demand them to deal with. Anything else they wish to add is superfluous. Judges are not given a free rein to deal with any other issues which spring to mind, or which appear to be important to them. Judges are not legislators, and should not use sitting and deciding on cases before them as a chance to depart from the issues that the facts of the case give rise to. This is why any statements, other than the judge's response to the material facts, will not be regarded as part of the binding precedent set by the court.

From the mooter's perspective, therefore, caution needs to be exercised when referring to authorities. When you are planning to refer the court to passages from a judgment to bolster your submissions, be careful to consider the status of those passages and to give some thought as to whether those comments are *ratio* or *obiter*. A mistake that is regularly made by weaker mooters is to refer to passages from dissenting judges, when their comments cannot possibly be part of the *ratio* of the case. There will be more on these issues in the chapter on dealing with authorities, but the key is to be prepared to put in hard work when researching your submissions. The lazier mooters tend to find a passage in a judgment which looks favourable to their submissions, and read it out in court, without investigating the status of the passage. They then often look surprised when asked a few awkward questions by the judge.

Secondary sources such as textbooks can be useful in helping you to locate the *ratio* or *rationes* of cases you are using; for example, in the context of *R v Owen Owens*, any criminal law textbook will tell you that that the reason why the appeal was allowed in *R v Woollin* [1999], and therefore the *ratio decidendi*, was that the trial judge did not use the correct direction based on virtual certainty, as laid down in the earlier case of *R v Nedrick* [1986].

Despite this, whilst textbooks can sometimes provide you with a valuable shortcut, it is strongly recommended that you get into the habit of trying to discern the status of comments in judgments yourself. Mooting is an excellent means of getting you to engage with primary sources, and there is a lot of confidence to be gained from knowing the *ratio* of a case because you have read it yourself, rather than simply because a textbook has told you. One good idea is to read the case yourself and to reach your own conclusions. After that, you can test your conclusions against what is said about that case in the secondary sources. In this way, you can feel your own way as far as case reading and interpretation is concerned, whilst, at the same time, having the safety net of being able to consult leading academic texts as to the veracity of your own conclusions.

2.5.2   Obiter dicta

One of the keys to knowing how to find the *ratio* of a case is to be able to distinguish them from comments made *obiter dicta*, or "by the way". Because of the fact that some judicial comments are made "by the way", they are, strictly speaking, superfluous, in that they were not necessary comments for the disposal of the case. The outcome of the case, and the legal principle(s) it lays down, is not dependent on such statements. As a result, comments made *obiter dicta* are merely persuasive and are not binding.

The **two** types of *obiter* comment are as follows:

First, a comment will be *obiter* if it is something that a judge says that is not in response to the material facts of a case. A judge who is deciding a case on, say, the law of theft will have the material facts, and these are the facts that he or she must respond to, and apply the law to, in their judgment. Sometimes, in order to explain the main point that they are making, judges will apply the law to a hypothetical set of facts. The purpose of this may be to provide an analogy that will make their judgment easier to understand. Clearly, comments like this are not strictly relevant to the material facts of the case, and are therefore not binding on any later court. If, in a theft case that turned on the meaning of dishonesty, a judge decided to clear up some issues on the meaning of appropriation, these comments would also be *obiter* if, according to the facts of the case, the meaning of appropriation was not a contentious issue.

Secondly, some statements in a judgment will be based on the material facts that the case brings up, but will still be regarded as *obiter* if they do not form part of the reason why the decision was made. The easiest example of this to spot is comments made as part of dissenting judgments. If a judge is part of the dissenting minority, then it follows that anything they say cannot be part of the *ratio decidendi*. At best, these comments can be regarded as *obiter*, and therefore persuasive. Another example of this type of *obiter* is statements made by a judge which lead to a conclusion other than the conclusion that the court eventually reaches. As these statements do not support the final decision of the court, they cannot be the reason for deciding the case.

Despite not being binding, *obiter dicta* comments can still have a massive influence on the development of the law. Possibly the most famous example is from Lord Atkin in *Donoghue v Stevenson* [1932], where the actual *ratio* of the case was that manufacturers of products owe a duty of care to eventual consumers in certain circumstances.

Lord Atkin's more general observations, about the meaning of duty of care, were comments made *obiter dicta*, but, nevertheless, have been, and still are, hugely influential in developing the law on the meaning of duty of care in negligence generally, and not just in product liability cases.

Because of this, mooters should not regard *obiter* comments as irrelevant when preparing. It should be remembered that these comments are persuasive and can be used in a host of situations. I will give **two examples of where *obiter* comments could effectively be used**.

First, if you are doing a moot set in the House of Lords and are arguing that the Practice Statement should be applied to overrule a previous decision, you may wish to use *obiter* comments to suggest a more attractive line of reasoning than that employed in the case that you are arguing should be overruled. The comments in that case may be persuasive to the extent of helping the court to see how justice could be better achieved if a different approach were used.

Secondly, if you are mooting in the Court of Appeal (Civil Division), and are arguing that one of the exceptions in *Young v Bristol Aeroplane* [1944] applies, you may wish to use *obiter* comments from another case to persuade the court to adopt an approach to the matter which suits your fictitious client. These two examples are far from exhaustive, and mooters are urged, where possible and desirable, to be creative in using *obiter* comments, especially where there is a shortage of binding authorities to support the submissions being made.

The key is to give some serious thought to the status of the judgments you use, before you use them. If there is a doubt about whether comments you are using are part of the *ratio*, or just *obiter*, you should at least be aware of them and be prepared to be questioned on the matter.

2.6 Ways of avoiding precedents: reversing, overruling and distinguishing

As will already be apparent, it is often necessary for you to be creative with case law and to deal with decisions that represent an obstacle to the submissions that the moot problem obliges you to make. In the textbooks, reversing, overruling and distinguishing are often represented as things that judges do. The reality is that, when a case is reversed, overruled or distinguished, it will often be as a result of submissions made by one of the counsel in the case. From your point of view as a mooter, these three ways of dealing with cases are a very useful tool when planning your submissions.

2.6.1   Reversing

Reversing occurs in an appeal case where the appeal court reaches a different conclusion to the lower court. As a result of this, the earlier decision is said to have been "reversed". In the context of *R v Owen Owens*, for example, Dr Owens is appealing to the Court of Appeal (Criminal Division) against a Crown Court verdict of guilty to a charge of murder. If he is successful in his appeal, we can say that the decision of the Crown Court has been reversed, and that his conviction has been quashed. It therefore follows that counsel for the appellant will always be submitting that the decision(s) of the lower court should be reversed. Counsel for the respondent, on the other hand, will be arguing the opposite, namely that the decision(s) of the lower court should be upheld.

2.6.2   Overruling

Overruling occurs when a court makes a decision, or Parliament passes legislation, which affects the rule of law in an earlier case. The actual decision or verdict that affected the parties in the earlier case remains binding on them, but the precedent set by the earlier court no longer has the binding effect that it previously did.

For example, in *R v G and R* [2003], as mentioned earlier, the House of Lords used the Practice Statement to overrule the earlier case of *R v Caldwell* [1982]. The effect of this was that the applicability of *Caldwell*, as a binding precedent on the meaning of recklessness in criminal damage cases, came to an end. However, this did not mean that, as far as the parties to *Caldwell* were concerned, the case was in some way considered again. The effect of the overruling is that the original decision still applies to the parties in *Caldwell*, but that *R v G and R* will now be the case that is followed in future cases on the meaning of recklessness in criminal damage. If cases had to be reconsidered every time a case was overruled and a new precedent were set, it would cause chaos in the justice system.

Obviously, it may well be the case that, in a moot, you will wish to ask the court to overrule a previous decision that does not suit your case. It goes without saying that any argument you raise on overruling of decisions must be done with regard to the court hierarchy. It may seem surprising, but it is not unknown for weaker mooters to ask the Court of Appeal to overrule a House of Lords decision, and so forth. Some of these mistakes can be put down to nerves, but often they are the result of weaknesses of knowledge and not knowing what can and cannot be argued. If you know your English legal system, these things are common sense. If you do not, then such mistakes are all too easy to make.

One final point on overruling is that the mooter must be aware that, in many instances, judges may prefer to leave changes in the law to Parliament. As mentioned earlier, judges are not legislators, and the courts often feel that major changes to the law are better left to Parliament, where the changes can be debated properly and drafted precisely by expert draftsmen. When suggesting that cases should be overruled, you need to be aware that considerations like this will possibly be used either by your opponents or by the judge in the form of questions. As with all lines of argument, you need to give some thought as to how realistic overruling is. Clearly, the doctrine of precedent and the court hierarchy do involve judges making and developing the law; however, there are some limitations on what judges will be prepared to do, and the argument that changes are better left to Parliament is one that is often used in the courts.

Nevertheless, just because a legal rule is well established, and the change you are arguing for would be a major one, should not necessarily deter you. As long as you are aware of the types of arguments you will face, it pays to be courageous in putting forward your arguments, so long as courage is tempered with realism. One example of a major change to a long-standing rule is to be found in *R v R (Rape: Marital Exemption)* [1992], where the old rule dating back to *Hale's History of the pleas of the crown* (1736), that a husband cannot be guilty of raping his wife, was finally changed. Counsel in this case was presumably not put off by the fact that the change being argued for was a major and historic one.

2.6.3   Distinguishing

As was mentioned in chapter **1**, the moot problem will give you cases that the lower court(s) either referred to or relied on in coming to their decision. Furthermore, your own research may turn up cases that you feel have a bearing on the moot. The authorities you find may all concur with the submissions you wish to make, in which case life will be relatively straightforward. As has been mentioned earlier, though, it is much more likely that you will be faced with some authorities which do not suit your case, and which you still need to deal with. One of the best ways of doing this, both for judges and for advocates, is distinguishing.

Distinguishing is one of the areas where the student mooter has to develop from somebody who is only expected to know what the cases say to somebody who can actually use cases to their own advantage in a creative way. By creativity, I do not mean that students should lie or be in some way unethical; merely that they should do what all lawyers do in court, and try to make the best of the materials they have at their disposal. It would be a very poor mooter indeed who, faced with some unfavourable authorities, simply gave up.

The essence of distinguishing is arguing that an authority, although perhaps correctly decided, does not, for some reason, apply to the case that you are dealing with. It is largely through the distinguishing of cases that the law manages to achieve its flexibility. Again, I cannot stress enough the importance of creativity and courage in using this method of avoiding a precedent. The best advocates are not "wallflowers", they have thick skins and are prepared to stand up in court and argue points that, to others, may seem an impertinence. Sometimes the law will be against one side in the moot. The judges will know that this is the case, and will therefore be looking for that side to show some imagination and pluck in doing the best they can, with limited materials at their disposal. As was mentioned in chapter **1**, it is for this reason that the party with the law against them, so long as they put forward credible arguments, can often emerge victorious.

The most likely ways that you will attempt to distinguish cases in a moot are by arguing that:

1) the facts of the moot case are materially different from a precedent case, meaning that the precedent should not be applied to the moot case; or

2) although the facts of the moot case bear a resemblance to the facts of a decided case, the decided case actually decided a point of law that is not applicable to the moot case.

For an example of the former, more common form of distinguishing, consider the sample moot problem, *R v Owen Owens*. In that moot, junior counsel for the appellant has to argue that the defence of necessity applies to the facts of the case on the basis of *Re A (Conjoined Twins)* [2000]. If you look at the facts of *Re A*, you will see that this is a fairly difficult task, as the cases, though similar in some ways, have some fairly major differences. The biggest difference is that the weaker of the twins in *Re A* was almost certain to die and was actually weakening the stronger of the twins.

As a result, junior counsel for the respondent already has an excellent argument to put to the court, namely that *R v Owen Owens* and *Re A* are distinguishable. Additionally, if you look at *R v Dudley and Stephens* [1884], you will see that an argument exists for junior counsel for the appellant, as this case is also arguably distinguishable from the moot case. In that case, the seamen chose who was going to die in order to save their own lives. In *R v Owen Owens*, the appellant was a doctor who was arguably exercising his best clinical judgment.

The key to all of these methods of avoiding precedents is that, in order to avoid a case, you have to know it well. If you really engage with the process of researching your moots, and the relevant case law, distinguishing is hopefully something you will become very much accustomed to.

2.7 Interpretation/construction of statutes

The moot problem may well refer to statutes, and the moot itself may well depend on the correct interpretation of legislation. If this is the case in a moot you are involved with, you therefore need to have a decent working knowledge of the various rules on how judges interpret legislation. Here again, the key words are creativity, courage and realism. Statutes are often open to more than one interpretation. Thankfully, at least for lawyers who have to make a living, language is not a precise tool. Sections of statutes can often be ambiguous or badly drafted, meaning that there are plenty of possible arguments to be had on the true intentions of Parliament in passing the legislation in the first place.

This section deals very briefly with three areas of knowledge:

1) aids to interpretation,

2) the approaches to statutory interpretation, and

3) the various rules and presumptions on the interpretation of statutes.

This section gives a brief introduction to each of these, but mooters are directed either to their own lecture notes or to a textbook on the English legal system for more detail on this topic. As a practical exercise, if you have not already done so, it is worth reading an Act of Parliament to get a feel for legislation and how it is set out, for example, to see what sorts of things schedules and interpretation sections etc contain.

2.7.1   Aids to statutory interpretation: what can be consulted?

When you are involved in a moot that hinges on a matter of statutory interpretation, you will be attempting in your submissions to persuade the court to adopt the interpretation most favourable to the case you are arguing. Over the years, rules have been developed as to what sources judges can consult in order to ascertain the correct interpretation of a statute. You need to be aware of these as a mooter, as you may wish to refer judges to them in the moot if it suits your submissions to do so. They appear in this section very briefly and as little more than a list.

A) Internal aids

Internal aids are aids that can be found within the statute itself.

1) The long title

The long title is the part of the Act which begins "an Act" and goes on to briefly describe the general aims of the legislation. For example, in the Fraud Act 2006, the long title states "An Act to make provision for, and in connection with, criminal liability for fraud and obtaining services dishonestly". Obviously, this is of rather limited use as an aid to interpretation, but it can be used to at least discern the general intention of Parliament in passing the legislation.

2) The short title

Again, this is available as an aid to interpretation, but clearly is of little use, as the short title seldom reflects in any detail the content of a piece of legislation. One example is the Crime and Disorder Act 1998, which covered a very wide range of subjects from the age of criminal responsibility, to provisions to do with "racially aggravated" offences. Anyone reading the short title would find it practically impossible to guess what the Act contained as a result.

3) The preamble

Modern Acts often do not have a preamble, but older pieces of legislation did, and often fairly detailed ones at that. Where this was the case, the courts would often set great store by what the preamble said when attempting to interpret the Act. If an Act does have a preamble, then it can still be used as an aid to interpretation.

4) Headings

Often, a section in an Act, or a group of sections, will have a heading.

This may also be of limited use when attempting to ascertain what those sections mean.

5) Schedules

These are usually at the end of an Act of Parliament, and can be used in the event of an uncertainty or ambiguity about one of the sections in the Act itself. Schedules normally deal with things like transitional provisions and lists of things that the legislation has repealed, for the avoidance of doubt.

6) Interpretation sections

Most Acts will contain at least one interpretation section, the aim of which is to give guidance on how certain words contained within the Act are to be interpreted. For example, section 5 of the Fraud Act 2006 contains some explanation of the terms "gain" and "loss", which are referred to in the offences created by sections 2 to 4. These are obviously of great use to the mooter, advocate or judge in deciding on the meaning of certain sections of legislation.

7) Marginal notes

These are written by statutory draftsmen, and are not part of the legislation itself. The traditional view is that they are therefore not permissible as aids to interpretation. However, there have been a limited number of cases where judges have clearly been prepared to use marginal notes, and you should familiarise yourself with such cases if it suits your submissions to refer to the marginal notes in a statute.

B) *External aids*

These are the aids that are not part of the statute itself. The use of such aids has always been something of a controversial issue, with purists arguing that, when interpreting legislation, only the legislation itself should be scrutinised. If there are ambiguities or uncertainties in legislation, then they should be solved by an analysis of the legislation, not materials other than the Act itself. The argument is that, once courts start looking beyond the legislation itself, it will open the floodgates so that all materials that have anything to do with the legislation can be considered.

Despite the above, there are some limited circumstances where certain external aids can be used to help determine the correct interpretation of legislation.

1) Reports of the proceedings of Parliament in Hansard

Since the decision of the House of Lords in *Pepper v Hart* [1993], a court can refer to parliamentary materials to determine the meaning of legislation if certain circumstances are present, These were laid down by Lord Browne-Wilkinson:

> "the exclusionary rule should be relaxed so as to permit reference to parliamentary materials where: (a) legislation is ambiguous or obscure, or leads to an absurdity; (b) the material relied upon consists of one or more statements by a Minister or other promoter of the Bill together if necessary with such other material as is necessary to understand such statements, and their effect; (c) the statements relied upon are clear."

From the above, it can be seen that the House of Lords was somewhat reluctant to allow the use of parliamentary materials and that they should be used only where absolutely necessary and subject to fairly strict conditions.

2) Explanatory notes

More recent Acts of Parliament will often contain a separate document of "Explanatory notes". These explain the main purposes of the legislation, and the sections contained therein, in relatively simple and straightforward language. Such notes, however, do not form part of the actual enactment. The case law on the use of explanatory notes is somewhat inconclusive, as the notes are not specifically approved by Parliament when the Bill becomes law. For more on this, if it is relevant in your moot, see the decisions in *Westminster City Council v National Asylum Support Service* [2002], where the court seemed fairly happy with the use of explanatory notes; and, for a slightly more conservative approach, *Wilson v First County Trust (No 2)* [2003].

3) Other materials

There are a few other types of material that are capable of being used as external aids to interpretation, subject to certain restrictions and conditions, including judicial precedents, and reports of law reform agencies such as the Law Commission.

2.8 Approaches to statutory interpretation

There are three main approaches to statutory interpretation which will be considered in the subsequent three sections of this chapter. There is no strict rule of law that tells judges which of the methods to use, and the choice is left to individual judges. Some approaches have been more prominent than others at different points in history, but there has never been any compulsion as to how judges tackle the issue of statutory interpretation. When making submissions on this in a moot, you can, as a result, be creative, provided that the interpretation that you are proposing has some logical basis and, therefore, some credibility.

2.8.1   The literal rule

Popular in Victorian times, the essence of this approach is to give the words in the statute their ordinary, everyday, plain meaning. This approach does not attempt to go behind the words in the Act to ascertain the intention of Parliament. The reasoning is that Parliament says what it means with legislation. As a result, any attempt to look behind the words that Parliament, as the supreme law-making body, lays down is not the job of judges. For an illustration of the literal rule in operation, see *Fisher v Bell* [1961].

2.8.2   The golden rule

This rule is basically where judges apply the literal rule in the first instance and see what the result is. If the result of applying the literal rule is a good one in terms of logic and justice, then all is well and good. If, however, the result is an absurdity, then the golden rule allows judges to depart from the literal interpretation and apply a meaning which avoids the absurdity. An example of this rule in operation is *Adler v George* [1964].

2.8.3   The purposive or mischief rule

The leading case here is *Heydon's case* (1584). The purposive approach is that, when passing legislation, Parliament has a purpose in mind in that it will be attempting to avoid a particular mischief. As a result, when interpreting legislation, the courts should look to the intentions of Parliament to try and apply the interpretation which puts right the mischief that Parliament was, in passing the legislation, trying to correct.

In recent years, the purposive approach has become the most popular, but when mooting, remember that there is no strict rule as to which method a judge should use. Also, judges do not specifically say which method they are applying when interpreting a statute. The reality is that judges may well use a mixture of all of the methods mentioned above.

2.9 Principles and presumptions on statutory interpretation

Over the years, a number of principles and presumptions have been developed which run alongside the various methods of statutory interpretation. The mooter should be aware of these before making any submissions on the meaning of a piece of legislation. Arguably, these rules are little more than common sense. However, whenever you are making submissions on the meaning of a statutory provision, make sure you do a check to see if any of the principles or presumptions apply. They include the following.

2.9.1 The principle that statutes should be read as a whole

This is because, when interpreting a particular section of an Act, you may find that what other sections say has a bearing on the correct interpretation. As a result, it can sometimes be problematic to try to interpret statutory sections in isolation.

2.9.2 The ejusdem generis principle

Ejusdem generis simply means "of the same kind", and this principle applies where a statute, which is intended to cover a wide range of situations, uses examples in the section rather than an exhaustive list. Therefore, if an Act referred to "Pigs, cows and other livestock", the rule would be engaged to say that the Act must also be referring to sheep, as they are of the same kind as pigs and cows, in that they are also livestock.

2.9.3 Expressio unius est exclusio alterius

This simply means "to express one thing is to exclude all others" and applies so that, where a statute specifically refers to something in a list but does not refer to something else, then it must mean that the thing not mentioned was intentionally excluded. If an Act said "Pigs, sheep, cows and goats", but did not follow those words with something along the lines of "and other livestock", then the correct interpretation must be that the Act does not apply to, for example, chickens.

2.9.4 The Interpretation Act 1978

This Act deals with common phrases and tells us how they should be interpreted. For example, section 6 of the Act states that:

> "unless the contrary intention appears: (a) words importing the masculine gender include the feminine; (b) words importing the feminine gender include the masculine ..."

Therefore, for example, when a statute uses the word "he", it should be interpreted to mean "she" as well, unless there is something in the statute that indicates that this would not be the correct interpretation.

2.9.5 The presumption against no fault criminal liability

All statutory criminal offences are presumed to require *mens rea*, or fault of some sort, on the part of the defendant. This presumption will only be rebutted where Parliament, in an Act, gives a clear indication that the offence is one of strict liability. For more on this, see the House of Lords decision in *Sweet v Parsley* [1970].

2.9.6 The presumption against deprivation of liberty

If Parliament wishes one of its Acts to carry powers whereby the liberty of persons may be deprived, it must make it very clear in the wording of the legislation. If the wording is not clear, this presumption will be engaged and the Act will probably be interpreted as not carrying the power to deprive people of their liberty. For this reason, criminal offences that carry possible terms of imprisonment usually make this very clear.

NB: There are a number of other presumptions which you may come across in a mooting context, including: the presumption against ousting the jurisdiction of the courts; the presumption that a statute does not bind the Crown; and the presumption that Parliament does not intend to violate international law.

It hopefully goes without saying that, as with other areas of the legal system, ignorance of these principles and presumptions can mean that you are making submissions that are completely unrealistic. It is therefore essential that you are aware of them if your moot involves a point of statutory interpretation.

2.10 Statutory interpretation and the Human Rights Act 1998

The enactment of the Human Rights Act means that there is now a further consideration when interpreting statutes. The effect of this Act is to give some meaningful status to the European Convention on Human Rights in English law.

Section 3(1) states:

"So far as it is possible to do so, primary legislation and subordinate legislation must be read and given effect in a way which is compatible with the Convention rights."

If a piece of legislation is clearly incompatible with one of the rights contained in the Convention, then the courts do not have to interpret the provision in a manner which the wording clearly will not allow for. Instead, they can issue a declaration of incompatibility under section 4. It is then for Parliament, if it wishes, to pass new legislation to remedy the incompatibility. For more on just how creative the judiciary have been prepared to be in interpreting statutes in line with Convention rights, see the House of Lords decision in *R v A (No 2)* [2001].

As with many of the aspects of the legal system that have been mentioned in this chapter, the Convention and the Human Rights Act provide lawyers and mooters with much in the way of fruitful avenues for argument. When the moot court will be involved in the interpretation of a statute, it is always worth trawling through the Convention rights to see if there might be an infringement of one of them, as a result of a certain interpretation of a statute. In that case, you can use the Human Rights Act, and cases like *R v A*, to argue an alternative, Convention-compatible, interpretation that suits your case.

2.11 Conclusion

As was mentioned at the beginning of this chapter, your knowledge of the legal system in which you are mooting can make a huge difference to your success and to the pleasure and benefit that you derive from mooting. If you are unclear on some of the key elements of the legal system, make sure you go back and look at it again. Knowledge of the legal system is, of course, only the beginning. It is the knowledge behind what will be the main knowledge required for successful mooting, namely the knowledge of the substantive law topics that the moot engages with.

When you first get your moot problem, it might be an idea to **list**, before you start your research, what you think are the main legal issues involved in the moot.

Here are some examples of lists based on *R v Owen Owens*:

Criminal law issues

1)   The meaning of intention in English criminal law (both direct and indirect).

2)   The elements of the defences of lawful force and necessity.

---

3) The grounds for appealing against conviction from the Crown Court to the Court of Appeal.

English legal system issues

These are sometimes harder to spot, as they may not be specifically disclosed in the moot problem. These may include:
1) Knowledge of the court hierarchy.
2) Ways of avoiding precedents, such as reversing, overruling and distinguishing.
3) An understanding of the status of judgments, such as dissenting judgments.
4) How to refer to authorities.
5) Correct modes of address for judges.

Mooters will clearly need to be able to start serious research from a position where they know the key elements of the law in these areas and what the leading cases and statutes in the areas are. Mooters are advised that, if they do not have a particularly good knowledge of the area of substantive law involved, then a basic textbook is a good starting point. However, after the basics have been acquired or remembered, it is essential to focus in detail on the primary sources of law and the more respected and narrowly focused secondary sources, such as articles in learned journals.

Note: these lists are for guidance purposes only, and are not intended to be exhaustive.

Once you have written a list of this sort, you can really begin your research in earnest. Be prepared for the fact that the list may grow and become more detailed as your research becomes more focused.

Part 2

The assessment of moots:

This part of the book deals with the assessment criteria for moots or, to put it another way, the things that judges will be looking for when they judge a moot. The organisers of different moots may give these criteria different names, and may put more emphasis on some of them than others. However, the criteria that are considered in the next five chapters comprise the main points that judges will be looking for you to impress them on. As will become apparent, there is some degree of overlap between the five criteria. Where appropriate, *R v Owen Owens* will be used to provide examples of issued raised in these chapters. Chapter **8** should also be referred to, together with the performance of *R v Owen Owens* online, as this provides practical examples and analysis of matters dealt with in a more abstract manner in this part of the book.

Chapter 3

Style and presentation

3.1 Introduction

Whilst this chapter deals with style and presentation, mooting obviously involves much more than this, and this should be borne in mind whilst reading this chapter. If mooting were just a matter of style and presentation, the legal side of mooting would be redundant. As a result, students could simply recite some poetry stylishly, whilst holding a long cigarette holder at a rakish angle, and expect to win the moot. Clearly, mooting requires a lot more in the way of substance than this.

The best advocates and, for that matter, the best mooters are a pleasure to listen to. They manage to make their submissions easy to follow, whilst dealing with often quite complex subject matter. They also manage to be persuasive and often quite charming, whilst at the same time appearing well organised and efficient. To the uninitiated, this can sometimes seem like an easy skill to acquire. In fact, many people, if asked, would probably feel that they already have many of the relevant skills needed to be a good courtroom performer.

One of the common mistakes made by many who start mooting is to think that the whole business is pretty straightforward, and that they can "blag" their way through a moot. The reality is that the polish and efficiency demonstrated by good advocates and mooters is, more often than not, the result of hard work and serious thought. When I first mooted as a law student, I thought that skill as a mooter was something I could take for granted. All I needed to do, I felt, was scribble a few witticisms from Oscar Wilde, or some such person, on the back of an envelope or cigarette packet, and the rest would follow. I did not hold this view for very long!

There is certainly an argument that the best advocates are born, not made, and it is certainly true that the vast majority of the best advocates start off from an advantageous position in that they are talented. Even so, talented people still need to work hard to make the best of their abilities and produce the end product that is seen in court. On its own, talent will only take you so far and, without the necessary hard work, judges may conclude that, whilst you have promise, you are far from the genuine article.

For the less-talented advocate or mooter, there is still a lot of improvement that is possible. It is true to say that even somebody starting from a very low level can make great strides, with hard work and a lot of careful thought. There are many students who have been involved in mooting and have started poorly, only for the penny to drop and for major improvements in performance and confidence to follow. Whether you are talented or not, the best advice is that you should initially work hard on your style and presentation in order to develop your technique and personality when appearing in court. To become a good courtroom performer, you need to give the matter your undivided attention. Watch moots and, wherever you live, go to court to watch good advocates plying their trade. A student who is serious about mooting should frequently attend the law courts.

The aim of this chapter is to provide some helpful tips on how to present your submissions in a stylish and persuasive manner, and to consider what the judges will be looking for under this assessment criterion.

3.2　Use of notes and scripts in court

For those starting off and finding their feet as a mooter, one of the most pressing issues is to find a technique that works for you in terms of what materials you will have in front of you when you stand up to speak in court. At one extreme, there is the fully prepared, verbatim script that can simply be read out. At the other end of the spectrum is the mooter who has no notes at all. For reasons that will be explained, it is probably best to fall somewhere in between these two extremes.

3.2.1　Having no notes and speaking "off the cuff"

In political speeches, it has long been the trend to speak off the cuff and without notes. The wisdom, if it can be so termed, behind this is that politicians will look like they are speaking from the heart. In the context of courtrooms and moot courts, there are a number of points that can be made about this. In terms of advantages, the speaker who has no notes will possibly speak persuasively and with conviction. They will possibly have good intonation and will vary the pace, volume and tone of their voice to suit what they are saying, as well as maintaining good eye contact with the judges. There is also something impressive about watching somebody who can speak well without having to look down at notes all the time, as it looks as though all the information they need is at their fingertips. Such speakers also appear flexible when questioned as they do not need to look at notes.

If all of this can be done well, the mooter will score highly in terms of style and presentation.

The problem is that political speech-making is very different from making submissions in a courtroom. Mooting is not about saying what you think or feel, it is about making submissions which refer to legal authority in order to persuade the court to adopt a line of reasoning. If you are going to do this, you will need case names, page numbers, paragraphs, citations from law reports, sections, subsections and paragraphs from statutes etc. As a result, unless you have a prodigiously good memory, you will at least need something in front of you to which you can refer, even if you are a good "off the cuff" speaker.

Additionally, there are many other problems associated with not having notes in front of you. The most obvious that will present itself to the nervous newcomer to mooting is the possibility of forgetting what to say, or running out of things to say during the moot. If you do not flesh your points out and structure them properly, preferably on paper, it is possible that you will forget parts or nuances of the point you are trying to make. This is especially the case if the point you are making is a complicated one. Why leave it all to memory when you can take advantage of a simple piece of paper to set your points out logically? Another aspect of mooting that was mentioned in chapter 1 is that mooting submissions are timed. You are advised to make the most of this time. If, because of poor memory, you fail to make your points fully and therefore do not use all your time, the judges will form a negative impression.

Because of the above points, you are advised to at least have some notes to give your submissions a basic running order that is well planned. This will also ensure that you do not forget to make important points. Remember, mooting can be a frightening experience, especially for the beginner, and memory loss is much more likely to worry you in situations where you are under pressure. Insulate yourself against basic problems, such as those mentioned above, by taking the time to prepare properly. If you leave too many matters to chance with the way you prepare, you may come unstuck in the moot.

3.2.2   Mooting with a verbatim script

Whilst the attractions of this are obvious, there are also many pitfalls. The **advantages** are that you will feel that your nerves are settled by having the security blanket of a script. You won't forget your arguments, nor will you have to grope for words. You will feel that you will be able to say everything that you want to say in the order in which you want to say it. Certainly, this added security can enhance your performance in many ways, as you may feel much more relaxed about the whole occasion. This is especially the case if you are new to mooting.

However, despite the above, there are many **disadvantages** to having a pre-prepared script. The first is that, in general, mooters with a rigid script present their arguments less stylishly than those who do not. The reasons for this are that, when you are reading a verbatim script, you tend to be less expressive. The variations in pace, volume and intonation, which otherwise make speech engaging, are reduced. As a result, what you are saying tends to be rather less interesting and, therefore, persuasive than it could be. The judges are much more likely to be bored by this sort of delivery, and are less likely to be persuaded to agree with your reasoning and find in your favour in the moot.

When reading from a script, the tendency can be to speak more quickly than you would if you were thinking of what to say as you said it. From judging many moots, I can say that judges often find the submissions of mooters with scripts too fast and, consequently, hard to follow. When added to the fact that an advocate who is reading is less engaging, this can have disastrous consequences on your chances of success.

Eye contact is also a problem for the over-scripted mooter. A submission is much more engaging and persuasive if the mooter is actually looking at you when he or she is speaking. A very negative impression is given if the mooter hardly makes any eye contact, but has their head buried in their notes. The mooter whose head is down looking at their notes can also sometimes be harder to hear.

One final problem associated with over-scripting your submissions is that, if you do have a very rigid script, then any judicial questions are highly unwelcome, as they can spoil the order of your submissions. Judicial questions are part of all moots, and you need to be prepared to be flexible in your submissions. If it looks as though, without your script, you cannot function, then the judges will notice this and draw negative conclusions from it. Sometimes, students who are over-scripted will respond to a judicial question by saying that they will deal with the point in due course. This is because they are afraid to depart from their script. Some judges will not let you do this, while others will simply note it down as a negative point.

3.2.3 A unified approach

So far, it has been argued that having no script is problematic, as is having too full and rigid a script. Each mooter will, of course, develop their own technique, but one good idea for the new mooter is to write out your submissions verbatim to start with, and then reduce it to more succinct **bullet points**. The benefits of this are numerous. It helps you, first, to formulate your preferred running order for the submissions you wish to make, and to find a preferred form of words to express them. The fact that you have reduced this to bullet points will then give you more flexibility in the face of judicial questions, and will mean that you will not need to be constantly reading from your notes. If you know your submissions well enough, the bullet points should jog your memory of the points you want to make. The fact that you have already considered a precise wording for your submissions will also mean that you are more likely to couch your submissions in appropriate language for a courtroom. Try practising with fewer and fewer bullet points as you become more experienced and confident. The less you have in front of you in terms of notes, the clearer your mind will be during the moot. It is very easy to become confused and inefficient if you have massive amounts of paper in front of you during a moot.

The great benefit of this sort of approach is that, at some point, if you want to become a good mooter, you are going to have to jump in at the deep end and speak on your own without just reading from notes. This allows you to do this in a reasonably secure way. This will improve the quality and persuasiveness of your delivery and will improve your eye contact with judges. You can even bring your original verbatim script with you to the moot, if it makes you feel more confident to have it with you, just in case.

3.2.4   Cards

Some students choose to write their submissions on small cards, which they put in a pile and hold in their hands. They then go through each card until they have finished the pile. It is much better to write your submissions in a counsel's notebook (or something like it) which can be bought at most legal stationers. This can then be placed on the lectern or the table in front of you.

It is important to remember that your notes should not be a distraction. If you are holding cards in front of you, it affects your whole appearance. If you are constantly having to change cards, this will be a distraction to the judges. Cards often make an advocate look defensive and nervous. At worst, you will look like a television game show host. I possibly stand to be corrected on this, but I have never seen a good advocate, either in court or in a moot, using cards. If you insist on using them, make sure that you do not clutch them in your hands whilst you are speaking. Make sure you simply have them in front of you on the lectern so that you can casually turn them over without it being too obvious.

3.3 Eye contact with the judges

This has already been mentioned briefly in the previous section, but it is certainly worthy of further mention in its own right. Time and time again, judges in moots comment that students appeared to be simply reading from a script, and that they maintained a poor level of eye contact. As was mentioned earlier, if you are a judge listening to a submission, you want to feel engaged by the mooter and persuaded by the submissions made. If the mooter is not looking at you, and you can only see the top of a head, then you will feel distinctly disengaged from the submissions that are being made. Just imagine a lecturer doing this at the front of a lecture theatre – it is unlikely that students would find the lecture an enjoyable experience. The same goes for general conversation: if the person you are speaking to cannot maintain eye contact, it can give the impression that the person is either shifty, untrustworthy, incompetent or just plain boring.

Despite the above, there are limits to how much eye contact is desirable. Obviously, you do not want to be fixing the judge(s) with a piercing and intimidating stare. The eye contact should basically be just enough to show the judges that you are not reading and to show that you are aware of the judges' reactions and of your surroundings. For example, when judges are about to ask a question they will show this in their behaviour in some way. Some students have to be stopped quite abruptly when a judge wants to ask a question, because they are completely unaware of the judges when they are speaking. Be aware at all times that you are trying to appeal to an audience, to persuade them. If you shut your audience out and occupy your own little world, you will not be successful in this respect.

3.4 Pace of delivery

One of the obvious ways in which good advocates in court, and in moots, make themselves sound professional and persuasive is by adopting an appropriate pace for the delivery of their submissions. Whilst some students will speak too slowly, the more common error is to speak too quickly in moots. The two most common reasons for this are nerves, as people often speak more quickly when they are nervous, and the fact that students are reading from a pre-prepared script. As was mentioned earlier in this chapter, this can cause mooters to speed up their delivery.

There are a number of reasons why too fast a delivery can cause problems for the mooter. Very fast speech, especially in a courtroom, simply sounds poor. Judges will expect mooters to speak in a manner befitting the court where the moot is set and to sound learned and professional. The chances of the judges forming this impression if your voice sounds like a machine gun are slim. Speaking quickly also makes it hard for the judges to follow what is being said. If a mooter is already halfway through his or her next point before the judges have digested the last one, the overall effect is that the points simply will not stick in the minds of the judges, if they are understood at all. If judges cannot follow your submissions, they are not going to be persuaded by them.

Your opponents, of course, also need to be able to follow what you are saying, so that they can respond to the submissions you make. The last point on pace is that, if you are speaking too fast, it probably means that you are not settled or relaxed in the moot. The art of good speaking depends very much on being relaxed and being able to breathe properly. If you are always trying to catch your breath and gulping for air and swallowing, you will struggle to speak well. If you do suffer from this problem, it is best to slow yourself down considerably, even if this involves a few slightly awkward pauses at the start. If you can control your breathing and relax, you will stand a much greater chance of speaking and mooting well.

There is nothing wrong with using **pauses** during your submissions in order to compose yourself, remember where you are in your submissions, or properly plan what you are going to say next. Nervous mooters often seem to feel that they have to maintain a continuous noise throughout their submissions, and that periods of silence are to be avoided at all costs. Do not worry about this too much. The judges will be impressed by the advocate who is able to think on his or her feet and compose themselves. Advocates who do not use appropriate pauses for this purpose will often lapse into waffle and, because they are not composed, say pretty much the first thing that comes into their head. As a result, a carefully planned submission on a complex point of law can be presented badly. When using this technique, it may be a courtesy to say something like:

"My Lords, can I just have a moment?"

If you ask something like this, most judges will give you a bit of time.

This will then give you time to consult your notes or to compose yourself, and, at the same time, the judges will know what you are doing. So long as these pauses do not become too lengthy and frequent, the judges will normally have no objection. From the mooters' viewpoint, they can be invaluable. In any event, frequent pauses are always going to be preferable to simply waffling.

3.5 Volume

It is often said that people who are engaged in public speaking in their professional lives, like lawyers, tend to speak too loudly on social occasions. If this is true, it is probably because such people are accustomed to projecting their voices in order to make themselves heard. It may seem like an obvious point but many mooters, especially when they are beginners, forget that they have to project their voice. Instead, some speak at roughly the same volume that they would if they were chatting to a friend who was sitting next to them. Some courtrooms are quite large and you need to speak loudly enough for everyone in the room to hear you. This includes your opponents who will often, depending on the layout of the courtroom, be sitting behind you. If you want to be heard by people sitting behind you, then the volume has to be increased even more, as your voice will not be directed towards those people. There is, however, no need to shout. You need to practise to find the right volume, bearing in mind your own voice. Some mooters will naturally have a feel for these things; for others, more practice and thought is required.

3.6 Intonation

Good speakers do not speak like Daleks. They vary the tone and volume of their voice, so that what they say is expressive and appropriate to the message that they are trying to convey. Good advocates and mooters, it goes without saying, have this skill. Those who read their submissions, or are too nervous, are much less likely to vary the tone of their voice and speak expressively. Some have this ability naturally; for others, it is necessary to observe good speakers in action and to attempt to learn from them. See the section later in this chapter about visiting court.

3.7 Accents and the use of slang

In order to be a good advocate, you do not have to be from an upper class background, nor do you have to speak in the sonorous tones of the great thespians. There is nothing wrong with having a regional accent; in fact, there are a number of high-profile barristers and solicitors who do. The main thing is that what you say can be understood and that you can speak in a manner that is appropriate to a courtroom. If, however, you are speaking in a way that can only be understood by people from a certain neighbourhood or social group, then this will not do in a moot. You need to be able to speak in a way that is intelligible to any person of a reasonable level of intelligence. As a result, the use of slang is not appropriate in court, unless slang is used in the moot problem and you need to repeat it to make your submissions. The same goes for abbreviations, although the reason for this is perhaps less to do with making yourself understood and more to do with the way that courtroom etiquette has evolved. For example, if you were referring to the "Royal Air Force", you would say just that, rather than abbreviating it to "RAF".

Unless you really want to, do not try to completely change the way that you speak simply to become a lawyer or, in the first instance, a mooter. Good mooters and advocates come in all shapes and sizes. It would be a sad state of affairs if all "good" advocates were clones, speaking in exactly the same way. Good advocates will certainly always have some characteristics in common, but they need not be identical. It will be much better for you in the long run if you can harness your own background and personality to become an effective advocate, rather than trying to change yourself too much.

3.8 Politeness and respect

Whilst the English legal system is, by its very nature, adversarial, this does not mean that advocates and mooters have to behave in an unpleasant manner when they are in court. Court proceedings, despite the underlying element of gladiatorial confrontation, should be conducted in a dignified and respectful manner. It is, therefore, not the point of mooting to be rude and disrespectful. This applies to your approach towards your opponents and, particularly, to the judges. Most English-based moots take place in the House of Lords or the Court of Appeal and, if you ever go and watch one of these courts, you will see that the proceedings are conducted quietly and with an element of calmness.

When referring to your opponents or the judges, make sure that you use the correct modes of address and are polite. Never appear to lose your temper or even to be irritable. Some students, perhaps because they are nervous or because they do not know the law well, have a tendency to look distinctly rattled when the judge asks questions or when the opposition disagrees with the submissions they have made. When you are sitting listening to the submissions of your opponent, you should, of course, be sitting quietly and taking notes so that you can respond. Interruptions are generally not permitted in moots, although you should check the specific rules with whoever is running the moot that you are participating in. The general rule, though, is that, if you wish to take issue with points raised by your opponents in their submissions, then you should wait for your turn to speak, rather than making interruptions. The use of "I object", as is common in many American films and television series, is not appropriate in a moot.

Remember, the judges will be deciding whether you have won the moot or, if the moot is assessed, what marks you will get. You need to keep them on your side as much as possible. There is more discussion of how to deal with judges in chapter **6**.

3.9   Body language

Whilst this is not a textbook on social psychology, it is worth saying a few words about body language. Obviously, the way that you carry yourself will have an impact on how well you come across to the judges. If you are slouching all over the lectern whilst you are speaking or sitting with your feet on the table, this will probably not look good. On the other hand, you may not wish to be standing rigidly to attention like a soldier on parade. The basic rule is that body language should be respectful and appropriate to the occasion. For more on relaxing yourself and dealing with your nerves, see section **3.19** below.

Too much movement can also look inappropriate for an advocate. It might happen in some of the films, but the reality is that advocates, certainly in England and Wales, do not wander around the courtroom while they are addressing the court. The general rule is that, whilst you can of course alter your stance and move your feet during your submissions, you should pretty much remain in the same place. If you do wander around during your submissions, this can look disrespectful to the court, as well as being inappropriate.

One of the modern practices is to record moots on DVD etc. The advantages of this are enormous, as mooters can see how they come across to others. Our body language is often something that we are not aware of, and it is often necessary for us to be shown what we are doing before we realise it. One particular area that judges pick up on is hand gestures. As far as this is concerned, there is a limit to what is acceptable in a courtroom. It is not theatre, and over-theatrical gestures are not appropriate. However, on the other hand, some hand movements can help to add to what the voice is trying to express and therefore get the message across more effectively.

The final problem with hand gestures arises when the mooter is nervous. As a result of nerves, mooters can do all manner of things, for example, tapping a pencil on the table whilst speaking, which are off-putting for the judges and detract from the performance and style of the mooter. The key is to calm yourself, slow yourself down and try to breathe properly. If you can do this, it is much less likely that these small things will be a problem.

3.10 Awareness of your surroundings

If you can, it is probably a good idea to visit the venue of the moot beforehand. The benefits of this are that you will have a mental picture of the moot venue in your mind whilst you are preparing, and will know what to expect when you arrive. If the room is very large or very small, you will have an idea in advance about what volume your submissions should be made at. You will also know how close the judges will be to you. Sometimes, if you are nervous, close proximity to the judges can be disconcerting, especially if you feel that they can see your notes. If you know about little problems like this in advance, you can plan how you will deal with them. You are also much less likely to be flustered than if these things are sprung on you at the last moment.

The most successful mooters are also the ones who are able to demonstrate that they are comfortable in the courtroom, and that they are aware of what is going on around them. Good mooters consider the judges, in the sense that they wait for them to find the appropriate pages and paragraphs in authorities that they refer them to. They are also aware of not speaking too quickly, and letting the judges take notes and digest the information given to them. Finally, the mooter who is aware of their surroundings will be constantly monitoring the response they are getting from judges throughout the submissions. This type of mooter will sense when a judge is about to ask a question or when the judges look like they need more clarification of a point. In conclusion, the mooter who is aware of his or her surroundings looks competent and professional, and makes the judges feel that they are dealing with somebody who is in control of what is happening in the moot. The importance of being able to be relaxed and comfortable in the court cannot be overstated.

3.11 Starting and finishing your submissions

This subject will be considered further in chapter **4**, but it is worth mentioning in this chapter, as the way that you start and finish your submissions may make a big difference to how the judges score you on style and presentation of argument. The main thing to remember is that you should be looking to start and finish strongly.

If you start well, then the first impression that the judges will have of you is a favourable one. First impressions are very important, and judges will often find that it takes a lot to negate that all-important first impression. As a result, once you have initially made a bad impression, it may be hard to reverse it. When beginning your submissions, you need to make it clear what you are arguing, and draw a signpost in the mind of the judges as to the structure of your arguments and why the judges should be persuaded by them.

When finishing your submissions, you have to remind the court of your best points and be sure to actually ask the court to do what you want them to do, namely allow or dismiss the appeal or, in the case of *R v Owen Owens*, quash or uphold a conviction. One of the things that disappoints judges is mooters who allow their submissions to end on a whimper, by simply staring at the judge when they have said what they want to say. Students who do this give the impression that they think the judge should be the one who brings an end to their submissions. This is for the mooter to control. If the judges wish to ask you some questions after your submissions have ended, then this is a matter for them, but you still need to be in control of the things that you have some control over. Don't just look to the judges when your submissions have finished, as it will appear weak. Try and finish with a flourish.

A) Starting your submissions. Seven stages to follow

Beneath are seven stages to follow which would get your submissions off to a clear and competent-looking start:

1) If you are leading counsel for the appellant, and therefore speaking first, you will need to introduce the other parties by giving their names and roles in the moot. For example:

"If it pleases the court, I appear as leading counsel for the appellant in this case, along with my learned friend Mr Smith. My learned friends Miss Jones and Mr Rigsby appear for the respondent as leading and junior counsel respectively."

2) If you are leading counsel for the appellant, you may wish to ask the judges whether they wish to hear the facts of the moot case. If they do not, just move on.

3) Say how many submissions you have (these should be clearly delineated so that the judges can recognise them as separate from each other).

4) State briefly what your submissions are. You could also briefly mention the main authorities that you are going to rely on in support of your submissions.

5) Tell the court what you will be asking them to do on the basis of your submissions, for example allowing or dismissing the appeal and/or upholding or quashing the conviction.

6) Inform the court that you will now begin your first submission.

7) Deal with your first detailed submission.

B) Finishing your submissions. Four stages to follow

1) When you have finished your last submission, make it clear that you have done so and that you are now moving on to your concluding remarks. The judges will like to know where you are up to, especially if the moot is timed and they are concerned that you are going to run out of time. They may also welcome the chance to hear a brief recap of your main submissions, especially if they did not hear or understand all of what you said.

2) Briefly restate your main submissions, with reference if possible to the authorities that you are relying on. You should particularly make sure that you end strongly by giving the judges your most important points again.

3) Tell the court once again what you want them to do as a result of your submissions. Take the lead yourself, don't just dry up – have some strong finishing lines well prepared. For example, in the context of a criminal moot like *R v Owen Owens*:

"My Lords, it is on this basis that I would submit that there was a material misdirection to the jury by the learned trial judge, and that the conviction in this case is unsafe. As a result, the appellant's conviction should be quashed and the appeal should be allowed. Unless your Lordships have any further questions, that concludes my submissions on behalf of the appellant."

4)   You should remain in your position until the judges indicate whether there will be any questions. Sometimes the judges may make you wait a bit while they think or finish writing notes. Try not to sit down or walk off to your seat until the judges have definitely finished with you. You do not want to spoil the effect by some kind of comic ending to your submissions, when the judges have to ask you to come back for questions. Your awareness of your surroundings is important here.

3.12 Dress codes

The normal dress for moots is a business suit for men and the equivalent for women, either a trouser suit or a suit with a skirt. Ask the organisers to see how strict they are about dress. Even if the organisers are not too strict on this, it may be worth trying to dress formally, as it makes the occasion feel more authentic. You may also feel more like a lawyer if you dress the part. If you do not have the appropriate clothes, and cannot buy them, then wear clothes that are as close an approximation to normal court wear as you can. Perhaps ask the organisers for guidance if your wardrobe or wallet is lacking in this respect.

Try to avoid wearing very casual clothes as these will look out of place, bearing in mind the nature of mooting. Some mooting competitions will also require that you wear a gown. If this is the case, wearing appropriate dress underneath is more important, as casual clothes could clash badly with a legal gown.

In spite of all of the above, it is highly unlikely that judges will actually mark down an otherwise good performance on the basis of dress. If, however, your performance is characterised by other faults, such as a disrespectful manner, or you are obviously poorly prepared, the judges may well see unsuitable clothes as an extension of these faults.

3.13 The use of humour and wit

If you are able to amuse the judges in some small way during your submissions, then this can be a good thing, as it will create a decent rapport between you. Unlike a real court case, mooting is fictitious and the use of humour is, accordingly, less likely to do harm than in a real-life case, where the parties are real people. The difficulty with using humour in a mooting context, however, is knowing when you can use it and how far you can go when you do.

Judges, like people generally, will vary enormously in terms of how receptive they are to the use of humour. Humour itself is a very subjective thing. There are two main cautionary notes that need to be struck about the use of humour. First, jokes can cause offence. Most jokes, especially the ones that people really laugh at, involve some misfortune on someone's part. If the judges, or others in the courtroom, don't like the joke, then it falls pretty flat and you can feel a bit of a twit. The second is that, if you get the wrong judge, or if you overdo the jokes and witty asides, you may give the impression that you are either making fun of the judge or are not taking the proceedings seriously. This is likely to cause annoyance and, again, will not be a very positive thing for you. The danger is that the judge will either not like the joke, or will feel that you are being disrespectful and not taking the moot seriously. Remember, mooting is not about you performing like a stand-up comedian or an actor. It is about you representing a fictitious client in an appropriate manner.

The best advice with humour in moots is for you to exercise extreme caution, and perhaps try to get a feel for your judges, to see whether they are likely to respond positively. On the other hand, if you can inject a bit of humour, wit or personality into the proceedings, then this can make mooting a more pleasurable and interesting experience for all concerned, as long as it does not go too far.

As far as the type of humour is concerned, you are best sticking to observational humour, and witty or dry delivery that has a direct relevance to the issues in the moot. Full-scale jokes of the "Englishman, Irishman and Scotsman" variety are clearly irrelevant and inappropriate to mooting.

3.14 Modes of address

A big part of mooting, as mentioned previously, is the ability to adopt an appropriate courtroom manner and to actually sound like a lawyer. One of the chief ways in which some mooters manage to look unconvincing in this respect is that they do not know the correct ways to refer to judges and their opponents.

3.14.1   Referring to your opponents

Never refer to your opponents by their first name. When you do refer to your opponents, always refer to them in one of the following ways:

"my learned friend"

"my learned friend Mr Smith"

"leading/junior counsel for the appellant/respondent".

When responding to your opponent's submissions, avoid falling into the trap of referring to your opponent as "he" or "she". Many mooters do this and it sounds very bad, albeit perhaps unintentionally.

The same rules pretty much apply when you are referring to your partner. The only difference is that you might want to reflect the fact that you are part of the same team when referring to your partner, for example "my learned junior/senior".

3.14.2   Direct references to the judges in your moot

This will depend on the court that the moot takes place in, as the correct modes of address are dictated by the status of the judge(s). As all English-based moots are likely to take place in the High Court or above, the correct reference is fairly straightforward. All judges sitting in the High Court and above, when you refer to them **individually**, are referred to as "my Lord" or "my Lady", as appropriate.

If you are referring to the judges **collectively** and they are all male, then "my Lords" is appropriate and "my Ladies" if it is an all-female group of judges. If there is a mixed-sex group of judges then, rightly or wrongly, the correct collective mode of address is "my Lords".

3.14.3   Indirect references to the judges in your moot

There are many circumstances in a moot where you will want to refer to the judges but a simple "my Lord" or "my Lady" would not be appropriate.

For example, if you wish to refer the judges to a passage in a judgment:

"If your Lordships now turn to the case of ..."

Another example would be if you feel that the judges are not persuaded by your first submission, you might say:

"If your Lordships are not convinced by my first submission, I would still submit that the appeal should be allowed in view of my second submission ..."

Basically, this deals with situations where, in everyday life, you would use the word "you". For example, as above, "If you would refer to the case of...". To use the word "you" in this context with a judge is regarded as a breach of etiquette, probably because it sounds too direct and could be regarded as not respectful enough to both the judge and the court.

If the judge asks you a question and you want to refer to him or her directly, for example, to indicate agreement, then the correct form would be simply "yes, my Lord" or "my Lady", as appropriate. These two forms of address can be mixed and matched in some situations so that you might properly say:

"My Lords, if I may now move on to my second submission. May I take your Lordships to the case of the Crown and Jones, reported at ..."

One final point that is worth mentioning is that you should always make sure that all of your submissions are addressed to the judges. Do not address your comments to your opponents – you do not have to convince them of anything. It is easy to fall into this trap, especially when you are responding to your opponents' submissions. Often, mooters will turn to face opponents when rebutting a point made by them. Don't do this. From the judge's perspective, it looks very bad.

3.14.4   Referring to judges from the law reports

During the course of moots, you will, of course, regularly be referring to the judgments of various types of judges from the law reports. The correct ways of referring to them are dealt with in chapter 7 (see section 7.5.11).

3.15   Going to court and watching

An absolute must for the mooter is regular visits to court to learn from real advocates dealing with real cases. Whilst mooting is not exactly the same as real court proceedings, you can still learn a vast amount from watching good and bad advocates in action. Ideally, you should become a regular at court during your student years, especially if you are seriously considering a career in the law. The benefits to the mooter are that you develop a feel for what is and what is not an appropriate courtroom manner, for the language that lawyers use, and for courtroom etiquette. For many newcomers to the legal profession and to mooting, these matters are not common sense. For many, these are matters that you have to develop a feel for over a period of time. From watching many different advocates in action, you will develop your own ideas of what is good style in court. Hopefully, you will be able to incorporate elements of the good advocates into your own courtroom personality. This method of learning is the perfect accompaniment to reading about advocacy and mooting.

You will, however, have to consider which courts to go and watch. Anything is better than nothing, but there are some courts that are perhaps better than others for the mooter to learn from. As was mentioned in chapter 1, mooting is not the same as mock trials. The mooter, therefore, is not generally involved in factual disputes and does not have to cross-examine witnesses or make speeches to sway juries. As a result, you may be best avoiding trials and concentrating on the type of hearing where lawyers make legal submissions. If you live in London, the Court of Appeal and the High Court are on the Strand, and are well worth many visits. If you live in a large city, then there may be a branch of the High Court in your area. Despite the above, trials are often the most entertaining hearings to watch. If watching a trial inspires you in terms of advocacy, then it is better to sit in on them than not to watch court proceedings at all. The point to bear in mind, however, is that whilst moots do have a degree of cut and thrust about them, they do not have the same type of cut and thrust as trials, where witnesses are being called and questioned.

3.16 Appropriate language

When you are making points in a moot, avoid using phrases like "I feel", "I think" or "in my opinion". In a courtroom, your opinions and feelings are irrelevant, and the court will only be interested in what your submissions are. As a result, the correct way to express yourself when making a point is, for example, "in my submission, the learned trial judge misinterpreted the case of *Woollin*", or "I would submit that the appeal should be dismissed". Initially, mooters can find this difficult, especially when combined with the modes of address mentioned above. A mastery of the appropriate way of speaking is essential, however, to becoming a convincing mooter.

3.17 Believing in your case

The simple point here is that you do not have to believe in the arguments that you are putting forward. As stated previously, you are making submissions on behalf of a fictitious client, not expressing your own personal opinions. It does, of course, help if you at least regard your arguments as credible, but lawyers would seldom earn much money if they only argued cases that corresponded with their own personal views. There is an argument that believing too strongly in the justice of what you are arguing is actually a handicap when appearing in court. Advocates are arguably at their best when they are cool and dispassionate. Any passion that is shown in court should be carefully simulated passion. When **showing** passion, it is worth exercising extreme caution. Mooting involves the making of submissions on points of law in an appellate court. As a result, highly theatrical, emotional delivery will seem out of place. Judges want to hear calm, coherent and eloquent submissions, not the ramblings of somebody who appears to be on the verge of a nervous breakdown. In a trial before a jury, there is perhaps more room for theatrics than there is in the calmer, more learned atmosphere of the appellate courts.

3.18 Practice

Adopting an appropriate courtroom manner takes hard work and serious thought for many who are new to mooting. You need to practise to perfect the skills needed to look the part when you get into the moot court. It may sound ridiculous, but a good idea is to stand in front of a mirror and make your submissions. You will see yourself in the mirror and develop a feel for how you will look to others. Additionally, you will get used to the sound of your own voice when it is being used in a public speaking capacity.

Modern students are also blessed with a range of recording equipment which was not available to past generations. Much of this equipment is to be found in the modern household. If you can lay your hands on such equipment, make sure you use it. It is far better than using a mirror. If you put in the necessary practice, you will start to develop some pride in yourself as an advocate. If you have pride in your performance, you will feel as though mooting is something that you really want to work hard at. That is the way in which the best mooters and advocates improve.

3.19 Nerves

Being nervous is a fact of life for anybody involved in public speaking. Actors, lecturers, politicians and lawyers, if they are being honest, will all admit that they have suffered from nerves at some time, if not frequently, during their careers. Being (generally) younger and more inexperienced, it follows that mooters are no exception to this. Nerves can, it goes without saying, have a great impact on a mooter's performance, particularly when it comes to the marks that are available for style and presentation.

The two main points that will be dealt with in this section are (1) how to perceive nerves, and (2) how to control nerves, assuming that they cannot be avoided.

3.19.1   Is being nervous for a moot necessarily a bad thing?

The first mistake that most new mooters make is to think that nerves are a bad thing. Of course, if you are absolutely crippled by nerves, this will not bode very well for your performance in the moot. In reality, however, few mooters get so nervous that they simply cannot function and go to pieces. For most, the experience is of a healthy and manageable degree of nervous energy before, during and after a moot.

As a result of the above, the first bit of advice, if you do become nervous before or during a moot, is not to try to get rid of your nerves. Whilst being nervous may not feel particularly pleasant, the reality is that, if you want to perform well, you cannot function without nerves. As long as they can be controlled, your nerves are actually a positive thing that you can turn to your advantage. The speaker who has no nerves and who stands stolidly in front of his or her audience, indifferent to their reaction, is unlikely to impress. Performances from public speakers that are impressive are usually those that have an element of dynamism, fuelled by nervous energy. Think of lecturers, lawyers or actors you have watched and consider whether they appeared completely relaxed, or whether their performances were characterised by a desire to please, persuade or entertain.

Being nervous produces adrenalin, which increases the power and alertness of the brain. As a result, you are actually more likely to remember the key points you want to make and think well on your feet if you are nervous. It also compliments the audience if the speaker shows a degree of nerves, as it demonstrates that the speaker cares about their reaction.

Being confident is fine, but it must be a quiet confidence with a nervous edge to it. The judges generally will not be impressed if you appear over-confident or arrogant. Advocacy is the art of persuasion. If you could not care less about the occasion or your audience, the chances are that you will be singularly unpersuasive.

3.19.2   How can nerves be controlled?

Assuming that nerves cannot be completely eliminated, the next question that you will want an answer to is, how can nerves be controlled and turned to your advantage? As noted previously, nerves can be destructive in some instances, but there is no reason why this has to be the case for the vast majority of mooters. Certainly, you are pretty much bound to encounter nerves of some form at some stage before or during your moot. How to avoid letting moots become your master will be considered in the following sections.

A) Preparation

It hopefully goes without saying that nerves are far less severe and far easier to cope with if you are well prepared for your moot. If you have prepared well, you will feel that you are reasonably content with the submissions that you are going to make. Your knowledge of the brief will not merely be the knowledge of somebody who has learned their lines. Instead, it will be knowledge coupled with the flexibility to adapt to events in the moot, such as judicial questions and points made by your opponents. Knowing that you have done the necessary hard work is, as a result, one of the best cures for cases of nerves. In fact, many mooters who do suffer from bad nerves do so because they know that they are not really prepared. Because of this, they know that they could easily be exposed in the moot. Even if you are prepared, you should still experience some nerves. If you are not, the chances are that your laziness will come back to haunt you.

B) Mental attitude

In the build-up to the moot, you may become more and more nervous. If this does happen, it is surprising how much of a positive effect you can have on yourself by the adoption of a good mental attitude. First, the time before the moot can be spent going over your notes, to make sure you are absolutely clear about what you want to say in your submissions. You can, in this respect, particularly concentrate on your opening remarks, so that you are confident that you will start well. A good start will probably give your performance a degree of positive momentum. In many cases, an early acquisition of some confidence can carry you through your entire submissions.

If you do get a bad case of nerves, the key is not to let it take you over. Panic is the last thing you need, so it is advisable in such cases to keep repeating to yourself that you can do this and be successful at it. Such a technique may sound ridiculous, but it is surprising how much of a positive effect it can have on you when you are going through a time of stress. Of course, it is not suggested that "techniques", such as the above, will get rid of your nerves altogether. They will, however, often provide you with the strength you need to control them.

C) The importance of breathing

The importance of breathing has already been mentioned in section **3.4** above. It is very hard to speak comfortably and effectively if, at the same time, you are struggling to breathe. If your breathing is poor, you will find that you often do not have enough air in your lungs to finish your sentence. You will look uncomfortable during the moot because you are struggling to swallow properly, and constantly gulping for air.

It is essential that you learn to breathe deeply from the diaphragm, without hunching your shoulders. Nervous people often hunch their shoulders, and the neck muscles are also tensed when this happens. The unfortunate effect of this is that a person's body language can appear rigid, tense and even hostile. Clearly, you do not want to create this sort of impression in a moot, but to look relaxed and in control.

A simple way of alleviating tension of this sort is to breathe in deeply a few times and then let the breath out slowly. As you are doing this, shake your shoulders gently to make sure that they are relaxed and let your arms fall to your sides. This technique is particularly useful before you get into the moot.

You may be worried about doing this in the moot itself, in case the judges or your opponents see you. Nevertheless, there are opportunities in the moot when the judges, in particular, will not be looking at you. An example of this would be when you have referred the judges to a case and they are trying to find the relevant volume or page. For a few seconds, the judges will almost certainly be looking down, and not at you. In any event, few judges will maintain piercing eye contact throughout the whole time that you are on your feet. As a result, there should be plenty of opportunities for you to take a few deep breaths and thus maintain, or regain, your composure. In reality, even if the judges do see you doing something like this, it should not have too drastic an effect on their assessment of you, especially if your performance is an otherwise polished one. As noted in section **3.4** above, it is better to slow yourself down a bit and get things right than to charge ahead and make a mess of your submissions as a result of rushing.

Chapter 4

Structure and content of legal argument

Introduction

As noted previously, the assessment and judging criteria dealt with in this book are not discrete entities that can be considered entirely in isolation. There is a considerable degree of overlap between them all. For example, if your submissions are well structured, then it is much more likely they will make sense to the judges. If your submissions are easily understood by the judges, it is much more likely that they will find them persuasive and, in turn, it is much more likely that they will feel like scoring you generously for style and presentation. Additionally, if the judges feel comfortable with what a mooter is saying, they are much more likely to ask detailed questions, which allow the mooter to score highly and impress with the answers.

Different judges have different ideas about how much weight should be given to structure and content on the one hand, and style and presentation on the other. There are some judges who will come down like a ton of bricks on a legal error, but do not seem to be overly concerned with issues of style. Others, however, will adopt the opposite approach, and be more relaxed about legal errors if a mooter has a good style and courtroom manner. The fact of the matter is that different judges will have different views as to what the purpose of mooting is. Some will hold that the primary function of mooting is to develop advocacy skills, while others will claim that it is primarily a test of the students' ability to apply their legal knowledge. The truth is that mooting is a mixture of all these things, and more besides.

If your mooting is an assessed part of your curriculum, the weight which is attached to the various assessment criteria will normally be advertised to students in course materials. The reality is that both style and presentation and structure and content are important, and that any mooter who has one without the other is unlikely to do very well. They are both vital. Without structure and content, mooting would lose its point as an exercise in legal education. As mentioned earlier, the mooter could simply recite some poetry in a stylish and polished manner and succeed on that basis. As a result, mooting would become divorced from the law. Without style and presentation, mooting would lose its point as a means of training students in the art of advocacy and persuasion. Because of this, you need to give careful consideration to all of the criteria on which moots are judged and assessed. On the one hand, you do not want the judges to think that you are all style and no substance. On the other hand, you do not want them to form the impression that you are a well-informed automaton, who merely reads out submissions in a dull monotone.

The aims of this chapter are to provide mooters with guidance on what their submissions should include, and how those submissions might be structured. It should be stressed at this point that there is no single right or wrong way to structure your submissions. Good submissions might be structured in many ways, as may bad ones. As far as content is concerned, what is appropriate will clearly be highly dependent on the area of law that you are mooting on. Notwithstanding this, however, there are certainly some useful tips that can help you to avoid some common errors. You should, therefore, feel free to be creative to develop your own style and structure, and use your own discretion in deciding what to include and what not to include in your submissions. There is no magic formula in mooting, but there are a number of things that the judges either will or will not find acceptable or impressive. What follows in this chapter is, therefore, not a strict guide. Instead, it is hoped that what follows will be used as useful guidance on how to impress the judges in this aspect of mooting.

4.2 The content of mooting submissions

As mentioned earlier, the content of your submissions will obviously vary according to the area(s) you are mooting on. However, whatever the area(s) involved, judges will be looking to give marks for mooters who can demonstrate a good grasp of legal knowledge, and who can be persuasive in putting forward a case using that legal knowledge. As far as legal knowledge is concerned, you will need a good grasp of the aspects of your legal system which are relevant to your particular moot. This is the one area of legal knowledge that you will need to demonstrate mastery of, no matter what substantive areas of law are engaged by the moot problem. As noted in chapter **2**, where some aspects of the English legal system were discussed in detail, knowledge of the legal system is something that some mooters tend to forget about.

In addition to the above, and perhaps more obviously, you will also need an in-depth knowledge of the particular area(s) of substantive law involved in the moot problem.

One helpful **preparation tip** is that it might be useful for the mooting beginner to make a list of all the English legal system issues and all the substantive law issues that are relevant to the moot. A preliminary list of this sort could be made when you first get the moot problem. You could then start your research and see if the list grows as your research becomes more detailed, focused and sophisticated. The advantage of this is that, during the research process, you can constantly monitor whether there are any gaps in your legal knowledge. A good general knowledge is highly beneficial here as, the more you know about a subject and the legal system in general, the more you will be aware of the limitations of your knowledge. If you have a good general knowledge before you start researching the moot, you are also more likely to think of good ideas for your submissions and dismiss bad ideas. If you start off with a poor knowledge base, it is very difficult to plan your research and assess it as you go along.

4.2.1   Checklist as far as content is concerned

The following **five headings** (A to E) deal with the main things that your submissions should contain. The ordering of them is a matter of structure and this will be dealt with separately later.

It should be borne in mind that you will have two main aims when you stand up to make your submissions. The first is that you will be hoping to persuade the judges that your submissions are correct and that they should adopt your line of argument. The second is that you will be attempting to refute points made by the other side and thus persuade the judges not to adopt the arguments of your opponents.

A) Opening remarks

The content of your opening remarks will vary according to your role in the moot. If you are leading counsel for the appellant, it will be your job to introduce the moot and the other parties. This will involve asking the judges if they would like a brief summary of the principal facts of the moot case. For more on the specifics of this, see chapter **3**. The judges will already know what the moot is about, but they will be looking to you to demonstrate the ability to show clarity from the outset in setting out your stall in the moot. This means that you have to make it clear that you understand your role in the moot, and what you are asking the judges to do.

For example, if you are counsel for the appellant, you will hopefully make it clear that you know who your client is, and that he or she is asking for the appeal to be allowed and the decision(s) of the previous court to be reversed. It may be surprising, but many weaker mooters seem to have difficulty in understanding who the appellant and respondent are, and which parties they were in any previous hearings. As a result, the first thing that you should do in terms of research and preparation is to familiarise yourself with the decision(s) of the lower court and consider how they impact on your client. This is the case, whether you are counsel for the appellant or the respondent.

As a result of the above, your opening remarks should act as a kind of **signpost**, which tells the judges where your submissions are going and why. Judges like to feel that they fully understand what is being said, and that they have a clear idea in mind of what you are submitting from the outset. Your opening remarks will be crucial to the judges in this respect. It is your chance to get them to really sit up and listen.

It therefore follows that, very early in your submissions, you should make it clear what your structure will be. You must stick to this structure and regularly remind the judges of it, and where you are up to in it, while you are speaking. You should also make it clear how many submissions you will be making, and briefly state in your opening remarks what each submission will involve. This way the judges will feel comfortable with you as an advocate, as they will feel that they can anticipate and understand your submissions from a very early stage.

Although mooting involves representing a fictitious client in a fictitious case, in order to be persuasive you need to be able to speak as though the outcome of the case actually matters. In the case of the sample moot problem, *R v Owen Owens*, the appellant, Dr Owens, has been convicted of murder at the Crown Court as a result of guidance given to the jury by Evans HHJ. Part of the skill of the advocate is to bring the law to life by helping the court to see how its operation affects their client. For example, counsel for the appellant may want to remind the court that the appellant is a doctor who was doing his best to act in the best interests of the patient. To be convicted of murder in such circumstances may be seen as somewhat peculiar. If you can weave this sort of comment into your opening remarks, then it will force the judges to sit up and listen to you, because you are bringing the issues to life by linking the law with the fate of an individual.

Some mooters, on the other hand, make their submissions in a slightly dry style which does not engage with the human issues that, were the case real, would be very important. As a result, it can seem as though they are treating the case as a purely intellectual or academic problem. This rarely has the effect of engaging the judges. In your opening remarks, you should therefore make reference to the potential injustice or problems involved in the court not adopting your arguments.

One slight note of caution is worth sounding here. As was mentioned in chapter 1, you are generally stuck with the facts of the moot problem. Please do not let the above allow you to feel that you have a free rein to invent facts and simulate emotions that cannot be justified by the facts. You should also bear in mind that, despite the above, it is generally not appropriate to present yourself as too emotional in court. You need to strike a balance whereby you have due regard to the human aspects of the case, whilst, at the same time, maintaining an appropriate courtroom manner. As was mentioned in chapter 3, you are appearing in an appellate court, not making a political speech.

Your opening remarks are a great opportunity to impress the judges and to create a strong impression. If you get this part of your submissions right, this will set you up for the rest of the time that you are on your feet.

B) The law and submissions on it

As mentioned earlier, all submissions made in a moot court should be based on legal authority or principle. The court will not be interested in your opinions or beliefs. You need, therefore, to ensure that your submissions are backed up by law or legal principle. To be successful at mooting, you have to learn to give the court sound legal, as opposed to moral, arguments as to why they should accept your submissions, and either allow or dismiss the appeal. There is nothing wrong with referring to the human or moral issues if they help your case, but any reference to them ideally should be backed up by legal authority or principle. The only possible exception to this is where you are mooting in the House of Lords and arguing that the *Practice Statement* [1966] should be used. Moral arguments may well carry more weight in this context, although, as noted in chapter 2, the Practice Statement is only used sparingly. Moral arguments alone may, therefore, not be enough.

One mistake which some students make is to give a very detailed general discussion of the law that is relevant to the moot, but not link it to the facts of the case. The judges will know the law. They do not need a general lecture from you on this. Instead, they will be looking for you to use the law to make a case for your client. General observations about the law in the area will not attract much in the way of marks, unless it is necessary for you to give some guidance as background to one of your submissions. This is more likely to be the case if you are referring to some esoteric point of law that the judges may not be familiar with.

In the example of *R v Owen Owens*, the judges will not want to listen to a lecture on oblique intention in criminal law. They will instead be looking for mooters to demonstrate not just general understanding of the law in the area, but to apply it to the facts of the moot and build an argument with it. In this moot, you would therefore need to look at the relevant case law and legislation, together with any relevant secondary sources, and see how these resources can be used to build a case for both the appellant and the respondent. The general rule is that, when you refer the court to legal authorities, for example, by reading from a case, you will need to add your own commentary to what you have read out.

For example, in *R v Owen Owens*, both leading counsel will probably want to read out passages from *R v Nedrick* and *R v Woollin* on the issue of oblique intention. Just reading passages out, however, is not enough. You then need to explain to the judges what your submission is on the basis of having read the passages in question. For more on this, see the discussion on the use of authorities in chapter **7**.

C) Your actual or positive case

This is closely related to B above. Your positive case is what you, as an advocate, are asserting and the reasons for it. The positive case is more easily identifiable if you are representing the appellant in a moot, as the appellant is the party who is arguing that something, namely the decision(s) of a lower court, should be changed. The appellant's positive case will be that the lower court's decision was incorrect and should be reversed. The reasoning behind this will be the authorities that you use to back up your submissions, and the way that you argue they should be interpreted.

If you are counsel for the respondent, it is easy to regard your case as a primarily negative or defensive one, as you will be arguing that the appeal should be dismissed and that the reasoning put forward by the appellants should be rejected. However, there is a positive side to all of this. As a respondent, you will be positively asserting that the findings of the lower court were correct, and that the authorities used by the court to arrive at the conclusion were the right cases and were interpreted correctly. To use *R v Owen Owens* as an example, the positive case of the appellant is that Evans HHJ's direction to the jury was incorrect on the issues of intention, necessity and the use of lawful force. The positive case of the respondent is that Evans HHJ was correct in the guidance he gave to the jury and that, as a result, the jury's verdict, in convicting Dr Owens, is safe.

In the above example, leading counsel for the respondent would clearly wish to look at the authorities relied on by Evans HHJ and the comments he makes on them. There are two ways that this can be approached. The first is to closely ally yourself to the arguments of Evans HHJ by arguing that he got it absolutely right. The second is to suggest that, even though the learned judge may have made some errors in his guidance to the jury, these were not sufficient to render the conviction unsafe.

In short, in your actual or positive case you are asserting something, rather than simply responding to something that has been said by the other side. There might be many issues, as counsel for the respondent, which you wish to address in your submissions that are never raised by the appellants.

D) Your response/reply to the other side's submissions

One of the things that judges will be looking at when marking or deciding a moot is the extent to which you have engaged with, and rebutted, the arguments of the other side. This can be described as your negative case, as it is the part of your submissions where you are not necessarily asserting something yourself, but are dealing with points raised by your opponents. You have to make sure, whether you appear as counsel for the appellant or the respondent, that you include reference to your opponents' arguments in your submissions. The timing of this will vary depending on whether you are counsel for the appellant or the respondent, as the appellant has a right of reply at the end of the moot. Counsel for the respondent, on the other hand, only gets one chance to speak, meaning that their reply has to be included in their submissions.

Mooting is not just about preparing your own submissions, ignoring those of the other side, and then crossing your fingers. You need to show the flexibility to respond quickly and effectively to what the other side are arguing. There will be much more on this in chapter 5.

E) Closing remarks

It should be apparent from the above that your submissions should have a discernible beginning, middle and end. As with your opening remarks, what you say in conclusion is an opportunity to finish strongly and thereby impress the judges. Unless you are very experienced and competent, do not leave these remarks to chance. Give some thought to the way you want to express yourself at the end of your submissions. It is the last the judges will hear of you, excluding any right to reply. You will want to finish on a high by reiterating your main submissions and asking the court to allow or dismiss the appeal on the basis of those submissions. See chapter **3** for some suggestions on how you might go about phrasing your concluding remarks in an appropriate manner.

4.2.2   The timing of submissions

Whilst it is certainly true to say that all of the above have to be included in your submissions, you must not lose sight of issues to do with timing. As was noted in chapter **1**, mooting submissions will always have a time limit, which will depend on the rules of whoever is organising the moot. The ideal situation is for you to finish your submissions close to the time limit, thereby making maximum use of the time available. At the same time, you will not want to go over your allotted time and have to be stopped by the judge(s).

When considering your content in the preparation stage, you must therefore rehearse your submissions to check whether you have too much or too little material, bearing in mind the time limit. If you overload and include too much material, you will have to rush through your submissions and will probably, as a result, score badly for style and presentation as well as structure. Submissions that are rushed seldom look stylish, professional or well structured.

4.3   Introduction to structuring submissions: your overall structure and the structure of individual points

Your main aim when you prepare your submissions is to make sense and to be persuasive. The judges will want to feel as though they are engaged by your submissions and they fully understand what is being said. One of the most obvious ways of achieving this is by adopting a sound structure for your submissions. As noted earlier, the assessment or judging criteria referred to in Part Two of this book are not to be viewed in isolation, but as overlapping. If the judges fully understand you, they are more likely to ask you meaningful questions, that will give you a chance to impress with your responses. If the judges find you hard to follow, then this limits what they can ask you. Many judges faced with this problem will simply question you in order to clarify your submissions. The chances of you impressing in these circumstances are remote.

This section deals with the two aspects of structure that you will need to address when preparing for moots. The **first** is the **overall**, or **macro**, structure of your submissions, namely the main, over-arching structure of your submissions. This should be a fairly straightforward aspect of your structure, but should not be over-looked. You should be able to think of your submissions in terms of them being a coherent whole that can easily be understood.

The **second** is the **micro** structure. This is the structure within a structure, which deals with how you structure the individual points which make up your overall structure, including your response to the other side's submissions. It is suggested that, in this aspect of struc-turing, you have more room for adopting your own more personal structure, but also more opportunities to make mistakes.

The reason for highlighting these two different facets of structure is that many mooters, while having a reasonable general or macro structure, fall down by not being well structured in the way that they deal with the minutiae of their submissions. As a result, judges will often feel lost and will therefore lose sight of the more general, macro structure. Students will sometimes complain when they get feedback saying that they lacked structure. They often feel that they did struc-ture their submissions, but were not given sufficient credit for it. You need to be conscious of keeping the judges with you in terms of them understanding your structure throughout the time that you are on your feet. To simply announce a nice, simple general structure at the beginning will not, on its own, achieve this, if you then lose the judges when you get to the detailed part of your submissions.

4.3.1   The overarching, general or macro structure of submissions

One of the first things to say about structuring mooting submis-sions is that there is no single right way in which your submissions should be structured. Having said that, at the risk of giving a sermon on the self-evident, there are certain things to do with your macro structure which do have to go in a certain order. As a result, your opening remarks will always be at the beginning, and your conclud-ing remarks at the end. Everything else mentioned in section **4.2** above will clearly go somewhere in the middle. Although this might seem obvious, the reality is that some mooters do not keep sight of the fact that their submissions must have **a beginning**, **a middle** and **an end**. Instead, some students get bogged down in the minutiae of their submissions, so that what they say when they stand up often just comes across like a list of authorities or submissions, rather than a structured argument.

For example, in *R v Owen Owens*, leading counsel for both sides could make many submissions on Evans HHJ's guidance to the jury on both direct and oblique intention, and on whether the conviction is "unsafe". In doing this, there are many cases and other authorities that could be referred to. If you are dealing with large amounts of often complex material, it is easy to lose sight of the basics as far as structure is concerned. It is therefore suggested that, throughout your preparation, and during the moot itself, you bear in mind your macro structure. This way, you will hopefully never lose sight of what you are trying to do in the moot and how, in general terms, you are trying to do it.

The table below provides a way for you to visualise a macro/over-arching structure.

Macro structure

1) Opening remarks (The content of these will depend on your role in the moot and whether you need to outline the facts and introduce the other participants)	How you order these opening remarks is a micro structure matter
2) Submissions ***Actual or positive case*** (the ordering of the submissions which make up your positive case will be an issue to do with your macro structure)	The way in which you structure each individual submission or point is part of your micro structure
Negative case or reply The point(s) at which you include your negative case or reply will be a macro structure issue, unless you are counsel for the appellants, in which case you will be allocated extra time for this after the respondents have made their submissions.	
Detailed reference to the law should be in this part of your structure; however, there is nothing wrong with referring to the law in your opening and closing remarks.	
3) Concluding remarks	How you order these remarks is a micro structure issue

In short, your opening remarks are your opportunity to say at the outset what you want the court to do and to introduce the judges to the reasoning that you are going to invite them to accept. The main body of your submissions is your chance to give the court the details of that reasoning, using appropriate legal authority to back it up, and (if you are counsel for the respondent) your response to the appellant's case. Finally, your concluding remarks are where you invite the court to allow or dismiss the appeal on the basis of the detailed legal reasoning that you will have supplied in your actual submissions. If the signposts in your submissions reflect what is going to be said and what has been said, then they will guide the judges to an understanding of your submissions. If your submissions and the regular **signposts** you give to the judges are consistent, this will mean that the message to the judges is consistent and regularly reinforced.

4.3.2   Macro or overarching structure and the ordering of your submissions

The likelihood is that you will have a number of submissions that you wish to make. Some of these points will be stronger than others, so you will need to decide how much time to allocate to them on the basis of their relative importance. You will also need to consider the running order of your submissions. Clearly, you do not want to start and end on a weak point, and for your strong points to somehow get lost in the middle. You also want to send a clear signal to the judges that you have an understandable and persuasive argument, which they can embrace from the outset. This section now deals with a number of issues that will help you to get this part of your structuring right.

Once you have made your opening remarks, you will need to make your actual submissions. As noted previously, it is likely that you will have more than one submission to make. If you engage in extensive research, there may be a number of arguments that present themselves to you as good submissions that you can add to your armoury. Nevertheless, the likelihood is that some of these submissions will be less significant than others in that they are less likely, on their own, to induce the judges to adopt the course of action that you are submitting they should. The question you need to ask yourself, therefore, is how to order your submissions to get the best out of them. Your aim will be to ensure that your submissions make a lasting impression on the judges, particularly the most significant submissions that you think are likely to be determine the outcome of the appeal.

For example, if you have three main submissions to make and one of them is the key submission that you feel is most likely to impress the judges, you will need to consider two things. **First**, how can you make the most of your main submission, so that it is a point that is really hammered home to the judges? And, **secondly**, how can you still use your less significant submissions to maximum effect, without them crowding out or obscuring your best submission?

There are many possible ways of ordering your submissions, but one good way of achieving your aims here is to make sure that you put your major submission to the judges first. In this way, it will be clear that this submission is the central argument you are relying on. The danger that you may be conscious of at this point, however, is that if you make your best point early in your submissions, then maybe the judges will have forgotten it by the time that you finish. They might only remember the less significant points you have mentioned later on in your submissions. The way to avoid this happening is make sure that you adequately mirror the submissions you have made in both your opening remarks and, more importantly, in your conclusion. By this, I am suggesting that you should return briefly to all of your main submissions in your closing remarks, particularly the strong ones. If you have done a good job of making your strongest points earlier on in your submissions, the judges will be impressed if you briefly, but strongly, hammer them home at the end.

The **benefits** of the above approach are, **first**, that you start your submissions strongly by dealing with matters that the judges will regard as crucial to the case. All too often, mooters will begin their submissions with rambling lectures about the general law in the relevant area, or with minor points which will not, on their own, win or lose them the case. As a result, the tendency of some judges will either be to switch off and miss the main points when you come to them, or to get irritable and ask when you are going to deal with key issues. **Secondly**, your submissions will be mirrored by what you have referred to in your opening and closing remarks. As a result, the judges will get the impression of a well-ordered symmetry in your submissions. **Finally**, by returning to your main points in your closing remarks, you will hopefully finish your submissions on something of a high, rather than with a whimper. The last thing the judges will remember is you making strong submissions on the key point(s) in the case.

Example of the above from *R v Owen Owens*

Senior counsel for the appellant in *R v Owen Owens* will be submitting that the appeal should be allowed due to a misdirection on the law by Evans HHJ on the issue of oblique intention. The most obvious submission to make is that the learned trial judge, in using the term "highly probable consequence" instead of "virtually certain consequence", gave the jury the wrong guidance according to the cases of *R v Nedrick* and *R v Woollin*.

Another point that could be raised by senior counsel for the appellant is that the judge stated that "the jury may infer intention". In *R v Mathews and Alleyne* it was held that the better direction is that the jury may "find" as opposed to "infer" intention. As a result, senior counsel for the appellant has at least two submissions that he or she can make as to why the conviction is unsafe and why the appeal should be allowed.

The second submission, whilst by no means wholly insignificant, is probably a far less serious example of a misdirection than the use of the phrase "highly probable consequence". As a result, this is a classic case of where you would want to make the *Nedrick/Woollin* point first. The point about "find" or "infer" from *Mathews and Alleyne* should certainly be made, but less time should be given to it and it should be mentioned after the other, far more promising point from the appellant's point of view. The prudent thing to do, as noted above, is then to return to the strongest point(s) during the concluding remarks, to make sure that the judges have not lost sight of what would be, for the appellant, a vital argument.

The key thing to bear in mind is that there is no single right or wrong way of ordering your points. The nature of the submissions might make it difficult for you to adopt the structure outlined above. For example, you may think that you have three submissions of equal value. Additionally, you may feel that you are dealing with a very esoteric point of law, and that the judges need a general introduction to some legal principles, before you can begin your submissions. An example of this would be if you were relying on a foreign case as persuasive authority in an area of law where there was no domestic authority. If this is the case, then clearly your introductory comments on the law will come before you launch into making any submissions on them. If your submissions are of roughly equal significance, then it may not matter which order you put them in, as long as they make sense in that order.

4.3.3   Mirroring and signposting

Mirroring is the process by which you ensure that all parts of your submissions are consistent with the whole. In your opening remarks, you will briefly state what you are arguing, what your submissions will be and, perhaps, how you are going to persuade the court that such submissions should be followed. It goes without saying that your opening remarks, your actual submissions and your concluding remarks should **mirror** one another. You should not be referring to matters in your closing remarks which were not **signposted** in your opening remarks, or which were not dealt with as part of your submissions. The only exception to this is if a matter arises as a result of a judicial intervention. Obviously, if this is the case, then you might not have referred to this elsewhere in your submissions.

Signposting is where you regularly, throughout your submissions, tell or remind the judges of:

A)   what you are asking them to do, for example, asking them to allow or dismiss the appeal.

B)   when you are:

  i)   beginning or ending an individual submission,
 ii)   telling the judges where you are up to in your submissions; for example, your second submission, your reply to the other side's arguments, or your concluding remarks,
iii)   referring to authorities or providing your own commentary on them.

Signposts in your submissions allow you to make all of these things clear. It is the advocacy equivalent of holding a signpost up to the judges and saying "this is what I am doing now", or "this is where I am up to in my submissions", or "this is what I am going to do next". As a result of signposting, you should make your submissions clear and easy to follow throughout. Most judges will appreciate your attempts to constantly communicate your structure to them and your place in it.

Example of signpost under A) above

"My Lords, as a result of the three submissions which I will make, I will be inviting your Lordships to allow the appeal and quash Dr Owens' conviction for murder."

You are telling the judges to expect three submissions and that these will be the basis of an argument to allow the appeal. The judges, therefore, know what to expect whilst you are on your feet, and can mentally prepare themselves for what is to come.

The **mirroring** here could involve saying something along the following lines towards the end of your submissions:

"My Lords, it is on the basis of these three submissions that I would respectfully submit that this appeal should be allowed and Dr Owens' murder conviction quashed"

What you have said in your opening remarks is mirrored by what you say in your conclusion. The detailed submissions that you make in the middle should also, it goes without saying, reflect your opening remarks and your conclusion. Because of this, your submissions will have a symmetry and tidiness about them.

Example of a signpost under B ii) above

"My Lords, that concludes the three submissions that I wish to put before the court. Unless your Lordships have any further questions at this point, I will now move on to my concluding remarks."

The mooter is clearly announcing that the main part of their submissions are over and that they will now move on to the conclusion. This could help the judges in many ways. They may wish to ask some questions at this point or at the end of the concluding remarks. Knowing where the mooter is up to in their submissions will allow the judges to make an informed decision. The judges may feel that the mooter is close to running out of time, but will now realise that the end of the submissions are imminent. Some judges are very strict on time limits, whilst others may give you a bit of latitude if they know you are about to finish.

Finally, if the judges know that your all-important concluding remarks are about to begin, they may pay an extra little bit of attention. This will particularly be the case if a judge feels they have missed or misunderstood part of your submissions.

Example of a signpost under B iii) above

"Bearing in mind Lord Steyn's comments on page x, paragraph x, it is my submission that the House of Lords in Woollin were intending to lay down something along the lines of a model direction. As a result, I would submit that any significant departure from the model direction must be regarded as a matter that would render any conviction unsafe. My further submission in respect of this passage is that …"

In this example, the mooter will have just read a passage from Lord Steyn's judgment in *R v Woollin*. As a result of the comments made, it is clear that the mooter is moving from reading out what the case actually says to providing their own commentary as to how Lord Steyn's comments should be interpreted. Sometimes, students struggle to make it clear that they are no longer reading from a case and are now back on their own submissions. This is especially problematic for those who are over-reliant on a script and who appear to be reading much of their submissions. Judges will often ask questions like "Are you still reading from Lord Steyn's judgment?" when the reality is that the mooter finished doing that some time ago. This example again illustrates the importance of signposts.

4.4   The structure of individual points or submissions or micro structure

Whilst the macro structure referred to above is generally going to be pretty much the same for all moots, your micro structure will vary enormously according to whether you are counsel for the appellant or respondent and according to the submissions you wish to make. It doesn't take a genius to work out that opening remarks should be at the beginning and concluding remarks at the end. How you structure your opening remarks, concluding remarks, submissions and responses in themselves is, however, potentially more complex. As noted previously, when you respond to your opponent's case will vary depending on your role. You will also have to give strong consideration to the ordering of the submissions that form the basis of your actual or positive case. If your submissions are ordered well, this can have a major effect on how well they are received by the judges and, consequently, on how well you do in the moot.

4.4.1 How to structure each individual submission you propose to make

As noted previously, you may have a number of submissions to make, which means you will have to put them all in a logical, persuasive order. This section, however, deals with the different issue of how each of those individual submissions should be structured as separate entities. It is clearly not enough to have your submissions in a good running order, but for them to be disorganised individually.

When you deal with each individual submission, you will want it to be persuasive, well organised and well structured. As a result, it follows that you need to have regard to structure not just in a general sense, but for each submission that you make. This is why the difference between macro and micro structure has been highlighted. What follows are **four simple steps** to ensure that your submissions include the right things and are structured in a way that will make sense to the judges. The sample problem, *R v Owen Owens*, will provide the setting for the four steps.

Step 1
Before you begin the submission, tell the judges briefly what it is.

In your opening remarks, you should have briefly stated how many submissions you are going to make and what they are. Nevertheless, when you come to each individual submission, you should make it clear to the judges that you are coming on to a specific point and say what it is. When you are addressing the judges in a moot, you are guiding them through your legal submissions. In order to do this persuasively and in a way that the judges will understand, it is therefore essential that you provide the judges with regular signposts so that they know where you are up to in your submissions and where you are going next. As a result, each time you start a new submission, you should announce it. Something along the following lines should suffice:

> "My Lords, if I may, I will now move onto my second submission and the second reason why I would submit that the appeal should be

allowed. In addition to the points made in my first submission, I would further submit that the learned trial judge misdirected the jury in stating that ..."

Step 2
Make reference to the law upon which you wish to rely.

As discussed earlier, any submissions you make should be backed up by legal authority or, if this is not possible, by some legal principle at the very least. Remember, you are making legal submissions, not giving your opinions. As a result, it will generally only be weak submissions that are made in the absence of reference to cases, statutes or other legal sources. The next step in making your submission is, therefore, to refer in detail to the sources that you are relying on in making your submissions. The reference should be detailed, in the sense that you should read directly from relevant passages of cases, statutes etc. It is not enough to simply say that a case says something and then expect the court to take your word for it.

An example of an appropriate reference to the law would be as follows:

"My Lords, in support of this submission, might I refer your Lordships to the Crown and Nedrick, 1986 volume 3 of the All England Reports for that year, at page 1. In particular I am referring your Lordships to the speech of Lord Chief Justice Lane at page x, paragraph x."

You should then read from the relevant passage(s) from the case. For more on referring to authorities, see chapter 7.

Step 3
Give your own commentary/interpretation on what you have referred to.

One mistake is to read from cases and other authorities, and then not follow this up with any comments of your own. The reason for this is perhaps that students feel that what they have referred to speaks for itself. This should not be taken for granted, however, and references to authorities should ideally be backed up with your own commentary on that authority. Something along the following lines may be appropriate:

"My Lords, in my submission it follows from Lord Chief Justice Lane's speech that ..."

or

> "Lord Chief Justice Lane clearly stops short of saying anything in this passage which would confirm that the appeal should be allowed in this case. I would submit that the correct interpretation of this passage is that …"

or

> "As a result, my Lords, it is my submission that the learned trial judge in this case materially misdirected the jury in a manner similar to the trial judge in the Crown and Nedrick. I would further submit that the conviction in this case is, accordingly, unsafe."

As will hopefully be apparent, the aim here is to ensure that you are not just reading out passages from authorities, but are making it clear that you are making submissions relevant to your fictitious client's case on the basis of legal authority. As was noted earlier, you need to help the judges to understand your submissions throughout the time when you are on your feet. The judges will not simply want to hear what the case says, but will be more interested to know what your submissions are, based on the passages you have read out. Because of this, it is not enough to simply read passages out and keep your fingers crossed that the judges will infer how they apply to your case. These points need to be properly hammered home.

Step 4
State clearly what it is that you are asking the judges to do.

When you have followed the steps mentioned above, you need to round your submission off by clearly saying to the judges what, as a result, you are asking them to do. As long as it does not become too repetitive, there is absolutely nothing wrong, at the end of each submission, with asking the judges to allow or dismiss the appeal on the basis of that submission. Obviously, you will also be asking for the appeal to be allowed or dismissed at the end of your submissions. However, the judges' understanding of your submissions will benefit from such signposting in the form of constant reminders of what you are asking for and why. Another benefit of this is that it makes it clear when one submission is ending and another is beginning.

For example, something along the following lines would be appropriate:

> "My Lords, that concludes my second submission. On this basis I would also submit that the appeal should be allowed and that Dr Owens' conviction for murder is unsafe. Unless your Lordships have any questions, I will now turn to my third and final submission."

Do not worry if you repeat yourself a little bit in your submissions by asking at regular intervals, after each individual submission, for the appeal to be allowed or dismissed. As long as you do not overdo this, judges will often be relieved by aspects of your submissions which make them easier to understand and, as a consequence, more persuasive. Regular signposts are a very good way of making your arguments more structured and more memorable. Often, judges will struggle to adequately recall what some mooters were trying to argue. This may be because lack of structure made the submissions difficult to understand, and unmemorable and unpersuasive as a result.

4.5 Structure of mooting submissions and your reply (counsel for the respondent only)

For more general comments on responding to opponents' submissions, see chapter 5. The following comments will, of course, only apply to those mooters appearing as counsel for the respondent. In a moot with a standard format, counsel for the appellants will know exactly when they should reply to their opponents, as they will be allocated extra time specifically for this purpose. Normally, this allocation will be about five minutes, but it will vary according to the rules imposed by the organiser of your moot. If you are counsel for the respondent, however, you will need to give serious thought in advance to where in your submissions you will want to make comments in response to the submissions of counsel for the appellant.

One key point to remember is that you will not have long to prepare your reply during the moot itself. This is why you should give serious thought to your response before you get into the moot court. Obviously, you will not know exactly what your opponent will say in their submissions. However, there are ways of anticipating this, and these will be considered in detail in the next chapter.

The key decision from a structure point of view is where to include your response in your submissions if you are counsel for the respondent. There is certainly no golden rule here. Some mooters will get their response in at the beginning of their submissions, some will leave them until the end, and others will respond as they go along. You might be able to make notes on each submission made by your opponent and them deal with them in the same order at some point during your submissions. You might be lucky in that the submissions of your opponent deal with issues in exactly the same order as you have planned to. This can often be the case, as many mooters will simply adopt the order given to them by the grounds of appeal. If so, you can simply make points in reply as you go through your own submissions.

The relative merits of these methods will be examined in the next chapter. The main point to remember at this stage is that, when structuring your submissions as counsel for the respondent, you really need to decide **when** in your submissions you are going to deal with response points in advance. This will limit the extent to which the response that you make will interfere with the structure of your main submissions, and will hopefully prevent you from panicking in the moot itself. When you become more experienced in mooting, you will learn that a little planning goes an incredibly long way in allowing you to perform in an impressive and efficient manner. The mooter who leaves these seemingly small things to chance is seldom impressive or efficient.

4.6   Ending one submission and beginning another

This has already been touched upon briefly earlier. It is vital that, if you want to move from one point or submission to another, that you make it crystal clear to the judge(s) that this is what you are doing. This can particularly be a problem with mooters who, because of nerves, are speaking too fast, or for mooters whom the judges are struggling to understand. It is very easy for judges, without the signposts referred to previously, to completely misunderstand your submissions because they do not know where you are up to in them. If it is not clear that you have moved on to a new submission, the judges may well interpret your comments on the current submission as though you are making some confused and rambling point on the previous one. They will not realise that you are now talking about something else. Needless to say, this completely undermines you in your attempts to be comprehensible, let alone persuasive.

Another problem is that judges will often decide to wait until you have finished an individual submission before questioning you on it. It follows that, if they do not realise that you have finished a submission, they will become frustrated and detached from what you are arguing. They may then start asking you questions about your first submission halfway through your second. This is not a good situation, either for you or the judges. As a result, when you do come to the end of a submission and start another one, make sure you make this clear in a manner such as that suggested in step four in section **4.4.1** above.

4.7   Avoid overloading your submissions

One of the problems that some mooters suffer from is that of overloading their submissions with too much material, by referring to too many cases and other sources.

Arguably, this is a point that could have been covered under the comments earlier in this chapter on the content of mooting submissions. Nevertheless, the issue of overloading is also highly relevant to structure. When you are preparing your submissions, you will no doubt be dealing with a large amount of material in the form of cases, statutes, articles, textbooks etc. One of the key skills needed for the successful mooter or practitioner is the ability to deal with large amounts of material. As noted previously, your submissions will have a time limit. This means that you have to be highly selective in the materials that you include in your actual submissions. If you had unlimited time for your submissions, there might be many things that you would want to include, but which time constraints force you to exclude. There will be more guidance on being selective, as to what materials to include, in chapter **7**.

The primary danger to bear in mind at this point is that your submissions are not so content heavy that they lose their structure. Some mooters' submissions tend to end up seeming like no more than a list of points, rather than an argument with a real shape and structure. It has been noted previously that all submissions should be backed up by legal authority or principle. This can, however, be taken too far by some mooters. If you refer to too many cases, or if you make overextensive references to the cases you choose, you will find that your arguments become obscured by too much detail. You will also feel under pressure to get through all your material in a very limited time. Additionally, excessive reference to legal materials can also affect the prestige of your submissions, in the sense that they can tend to become somewhat trivialised.

You will recall from section **4.4.1** above the four steps involved in making an individual submission. It is in steps 1, 3 and 4 that you create your structure for your submissions. Simply stating the law without reference to the other three steps means that your submissions will have little or no meaning.

4.8 Conclusion

It will be clear from this chapter that the material that you include in your submissions, and the way that you structure it, is crucial to your success as a mooter. If your content is poor, you will probably struggle to develop a good argument, answer judicial questions or respond to your opponent's submissions.

If your structure is poor, it is unlikely that the judges will understand you well or be persuaded by you. As a result of this, it is unlikely that they will be able to enter into advanced dialogue with you in the form of asking questions. It is also unlikely that they will score you highly for style and presentation, because they will have found your submissions hard to follow. Finally (for counsel for the respondent only), it will be harder for you to fit a response to your opponent's submissions into your structure if your structure is poor in the first place. The only way to avoid such problems is by hard work in preparation.

Chapter 5

Responding to your opponent's submissions

When will you have to respond to your opponent's submissions?

As has been noted previously in this book, when you have to respond to your opponent will depend on your role in the moot. If you are **counsel for the appellant**, be it leading or junior counsel, your right of reply will be separate from your main submissions. This is because counsel for the appellant are given a specific time slot for replying at the end of the moot, after the respondents have made their submissions. If you are uncertain about the running order of speeches and replies, then the simple thing to do is to check with the organiser of your moot, as they will give you a definitive answer. The right of reply for counsel for the appellants will normally be given a time allocation of around five minutes, but this varies between institutions, so make sure you check with whoever is organising your moot.

If you are **counsel for the respondent**, be it leading or junior counsel, you will not be given specific time for a right to reply. This means that you will have to find a way to weave your responses to points made by the other side into your main submissions. Obviously, as you are counsel for the respondent, you will already have heard the submissions made by counsel for the appellant. In theory at least, counsel for both the appellant and respondent should therefore be in a position to respond to the other side's submissions.

Why is responding to your opponent difficult?

Demonstrating your ability to respond to your opponent's arguments is a key aspect of the way in which moots are judged and assessed. This ability is something that all judges in moots will be looking for clear evidence of. Despite the fact that most mooters know this, many still perform surprisingly badly when it comes to responding to their opponents. There may be a number of reasons for this:

1) Some students may be reasonably comfortable when it comes to preparing submissions and then going through them in court. They will have time to prepare these submissions and to structure them appropriately. As noted earlier, some mooters, unadvisedly, use a

verbatim script so that they can feel comfortable in this respect. A much more difficult aspect of mooting, however, is involved in having the organisational powers, the speed of thought and the intellectual flexibility to respond adequately to your opponent's submissions. As will be noted later in this chapter, during the moot itself you will only be given a very short period of time to cobble together something which is comprehensive, coherent and persuasive in reply. This is not an easy skill to acquire, as many mooters discover.

2)   Many mooters, quite rightly, spend a lot of time preparing their main submissions. Many do not, however, give enough thought to how they are going to organise themselves when it comes to responding. Because of this, mooters who look quite good at putting forward their main submissions can sometimes look quite poor at responding to the other side. The security blanket of having lots of time to prepare is taken away, and the mooter feels exposed. One of the aims of this chapter is to provide advice on how you can safeguard yourself against such difficulties.

3)   Some students seem to suffer from a mindset which means that they feel incredibly relieved when they have got through the main submissions that they have prepared. In this relieved state, they seem to lose the impetus to carry on the fight and really have a go at their opponent's submissions. This, to an extent, is understandable, as a mooter may feel that they have done a good job with their main submissions. In this euphoric state, they are prepared to sacrifice what they see as merely one aspect of what the judges will be looking for. Please avoid this sort of approach. If you are going to moot well and score highly, you have to be prepared to see it through to the end, and not make concessions to your own feelings during the moot hearing. This will be even more important if you ever go into practice as a lawyer, where a real client is relying on you to represent their interests to the best of your ability.

Another related problem can be over-confidence, or a false sense of security. Mooters can think that the response is only a very small matter compared to their main submissions. As a result, some feel that responding is something that can be done in an ad hoc manner. Such students, when they receive feedback, are often surprised when the judges explain the importance that was attached to the ability to respond.

4)   As noted previously, knowledge of the law is a key aspect of mooting, and is a key factor that judges will be looking for when they

judge or assess your performance. Generally, a student who does not know the relevant law really well will not make a very good job of responding to their opponent. Only a really sound knowledge provides you with the platform to have the intellectual flexibility to see the same law from a different angle. Some mooters only know the law just well enough to deliver their own submissions. When they are forced to respond to the other side or, for that matter, respond to a judicial question, they often discover that they do not have the depth of knowledge that would enable them to respond quickly and effectively.

An example of this is where the other side read out and comment on a different passage from a judgment that you are also using in your submissions. If you only know the passages that are of assistance to you, but have little knowledge of the rest of the judgment, then it is very hard for you to deal with the points raised in the short amount of time available to you. In this situation, you will probably just be reduced to repeating your own points on the case in question, rather than truly rebutting the points raised by the other side.

5) Linked to the above point is the possibility that some students will simply not spend enough time preparing for their moot. Lack of preparation shows itself right through the assessment and judging criteria for moots. Arguably, however, it is even more pronounced when considering a mooter's ability to respond. If you are not prepared, you will not have taken steps to anticipate and neutralise your opponent's arguments. You will probably not even adequately understand your own submissions, let alone your opponent's. In such a state of confusion, you will be in no position to respond in a convincing way. There is more later in this chapter on how to prepare your response to the other side's submissions (see section 5.4).

5.3   Why is responding to your opponents an important part of mooting?

Quite apart from the fact that it is something that the judges will be looking for, the ability to respond well to your opponent's submissions is important for a number of other reasons. As noted in chapter **3**, making submissions in a court of law or moot court is not the same as making a set-piece political speech. You are required to do more than simply say the things you want to say and then keep your fingers crossed that the judges will adopt your line of argument instead of your opponent's. Successful advocacy requires you to engage with the other side's submissions and attempt to rebut them.

5.3.1   The adversarial nature of mooting

The English legal system is essentially adversarial in its nature. This means that court proceedings can often have something of the feeling of a gladiatorial contest about them. An adversarial system means that the two sides in a case directly confront one another, in the sense that they will both seek to make the most of the evidence and law at their disposal. Advocates will have two aims in mind in this respect. First, the mooter or advocate aims to use all available materials and evidence in a manner that will hopefully persuade the judges to adopt the submissions that they are proposing. Secondly, the mooter or advocate aims to rebut the submissions made by the other side to persuade the judges not to adopt that particular line of argument. As mentioned in chapter **3**, although the system is adversarial, proceedings in court should still be conducted in a polite and respectful manner.

5.3.2   The importance of quick thinking and intellectual flexibility

Mooting and advocacy generally are all about showing the flexibility to deal with arguments put to you. If, as soon as you are faced with a decent opposing argument, you completely give in, this will not bode well for your chances of a successful career as a mooter, or as a practitioner thereafter. When you get involved in mooting, just like a lawyer, you have to get used to what you say being challenged and meeting such challenges. It is often said that good advocates are those who can think on their feet when under pressure. Most law students, if given adequate time to reflect and to weigh their reaction to a nicety, can get their heads around some fairly complex material. In the pressured atmosphere of a courtroom, however, it is much more difficult to think clearly and respond to submissions efficiently.

5.3.3   In order to know your own case well, you need to know it from the other side's point of view

Another reason why your ability to respond is important is that you cannot really say that you know your own case unless you can apprehend the weaknesses in it. As a result, a large part of your preparation for a moot should be dedicated to attempting to spot the weaknesses in your own argument and trying to insulate yourself against the attacks that might be launched by the other side. As a result, you should ideally dedicate some preparation time to preparing the case as though you were representing the other side.

5.3.4   Ability to respond as a means of testing your suitability for life as an advocate

As discussed in chapter **1**, mooting originated in the Inns of Court as a means of training aspiring barristers for life at the bar. Although times have changed, mooting still remains a means of testing your suitability for a career in the legal profession. The only major difference is that your client will be fictitious and, as a result, what you say in the moot will not have any dire consequences. Nevertheless the likelihood is that, if you have the ability to use the law to respond well to the arguments of others, you will at least have the seeds of what could be a decent career in the law. Do not just leave this key aspect of mooting to chance. Preparation and hard work will be vital to your chances. These issues are now considered further in the following sections.

5.4   Preparing your response

Some mooters will get themselves very worked up, worrying about what their opponents are going to say in the moot. Such students will often approach lecturers at the institution where they study, to ask them about how they can anticipate this.

It was made clear above that, contrary to the beliefs of some mooters, your response or right to reply is something that can to a large extent be prepared before you even get into the moot court. The tendency is to think "How can I prepare my response before I have even heard my opponent speak?". Whilst this is an entirely reasonable question to ask, the reality is that there are a number of ways in which you can make yourself ready to respond before your opponent even rises to their feet. Obviously, you will also want to wait until you have heard your opponent speak before you finalise your response, but there is so much more that you can do than just wait. The aim of this section is to give you guidance on steps you can take before you get to court. The following sections will deal, **first**, with what preparation can be done before the moot, and **secondly**, with what you can do when you are in the moot itself, to finalise the response points that you wish to make.

5.4.1   Preparing your response before the moot

Some mooters hardly give any consideration to their response until they actually get into the moot. By this time, it is often very difficult to prepare a good response, due to the time constraints and the fact that you will be under considerable pressure in the moot. The following paragraphs will hopefully show that there is much that can be done to prepare your response before you get into the moot court.

A) Using the moot problem and the grounds of appeal as a source for your preparation

When considering what the likely submissions of their opponents will be, many mooters miss the fact that they have a highly valuable clue right in front of them, in the form of the moot problem. As noted in chapter 1, the moot problem will contain the settled facts of the case (including any facts where there is room for dispute). The moot problem will also often include details of the findings of the lower court, and will always include the grounds upon which the appellant wishes to appeal to the moot court.

This information is absolutely vital when it comes to predicting what your opponents will say in the moot, as it delineates the acceptable matters that the parties can dispute.

1) The facts contained in the problem

If some facts are absolutely clear, then you are stuck with them. Other facts may be more open to interpretation and dispute, but there will still be limits as to how far you or your opponent can go without looking ridiculous. Sometimes your opponent, particularly if they are not a very strong mooter, may raise arguments about the facts which are unrealistic, bearing in mind what the moot problem says. This is particularly likely to be a problem if you have an opponent who has not researched their legal arguments very well. If they feel that they are short on legal arguments, they may attempt to bend the facts to suit what they wish to argue. Such arguments may well seem foolish to you. Whether they are foolish or not, you still need to know how to deal with them courteously and firmly.

Example 1

Counsel for the appellant in *R v Owen Owens* could attempt to argue that Dr Owens had, for some reason, not caused the death of the weaker twin or, even worse, that there is no proof of a death at all. This would clearly be a ludicrous argument. Although the moot problem does not contain a death certificate, or deal with issues of causation in any detail, it is clear from the wording of the problem that the weaker of the twins died, and that the separation operation was the cause of that death. To argue contrary to this would be to contradict the moot problem. It would also be an argument which is outside the grounds of appeal.

If your opponent attempts something along these lines, and you are counsel for the other side (in this example, if you are counsel for the respondent), it should be a simple matter to respond along the following lines:

> "My Lords, my learned friend has attempted in her submissions to question certain facts which are not, and have never previously been, in dispute. At the trial of Dr Owens, it was accepted that Glen had indeed died, and that the significant cause of his death at that time was the separation operation, carried out by Dr Owens. Apart from that, I have no submissions on this matter as they are not issues which are in dispute. Furthermore I would submit that such matters clearly fall outside the grounds of appeal."

Your opponent may also attempt to argue a point on the facts that is not as obviously wrong as in the example set out above. Instead, they may try to dispute facts that are disputable, but nevertheless go too far in doing so. If you look at the moot problem in R v Owen Owens, you will see that there are possible arguments that both sides could raise in respect of the expert medical evidence. More than one expert has been consulted, and there is also the fact that Dr Owens thought that the operation should be carried out and that his colleagues disagreed with him.

Example 2

Imagine that counsel for the appellant made the following comments on the expert medical evidence:

> "My Lords, the expert medical evidence before the court is broadly supportive of Dr Owens' decision to carry out the separation evidence at the time that he did."

In these circumstances, a response along the following lines might be appropriate:

> "My Lords, in her submissions, my learned friend, counsel for the appellant made reference to the expert medical evidence before the court in this case. Her submission was that the expert evidence 'clearly supports' the decision by Dr Owens to carry out the separation operation. My Lords, I would submit that, when taken as a whole, the expert evidence cannot be interpreted in this way. At no

> point do any of the medical experts, including the defence expert, say that it was right to perform the operation at the time that Dr Owens did. In my submission the weight of medical opinion before the court in this case is clearly against the decision to carry out the operation.
>
> My submission here is based on the comments of the Crown's expert, the defence expert and on the objections raised by all of the appellants' colleagues at the hospital. If your Lordships wish me to do so, I can go through these comments again for clarification."

It follows from the above that you should master the facts of all moot problems that you deal with. As a result, if you do have an opponent who tries to argue on the facts, you will at least be in a position to see when they have gone too far. If you have the knowledge to spot erroneous arguments on the facts of the moot, you will obviously be in a good position to deal with them properly if they arise.

2) Using the grounds of appeal

As with the facts of the moot problem, you are also stuck with the grounds of appeal. Although there may be some room for disagreement as to how the grounds of appeal should be interpreted, the reality is that the grounds of appeal provide you with a huge clue as to what your opponent should actually say in the moot. The reason for this is that the grounds of appeal, both in moots and in practice, are designed to set out what the contentious issues are. The real courts, and this applies in moot courts as well, do not want a situation whereby advocates and mooters can unilaterally decide to argue some new point that nobody was previously aware of. The grounds of appeal, therefore, control the subject matter which is in dispute, and they also control the particular aspects of that subject matter which should be argued.

As a result, if you read the grounds of appeal carefully and, from your research, gain a good understanding of the issues, you should be fairly successful at predicting most of what your opponents will argue. If their arguments cause you major surprise, then it may be that they have argued outside the grounds of appeal. Often, the judge will raise these issues with your opponent. Whether this happens or not, it gives you a good point to make during your right to reply (if you are counsel for the appellant) or in the part of your submissions where you respond to the other side (if you are counsel for the respondent).

Example

As noted in the previous section, in the example of *R v Owen Owens*, counsel for the appellant may, rather foolishly, try to argue that there is no proof of death and that, in any event, Dr Owens has not been proven to be the cause of the death. In the event of such an argument, counsel for the respondent could point out in his response that such arguments fall clearly outside the grounds of appeal. As will be discussed later in this chapter, weak opponents can be very difficult to deal with in a moot. Nevertheless, you may often have a weak opponent and you will have to deal with them.

In such a case as that mentioned above, something along the following lines would be appropriate:

"My Lords, I have already submitted that my learned friend has attempted to go behind facts which are not open for dispute, in claiming that there is no proof of death and no proof of Dr Owens being the cause of death. I would further submit that such arguments fall well outside the grounds of appeal in this case.

The grounds of appeal were, of course, drafted by the appellants. As counsel for the respondent, the Crown, I have had no notice of any additional arguments, other than those contained in the grounds of appeal. The court has not had any notice of these additional arguments either. Such arguments were not, as far as we are told, raised at the trial. The grounds of appeal state clearly that the reasons why Dr Owens is arguing his conviction is unsafe are the alleged misdirections to the jury on the issues of intention, private defence and necessity. There is no mention of any other legal issues, such as causation. As a result, I have no submissions to make on these points, other than that they are not issues that this court is here to deal with today."

The effect of the above is that you are clearly telling the court that your opponents' arguments are irrelevant. As a result, you do not have to make any submissions on them, and the court does not need to give them serious consideration in order to dispose of the appeal. The key point to remember here is that, if you know the moot problem well and if you understand the grounds of appeal and the law on them, you should not be too surprised by the submissions raised by your opponent. Occasionally, unrealistic points will be made by your opponents, however, and you will need to be ready for this possibility.

3) Use of authorities used in the moot problem

As in the sample moot problem, *R v Owen Owens*, the moot problem itself may well refer to some authorities, such as cases and statutes. These authorities will also provide you with several clues as to what your opponent may argue. You must remember that your opponents will be in pretty much the same position as you, in the sense that they will be using the moot problem as the initial basis for ideas for their submissions. They will naturally gravitate to the authorities used in the moot problem in order to see whether those cases help them at all.

Example

In *R v Owen Owens*, Evans HHJ refers to a number of cases in his guidance to the jury, at the point where the problem says "Evans HHJ held that:".

As counsel for the appellant, you will clearly be aware that counsel for the respondent's main task is going to be to argue that Evans HHJ was correct in using these cases in the way that he did. Counsel for the respondent is clearly going to try to find passages from these judgments which supports what Evans HHJ said at the trial. As a result, you will immediately expect to see these cases in your opponent's list of authorities. You must also read these cases and be prepared to respond to the points that are likely to be mentioned. There may be passages in these cases that contradict what Evans HHJ said. There may be passages which could be reasonably interpreted in a different way to how Evans HHJ must have done.

Alternatively, counsel for the respondent would also expect these cases to be on the appellant's list of authorities. Counsel for the appellant is clearly going to submit that Evans HHJ was incorrect in his use or interpretation of these cases.

The chances of either side using vastly different authorities from those mentioned in the moot problem are pretty remote. As a result, you should have a good idea from the outset about what your opponents are going to argue. This will become even clearer as your research progresses and you become more familiar with the moot problem.

B) Using exchange of authorities and preparing your response

As was mentioned in chapter **1**, most mooting competitions will require that all participants in moots should send a list of the authorities that they intend to rely on some time before the moot. This is known as exchange of authorities, and should be used as a key part of your preparations.

Whilst the moot problem will disclose a number of authorities which you strongly suspect will be used by your opponent, the list of authorities provided by your opponent will give you the most certain indication yet of what materials you will be up against and what arguments will be employed.

The general rule is that mooters should only include authorities on their list if they genuinely intend to use them in the moot. Any attempt at including bogus authorities in lists will be met with strong disapproval from the judges and could, depending on the organiser's rules, result in marks being deducted.

The benefit of exchange of authorities is that the cases used by your opponent should confirm what your opponent's case is going to be. If your research has gone well, you will probably already have a good idea about what your opponent's arguments are going to be. If the list of authorities provided by your opponent surprises you, at least you will have time to do some research to retrieve the situation. Exchange of authorities generally takes place a week or so before the moot. As a result, you will normally have time to read the cases that your opponent has submitted on their list.

As noted earlier, some students will not use the opportunity that exchange of authorities provides them with, and will not use the information that they get to prepare their response in advance. The lazy option is to simply wait and see what the opposition says, and worry about it when the time comes. Mooters who do this are more likely to respond to the opponent's submissions poorly.

If you do use your list of authorities from the other side properly, there are **five simple steps** that you can follow.

Step 1

Write a list of all the arguments that you feel your opponent may raise, on the basis of the authorities you have been given.

Step 2

Write a list of responses to all the points that you have included on your first list. Some of the points you come up with may not be referred to by the other side. For those that are referred to, you will have some ready-made responses lined up for the moot.

Step 3

If you are really well prepared in this respect, you could also back up your responses with reference to relevant authority. This sounds far better than simply responding off the top of your head, without referring to the law. If your actual submissions should be backed up by legal authority, the same should apply to your responses.

Step 4

In order to avoid confusion, it might be an idea to tick off the points that you have anticipated which are subsequently made in the moot by your opponent. If your opponent does not refer to a point that you anticipated, then, obviously, you will not want to raise it in your reply. The time spent preparing these points should not be regarded as time wasted, as any work which helps you to understand the limitations of your own submissions will help you. There is also the chance that such points may be raised by the judges when they put questions to you.

Step 5

There may be some points that are raised by your opponent which you do not anticipate. This is not the end of the world, as some responses can be prepared in the heat of the moment during the moot. If you have anticipated the bulk of your opponent's submissions, this will make life far easier for you during the moot itself.

Obviously, all of the above requires a considerable amount of work. Because of this, it is far better if the bulk of your main submissions are prepared just before exchange takes place. In that way, you can spend the remainder of the time, after exchange, fine-tuning your submissions and working on the five steps above, so that your response will be impressive. The benefit of following the five stages above is that you will have large parts of your response ready-made for the moot. This will take the pressure off you and give you a greater chance of impressing the judges with your response. It will also mean that, whilst your opponent is actually speaking, you will be able to concentrate on listening instead of frantically trying to write down all that they say. The list referred to above will mean that you should already have written down most of the points that your opponent will refer to. It takes a lot less time to simply tick points off as they are mentioned.

5.4.2   Preparing your response during the moot

Whilst there are many things that can be done to prepare your response before the moot takes place, logic dictates that you cannot be completely prepared to respond until you have actually heard what the other side says. As a result, no matter how much preparation you have done before the moot, you will have to wait until your opponent is on their feet before putting the final touches to your response. As mentioned in the previous section, however, hard work before the moot can put you in a much stronger position in this respect. What follows are a number of points to help you finalise your response during the moot itself.

A) Listen to your opponents whilst they are speaking

For some mooters, this point may represent something of a sermon on the self-evident. However, it is surprising how many students appear not to be listening or taking any notes whilst their opponent is speaking.

One can only speculate on the reasons for this. Perhaps some students do not think that their response is a particularly important part of the moot. Counsel for the appellant may be so relieved when they sit down that they forget to take much notice when their opponent is speaking. Counsel for the respondent has the difficult task of listening to their opponents' submissions before they have got their own out of the way. As a result, nerves may play a part, meaning that worrying about responding may be sacrificed in favour of fine-tuning the actual submissions that are about to be made.

Whatever reasons there may be for not paying adequate attention, you must resist them. The time when your opponent is speaking is vital to you so that you can finally put your response down in the form and order in which you will say it. If you have followed the five steps mentioned in the previous section, you will use this time to tick off on your list all the points that you anticipated and to organise and put in order your response(s) to them. If your opponent raises points that you had not anticipated, you need to decide quickly what, if anything, you are going to say in response to them.

One final point worth mentioning is that, just because you are not speaking, it does not mean that the judges cannot see you. Judges will normally keep an eye on the other participants during the moot, as well as the person who is speaking. They will take a dim view of a mooter who appears to be miles away whilst their opponent is speaking, especially if the response to those submissions is subsequently a poor one. Some students also make the mistake of looking disrespectful or scathing whilst their opponent is speaking. Such mistakes should be avoided at all costs. It is far better to remain impassive than to pull ironic or sarcastic faces whilst your opponent is speaking.

B) Use bullet points

In chapter **3**, it was recommended that, if possible, you should avoid being over-reliant on a prepared script. This is even more of a valid point when you are in the moot, putting the final touches to your response. At least with your main submissions you have plenty of time before the moot to prepare a verbatim script, if you are minded to do so. As far as your response to the other side's submissions is concerned, you only have a very short amount of time to decide exactly what you are going to say.

> ### Example
>
> If, in a moot with four participants, you are junior counsel for the respondent, you will be listening and responding to the submissions of junior counsel to the appellant.
>
> According to the order of speakers referred to in chapter **1**, your opponent will speak second and you will speak last.
>
> As a result, at the end of your opponent's submissions, there will only be one speaker (senior counsel for the respondent) left before you have to begin your submissions.
>
> If each speaker, according to the rules of your moot, is given 15 minutes for their submissions, then you will see that there is a very tight time limit on your preparation.

As a result of the above, it is clearly highly undesirable that you painstakingly attempt to write out your responses to the other side in a verbatim way. You simply will not have the time. You should also bear in mind the potential pressure that you will be under. Writing out full sentences in longhand will be too time consuming, and will require more concentration than you are able to give in the circumstances. The likelihood is that you will be writing whilst you are listening to what your opponent is saying. If you are writing out your responses in longhand, you will probably, unless you are very competent at this, be unable to keep up. The chances are that you will miss points or become confused at what your opponent is saying, because you have not heard it all. It is much better to master what your opponent is actually saying, and to get your head around the legal issues raised, than to worry about writing it all down verbatim. Finally, as discussed in chapter **3**, it generally makes your submissions sound more lucid, expressive and, therefore, persuasive if you are not simply reading them out from a verbatim script. It is for these reasons that, with both your main submissions and your response, you are advised to confine yourself to relatively short bullet points.

The bullet points for your response should include the following:
1) The particular comments or submission(s) of your opponent that you are responding to.
2) What your response to it actually is.
3) The reason why you are responding to it in the way you are. This would ideally include reference to authority, such as cases or statutes.

The reason why you should include **point one** above is that you are attempting to rebut an argument put forward by your opponent. As a result, you need to make it very clear, with the use of signposts, which particular bit(s) of your opponent's submissions you are attempting to deal with. Hopefully, the judges will be able to quickly recall the part of the submissions that you are referring to. Because of this, the response that you make will be more comprehensible. You also have to be aware of the possibility that the judges might not have properly heard or understood your opponent's submissions. If this is the case, it is important that you give an indication of what you think your opponent was arguing and put this to the judges before you give your response.

Point two is obviously important, because this will be your actual response to the submissions that your opponent has made. The judges will only give you credit for responding if they can really understand what you are saying about the other side's submissions. You must, therefore, make this point very clearly.

Point three is clearly linked to point two, as here you are providing the court with the legal justification for your response. Without legal reasoning or authority to back them up, all submissions are of limited persuasiveness. This is equally true of your responses as it is of your main submissions. One of the reasons why many students score badly on their ability to respond is that they omit to use authorities at this stage.

Example

In *R v Owen Owens*, senior counsel for the appellant, in their right of reply, might appropriately say something like:

"My Lords, I would like to deal briefly with my learned friend's first submission. This was that His Honour Judge Evans did not misdirect the jury on the basis of the Crown and Woollin, as the phrase 'highly probable consequence' has the same meaning as 'virtually certain consequence'. If I can go back to the judgment of Lord Steyn in Woollin at page ... of the volume that I think your Lordships still have before you ..."

5.5 Other points to bear in mind when responding to your opponent

The rest of this section deals with a number of other important points to remember when you are responding to the submissions made by the other side.

5.5.1 Address the judge and not your opponent

A common mistake that mooters can make is to address their response or reply to the other side rather than to the judge. This is a perfectly natural mistake to make. If you are dealing with points that the other side has made, it seems normal to address them directly whilst you are doing so. From a judge's viewpoint, however, this can look awful. It can also look ludicrous to the other participants in the moot. Opinion amongst judges is divided as to whether this looks simply incompetent or whether it is rude. Some judges take the view that it is both.

Always address your responses to the judges, and maintain proper eye contact with them. There is nothing wrong with glancing sideways at your opponent, but it should always be clear that you are addressing the judges. You are trying to persuade the judges. You do not have to convince your opponents of anything. It is probably best not to think of mooting as some kind of personal tussle between you and your opponent. It is much better to think of it as you attempting to persuade the judges of the veracity of your own submissions.

5.5.2   Remain courteous to your opponent

As noted in chapter **3**, one of the hallmarks of a good advocate is the ability to remain calm in the face of opposition and to retain a certain dignity throughout the proceedings. One place where the mask can slip with mooters is during their response or right of reply. Not surprisingly, some mooters become distinctly rattled when they hear their carefully prepared arguments traduced by their opponents. It is not uncommon for mooters, anxious to respond, to forget basic manners.

One of the ways in which this often manifests itself is in referring to opponents as "him" or "her", or by using expressions such as "he said" or "she said". Always refer to your opponent in a polite but formal way, either as "my learned friend" or as, for example, "senior counsel for the appellant".

You should never get personal, or accuse your opponent of lying. If you strongly disagree with a submission or comment made by the other side, confine yourself to polite but firm responses.

Example

"My Lords, my learned friend has strongly contended that the case of the Crown and Mathews and Alleyne is not relevant to this ground of appeal. I would equally strongly respond that this case is indeed relevant. Can I refer your Lordships back to page ... of the judgment ..."

5.5.3   Do not just repeat your submissions

These comments apply primarily to mooters who appear as counsel for the appellant and who, as a result, have a separate allocation of time in which to reply.

A common default position for mooters, who have not properly prepared a response, is to simply repeat the submissions that they have already made. You should remember that your response or right of reply is just that: it is your chance to deal with points raised by your opponents in their submissions.

As a result, the general rule is that you should not be mentioning points unless the submissions of your opponent oblige you to do so, or give you the right to do so. You should not be storing up good points of your own, which could have been mentioned in your main submissions, for your reply. If you mention things in your reply, which were not brought up by your opponent in their submissions, a judge who is really paying attention will ask you why you are referring to it at that point. If you cannot answer the question satisfactorily, then the judge may refuse to let you continue with that point.

On the other hand, the above comments should not be interpreted as meaning that you should never repeat any of your submissions in your reply. Your opponent, counsel for the respondent, will already have replied to your main submissions. In order to defend your submissions against the comments made by your opponent, you may need to reiterate them to some extent.

Example

"My Lords, in her submissions my learned friend made a number of references to my first submission, namely, that the learned judge misdirected the jury on the issue of oblique intention. It was my learned friend's contention that there was no material misdirection to the jury which could render the conviction unsafe. I would respond to my learned friend's comments by submitting that, in light of the Crown and Woollin, this must be incorrect. Could I refer your Lordships back to that case, in particular, to page ..."

Additionally, your opponent may, either deliberately or otherwise, have twisted or misinterpreted your submissions. If this is the case, there is nothing wrong with briefly reiterating the relevant submissions, so that the judges are sure about what you are submitting. At the end of your reply, you may also wish to finish strongly by hammering home your main submissions. The problem with this, however, is that you may already have done this at the end of your main submissions. Doing it again at the end of the reply can seem a bit repetitive. The other obvious danger is that it might test the patience of the judges, just before you are about to sit down. As a result, the last impression the judges will have of you could be a negative one.

°<AQ5 **5.5.4** Timing issues

As noted previously, counsel for the appellant will normally get an extra period of time in order to reply. This will usually be in the order of five minutes. Weaker mooters often feel that they will never be able to fill five minutes, bearing in mind how little they will have prepared. For the better mooters, however, five minutes is no time at all. If you are well prepared for your response, the chances are that you will need to be careful that you do not go over the allocated time.

Similarly, counsel for the respondent will have to leave some time spare in their allocation of time, so that there is space for a decent response. As noted in chapter **1**, you need to use the time available to you to the best advantage. If you have five minutes available for your reply, you will want to fill as much of that time as possible with good responses to your opponent's arguments.

5.5.5 Responding to a poor opponent

To the uninitiated, this may seem very straightforward indeed. What, you may think, could be more simple than responding to a poor opponent? Surely they will have made many mistakes which you will be able to pick up on. Whilst this is obviously true in some cases, in others, responding to a poor opponent can be a very difficult proposition.

A) The opponent who cannot be heard

Some weaker mooters will deliver their submissions in a timid whisper. Whilst you can be happy about this in terms of the impression that they will make on the judges, it can play havoc with your ability to respond.

This can be even more problematic depending on the layout of the court. In many moot courts, the person speaking may stand at a lectern or desk in front of the other participants. If your opponent has their back to you, and speaks very quietly, it will be very difficult for you to hear what is being said. The judge(s) should be aware of this as a potential problem, and should ask the person speaking to increase the volume of their submissions. However, this does not always work. A weaker mooter, who is also perhaps very nervous, may increase the volume for a few moments before reverting to the old, inaudible delivery. Most moot judges will be able to recall occasions where they have repeatedly asked mooters to speak up, but to no avail.

From the mooter's perspective, this creates a huge problem in terms of your ability to respond. How can you respond to something that you cannot hear? Earlier in this chapter, guidance was given on how to prepare your response before the moot takes place. If you are struggling to hear your opponent in the moot, you will still have the moot problem, the grounds of appeal and the list of authorities that they have submitted.

If you really cannot hear anything, which is unlikely, the only option is to use these sources to respond as best you can to what the submissions of your opponent should be, based on the moot problem and the authorities they have sent you. Hopefully, you will be able to hear something of what your opponent says. If so, you can use the moot problem and the list of authorities, together with what you can hear, to get a flavour of what is being said. Earlier in the chapter, it was suggested that, in preparing your response in advance, you could write a list of the most likely submissions your opponent will make. If you have done this well, such a list is just as valuable to you in dealing with a poor opponent as it is with a brilliant one. Even if you are struggling to hear, you are more likely to spot a familiar and antici-pated argument than you are one that is completely new to you.

Finally, and perhaps most obviously, there is nothing wrong with telling the court that you struggled to hear what your opponent was saying. As long as you do this in a courteous manner, it is perfectly proper. Where you do this it is, however, much better, if possible, to combine it with having a go at discerning what your opponent was saying. If you simply say that you could not hear, this will be a very short response. You will encounter further problems if the judges feel that it was not as difficult to hear as you suggest. One thing you should not do, unless the rules of your moot say it is acceptable, is jump up and object whilst your opponent is speaking.

Example

Something along the following lines would be an appropriate way of dealing with the above situation:

"My Lords, unfortunately I found large parts of my learned friend's submissions fairly difficult to hear. This makes it rather difficult for me to respond adequately to all the submissions made. Nevertheless, I believe that my learned friend's first submission, in line with the grounds of appeal, was that there was no material misdirection by the learned trial judge on the issue of oblique intention. If I have under-stood my learned friend's submission correctly, I would respond by asking your Lordships to look once again at the judgment in the Crown and Nedrick, in particular page ..."

The benefits of the example above are that you are showing the courage to say that you could not hear your opponent, but at the same time being courteous in doing so. Additionally, whilst you are not sure of the precise nature of the first submission made by the other side, you are still attempting to respond to it as best you can.

In these circumstances, the judges might help you out and say what they think the submission was. If this happens, accept what the judge says and respond to it; but if you have a credible alternative idea, put that to the judges as well.

B) The opponent who cannot be understood

With some opponents, you might be able to hear them loud and clear, but will not be able to understand the logic of what they are submitting. This could be caused by a number of factors: the content of the arguments used may simply be wrong, or it may be structured in a way that makes it hard to follow, or appear to have no structure at all. Additionally, the presentational skills of your opponent may be poor, so that it is hard to engage with what they are saying. This can particularly be the case with mooters who are simply reading from a script. It can sound very boring and, consequently, be hard to follow. You must also be prepared to examine yourself, and consider whether you might have something to do with the misunderstanding.

As with the opponent who is hard to hear, you must not stand up and object whilst they are speaking, and you must remain courteous when pointing out the difficulties you have experienced. As with the inaudible opponent, the best way to insulate yourself against this problem is to prepare your response well in advance, so that you are familiar with the likely arguments to be raised. This way, you will be far more skilled at spotting the submissions that your opponent is making, irrespective of their deficiencies as an advocate.

As with the situation where you cannot hear your opponent, there is nothing wrong with explaining that you were unable to follow your opponent's submissions, as long as there are reasonable grounds for having such difficulties. In this situation, to avoid too short a response, you should always attempt to respond to the other side. If you simply stand up and say that you did not understand, your response will seem far too short and perhaps lazy. This will especially be a problem if the judges found your opponent's submissions easier to understand than you did.

A good mooter should always be slow to attribute lack of under-standing on their part to the inadequacies of their opponent. It is only in rare cases that you should attempt to claim that you find it difficult to respond because of the way your opponent presented their submissions. If the judges found your opponent's arguments fairly easy to follow, and you are claiming otherwise, the likelihood is that the judges will not look favourably on you. The judges may give you a clue in the way they question your opponent. If they seem very dissatisfied and confused, then this will reinforce your own impression of your opponent's submissions. However, even if the judges do adopt a hard line with your opponent, you must remember that you are not a judge and that you need to remain courteous to all participants in the moot, not just the judges.

5.5.6   Dealing with a strong opponent

In mooting, as in practice, you will come across some very bright people. Some will appear to have a wonderful grasp of the law and will deliver their submissions in a highly appropriate and professional manner. Having a good opponent can actually be an advantage in a number of ways. As far as responding is concerned, it is much easier to follow, and therefore respond to, the submissions of a highly competent mooter. This only applies, however, if you are well enough prepared to follow the more sophisticated arguments that might be put forward.

One final point about dealing with a strong opponent is not to allow yourself to be intimidated. Most mooters are people who want to practise law. Very good advocates exist; this is a fact of life. If you want to be a lawyer, then you have to aim high and be prepared to take on the best. If your opponent's submissions are brilliant, do not let this take the wind out of your sails. You will need to decide whether you really want to compete with such people and whether you really feel that you can. One of the best ways of learning mooting and advocacy skills is to watch those who have mastered the art. If you do come up against good opposition, do not let this put you off. Treat it as an opportunity to learn and improve your own advocacy skills.

Mooting is a learning method, a preparation for your future legal career. There will always be somebody out there who is better than you are. Do not take yourself too seriously too soon. You need to learn to take a pride in your advocacy skills, but still not be too proud to learn.

Chapter 6

Dealing with the judges in a moot

6.1 Introduction

One of the key things that judges will consider when they come to judge or assess a moot is the way in which the participants interacted with them. There are many issues that the new mooter will be uncertain about in dealing with the judges. This chapter considers the main questions that the new mooter will need guidance on in order to deal with judges in an appropriate and professional manner. As noted previously, mooting is all about persuading judges to adopt your submissions over those of the other side. You are far more likely to do this if your interaction with the judges themselves is successful. If the way that you interact with judges is maladroit and characterised by infelicities of behaviour, it follows that you are less likely to be persuasive.

As far as the scoring of moots is concerned, either for competition or assessment purposes, one of the criteria that judges will often use is how well the mooter responded to judicial questions. As noted previously, a moot is not just an opportunity to make a pre-prepared speech, with no interruptions. It is also about responding to your opponents and interacting with the judges. In order to do this successfully, you need good knowledge of the area(s) that you are mooting on and the flexibility to consider the other people involved in the moot, and what they have to say about the moot case.

As a result, this is another area where students sometimes score badly in moots. If you are poorly prepared, the chances are that any judicial questions will not provide you with a chance to shine. Instead, they can provide some poorly prepared mooters with a chance to look bad. The aim of this chapter is to enable you to prepare adequately for your interactions with the judges.

6.2 Dealing with questions from the judges

Questions from the bench are inevitable. This section deals with a number of issues to do with judicial questioning, and helps you to avoid the many problems that some mooters encounter when the judges intervene with a question.

6.2.1   Allow the judges to interrupt you

As noted previously, judicial questions are a fact of life for mooters. As a result, you should be expecting them. When you are making your submissions, you need to be prepared for the possibility that, at any given time, the judge(s) could decide to stop you and ask a question. One of the mistakes that some students make is to carry on speaking, even though the judge has already begun to ask a question.

Part of the problem here is that some students are not sufficiently aware of what is going on around them (for more on awareness of surroundings, see chapter 3). Often, judges will indicate by their body language that they are about to intervene with a question. If you are watching a person, there are many possible clues that help you to see that they are about to speak, for example, a sharper intake of breath or a hand movement may indicate that a question is coming. If you have your head down and are just reading from a script, you probably will not notice things like this. As a result, you are more likely to have to be rudely interrupted by the judges whilst you are in mid-sentence. If you are speaking without undue reliance on notes, you are more likely to be aware of the judge(s) and when a question is imminent. Because of this, you can stop at a more appropriate moment to allow the judge to ask the question.

Alternatively, some judges may have a slightly more abrasive manner, and will ask a question without giving any warning that they are about to do so. This is something that you also need to be prepared for. The moment that the judge starts to speak, you should stop speaking. There should not be a few awkward seconds where you and the judge are effectively competing to be heard. You must remember that the judge is in charge of the proceedings, and this must be reflected in the way in which you conduct yourself. It is never appropriate for you to try to drown a judge out when they are attempting to address you.

6.2.2   Listen carefully to the questions that the judges ask

This may seem like something of a sermon on the self-evident to most mooters. However, the reality is that making sure that you concentrate and listen to judicial questions is not always as easy as it may sound.

Sometimes, you may be so engrossed in what you are trying to say in your actual submissions that you will find it difficult to concentrate on what the judges are saying. This can be particularly problematic if you are not well prepared for a moot and, consequently, all of your mental energy is taken up in understanding your own submissions. Because of poor preparation and consequential nerves, some mooters find it hard to properly focus on what judges are asking them. As a result, it can often be the case that such a mooter will not have even properly heard the question. In these circumstances, a good answer to the question is a remote possibility.

The obvious way that you make listening effectively easier for yourself in the moot is by attempting, in your preparation for the moot, to anticipate the possible questions that the judges may ask you (for more on this, see 6.2.10). If you have a good idea of what the likely questions are going to be, you are much more likely to understand them properly when they are put to you. This will especially be the case where the judge phrases a question slightly differently from how you might have done. What you do not want is a situation where you have to strain every intellectual sinew in order to follow the drift of judicial questions.

6.2.3   Avoid becoming annoyed or impatient with judicial questions

As noted previously, your rapport with the judges is vital to your chances of success. If you have a good rapport with the judges, this can be your launch pad to persuasiveness. If your rapport with the judges is strained, quite the reverse is the case. If, or when, you get into practice, you will see that questions from the bench are an accepted part of everyday life. The same is the case with mooting. If possible, you must learn to welcome questions and embrace them as an opportunity to score well and impress the judges.

Unfortunately, some mooters sometimes give the impression of being irritated at judicial questions. Not surprisingly, this goes down very badly with the judges. To be genuinely irritated by a judicial question in a moot is inexcusable. The judges are in charge of the proceedings and have the right to ask questions of you. Indeed, some of the higher marks are available to mooters who can answer questions well. As a result, this is not something that mooters should be annoyed about, if they want to do well. If the judges do not ask you enough challenging questions, they are not giving you the opportunity to impress them. If you ever do become irritated in a moot, you must do your best to control and hide your feelings. This can be particularly difficult where you feel that the judge has been rude to you (for more on this, see later in this section).

Most mooters, however, do realise that the judge is in charge and that it is inappropriate to become irritated during the moot. A far more common reason why mooters can sometimes look annoyed or irritated during a moot is nerves. If you are nervous, then you can often seem tense to observers. Sometimes, this tension makes it harder to think clearly about everyday things like politeness. As a result, the tension transmits to others and can frequently be interpreted as unpleasantness of some sort. Additionally, one has to consider that speaking in a public context such as a moot is a daunting prospect to many, especially if it is for the first time. Then to be challenged by an expert on your submissions can be a lot for some mooters to cope with. Most students who are new to mooting are not even accustomed to public speaking, let alone to having what they have said challenged or attacked.

It is, therefore, not really surprising that some mooters show signs of strain when dealing with questions. Nevertheless, you need to give this some serious thought before you moot, because of the negative effects it can have on the judges' perceptions of you.

One way of preparing for this is by giving some thought to the manner you wish to adopt when questioned by the judges, and practising it, preferably aloud, to yourself. Ask yourself some questions which you think the judges could put to you, and then answer in what you think is an appropriate, professional manner. At all stages, you should determine that the manner you adopt with the judges should be calm and courteous. There is nothing wrong with disagreeing with the judges and sticking to your arguments. However, whilst you can be firm in doing this, you should never allow yourself to betray signs of anger or hostility.

6.2.4   What will the judges ask?

Unfortunately, there is no definitive answer to this question. Logic dictates that the judges will be keen to ask you questions that they deem to be directly relevant to the moot problem and to the grounds of appeal. However, what the judges will deem to be directly relevant is less easy to predict. The only way that you can ensure you have a good chance of predicting this is by engaging in proper, painstaking research for your moots. If you do not do this, there is every chance that things that you are not aware of will be the subject of questions from the bench, or, for that matter, submissions from the other side.

If you go into practice as a lawyer, you will discover that counsel are supposed to assist the judge with questions of law. In moots, judges will sometimes try to test your depth of knowledge on the law, by asking questions about things that you may not have even made any submissions on.

In the above situation, it is not enough to simply say you are not interested in the issue, because it is not part of your submissions. The judge might press you on the issue regardless, making you look like you are poorly prepared and defensive in the process. By far the best situation is where you are so well prepared that you are able to answer questions on the relevant legal subject, even if you think it falls outside what you should be submitting. Students who really know the law well tend to be those who have read around the subject, rather than those who know little outside the parameters of the narrow submissions that they wish to make.

Example

In the context of *R v Owen Owens*, the judge might ask one of the participants to explain the two limbs of the *Nedrick/Woollin* direction on oblique intention. That particular participant may not wish to raise the issue of oblique intention, perhaps preferring to base their submissions on the issue of direct intention instead. If this happens, you must do your best to answer the question. If you have read widely around the subject, you will, more often than not, be in a position to answer questions such as this.

If you are not in a position to answer a question, because it is not on a case or subject that is part of your submissions, there is a way of dealing with the situation, although it is far from ideal.

Something along the following lines would probably be the least damaging option for senior counsel for the respondent:

> "Regrettably, my Lord, I am unable to be of assistance on this particular issue. I am not submitting that this appeal should be dismissed on the basis of oblique intention issues, but am confining my submissions to the issue of direct intention."

As noted above, this is no more than damage limitation, and a mooter answering a question in this manner may still be vulnerable to supplementary questions from the judge, for example, on why they are not dealing with the issue of oblique intention.

Nevertheless, if you really do not know the answer, this approach is far better than simply floundering and waffling. At least here the mooter may retain something of an aura of control over the exchange with the judge.

For more on what to do when you do not know the answer to a judicial question, see 6.2.7.

6.2.5 When will the judges ask questions?

Mooters who are well prepared should be prepared for judicial questions at any time whilst they are on their feet. Judges will vary enormously in their approaches to questioning. Some judges are far more proactive and aggressive in asking questions than others.

Some judges will ask you a barrage of questions fairly early on in your submissions, and then leave you in relative peace for the rest of the time. Other judges will allow you to complete most, or even all, of your submissions before giving you a fairly testing time with questions at the end. Such judges will often prefer to really listen to what you have to say and to make a note of queries and questions as they go along.

Finally, there are judges who will ask you questions throughout your submissions as and when they feel like it. In terms of maintaining your structure and not missing out points that you intended to make, this type of judge is the most difficult to deal with. This is also the most common judicial approach to questioning in moots.

There are two reasons why most judges adopt the latter approach: first, asking questions when you feel like it is generally much easier for judges than writing the question down and remembering it later; and, secondly, judges will be trying to give you the chance to demonstrate the flexibility to answer questions at any point in your submissions, no matter how inconvenient it might be for your structure. If you can demonstrate this ability, you are much more likely to have impressed the judges and scored highly. Generally, judges will not bully you. They will only ask regular questions throughout your submissions, and persistently try to disrupt your structure, if they feel that you cannot cope with the ordeal. As a result, if the judges do seem to be asking you lots of challenging questions throughout your submissions, treat it as an opportunity to do well, rather than as a problem.

6.2.6 What if the judge asks you a question that you do not want to answer at that point in your submissions?

Normally, when judges ask a question, they will require an immediate answer. This can be inconvenient for some mooters, especially if the answer to the particular question is something that they intend to deal with anyway at a later point in their submissions. If you end up in this situation, there are a number of ways in which you can respond. The main thing to remember, however, is that the judge is in ultimate control of the situation, and whatever you do will depend on how much latitude the judge is prepared to give you.

A) Three alternative approaches

There are probably three ways of tackling this situation. They are dealt with below **in order of preference.**

1) The **first**, and undoubtedly best, response is to give the judge an immediate answer to the question. This has two principal advantages. First, the judges will be gratified and impressed with the fact that you have responded immediately to the question put. They will not feel that you are evasive and trying to avoid answering the question. If you give a good and immediate answer, the judges will obviously be impressed and feel that they are dealing with an advocate who has mastery of the moot problem and the relevant law. Secondly, the judges will also be impressed that you can demonstrate the flexibility to think on your feet and make adjustments to your structure.

The above applies if the matter raised by the question is something you are going to deal with later in your submissions. It is particularly difficult if you are later going to make several points on that issue, but the judicial question, and therefore your answer to it, doesn't cover all of them. To make adjustments like this as you go along, and not get muddled with the structure that you will have prepared in your notes, requires good knowledge of the relevant law and a lot of flexibility. The weaker mooters will cling like limpets to the structure that they have prepared and which appears in their notes. This is why many mooters ask the judge if they can deal with questions later. They are afraid of what will happen to them if they depart from the structure and script that they have prepared.

2) The **second** way of dealing with this situation is to explain to the judge that you will be dealing with the issues raised by the question later in your submissions, and to ask if you can deal with them when you get to them. If you do this, and the judge says that they want an immediate answer, you must accept the situation gracefully and do your best to answer the question there and then. Some judges will take a hard line on this sort of issue and will always insist on an immediate answer. With other judges, the politeness and persuasiveness you demonstrate in asking to deal with the issue later may persuade the judge to show you some leniency on this.

One note of caution needs to be sounded about asking the judges to let you answer a question later. If the judge accepts your request, it may be on condition that you will deal with the issue very soon. Normally, a judge will not be happy to ask a question at the beginning of your submissions, to only get the answer 15 minutes later, when it is convenient to you. As a result, if you do adopt this approach, it is best to do so only if you are coming to the issue, or can come to it, very shortly in your submissions, rather than at some unspecified time in the future. It is also best, when you do come to the issue raised by the judicial question, to refer to the fact that it was the subject of a question.

Something along the following lines would be appropriate:

"My Lords, I will now turn to the relevance of the Nedrick/Woollin direction. This, of course, was the subject of a question from your Lordship a few moments ago."

It is also advisable to show respect and gratitude if the judge allows you to delay your answer to a question. Do not just take it as something you are entitled to.

The **advantages** of this second approach are that it takes a little bit of courage to not simply cave in to every request from the bench. If you ask to deal with an issue later, you are effectively saying to the court that you have a structure and, as far as possible, you want to stick to it. Your structure will also not suffer in the ways that it can if the first approach, above, is adopted. You will not have to make difficult adjustments to your running order of submissions and their content.

The **disadvantages** of this approach have already been outlined. The judge(s) may come to the conclusion that you are too reliant on your notes, and do not have the flexibility to answer questions when they are put. If you ask the judges for permission to answer the question later in an impolite or defensive way, the judges may well take a pretty dim view of you. Some mooters do this in such a clumsy way that it almost looks as if they are refusing to answer the question. Beware of this, and remember that the judge is in charge of the proceedings at all times.

3)   The **final**, and certainly the worst, way of dealing with this situation is to ask to answer the judicial question later in your submissions, and then fail to do so. There will be more on how to deal with questions when you don't know the answer later in this chapter; however, you should never say you will deal with an issue later to try to cover up the fact that you do not know the answer. First, it is unethical to deceive the court in this manner. Secondly, the judges will almost certainly remember if you do not answer a question that they

have asked. Thirdly, if the judge insists on an immediate answer, and you have already indicated that you are capable of answering the question later, it will look pretty awful if it turns out that you cannot do so.

Dealing with questions where you do not know the answer

This issue has partially been covered in other sections of this chapter. However, a big problem for many mooters, and the subject of many nerves, is the issue of what to do if you do not know the answer to a judicial question.

There may be some questions which, even though you are somewhat surprised by the question, you can still have a go at answering. For example, a judge may ask you for your submissions on a case that you have never heard of. He or she may help you a bit by, rather than simply giving the name of the case, telling you what the case actually decided. In this type of situation, as long as you know your own submissions well, there is no reason why you should not be able to think quickly to find a way of reconciling the case raised with your submissions. For example, if the case raised by the judge is a Court of Appeal decision, you could point out that it could not take precedence over House of Lords decisions that you are using on the same issue.

The much more difficult situation is when the judge asks you a question which you are completely unable to answer. With this situation, there will either be no clues in the question that might help you, or any clues given are of no use to you because you are not sufficiently prepared to exploit any lifelines that the judges may throw you. Faced with this situation, some mooters attempt to waffle or "blag" their way out of trouble. Others simply crumble and lose their composure for much of the rest of their submissions. You should be looking to do neither of these things.

As far as waffle is concerned, some mooters take the view that it is better to make some comments, no matter how poor, rather than simply dry up. The problem with this approach is that most moot judges will be highly knowledgeable about the relevant law. As a result, they can see through waffle very easily. If your responses to a question do not make sense, or are not backed up by any legal authority or principle, the judges will realise that you are making your response up as you go along. A further problem with this approach is that, when you are speaking in this way, without any real knowledge to give substance to your words, or any preparation, there is a risk that you will say something foolish, or something that contradicts something you have already said or intend to say later. A small number of mooters have a talent for waffle. Even the talented ones do not get much benefit from their efforts and are generally easily seen through by judges.

If you really are unable to answer a judicial question, it is suggested that **the best way to deal with the situation is to come clean and admit it to the judges**. Obviously, to adopt this course of action too often in a moot will look poor. You should also only adopt this course if you really are sure that you cannot say anything of value in answer to the question.

It is suggested that there are **three main advantages** to this approach:

1)   If you know in advance that you are going to adopt this approach when you cannot answer a question, you can plan in advance the form of words that will limit the damage done to the greatest effect. For more guidance on what you could say in this situation, see the end of this section. Because you are to some extent prepared, you at least retain some control of the situation and make a good job of what is merely an exercise in damage limitation.

2)   The judges may well be impressed that you have at least shown the honesty and courage required to admit that you do not know the answer to a question. Certain wise men (probably French) have, over the years, claimed that one of the signs of wisdom is knowing what you do not know. As a result, it is possible to admit you do not know the answer to a question, and to look reasonably good and in control of the situation in the process.

3)   The embarrassment and unpleasantness of not knowing the answer to the question ends much more quickly if this approach is adopted. By a simple admission, you are, to some extent, taking control of the situation back and drawing a line under the matter. The hope is that you will then be able to regain your composure and carry on with your submissions in an unflustered way. This is not the case with the mooter who waffles or simply crumbles. Here, the agony is prolonged and the composure is consequently harder to regain. As a result, the damage done by your being unable to deal with a question properly is limited. If you do adopt this approach, try to keep your

comments short and confident, but also polite. You are not advised to enter into lengthy, grovelling apologies, although some sign of contrition is obviously appropriate. If you look like you are perfectly at ease with not knowing the answers to judicial questions, the effect created will be very poor.

Example

"I am very sorry, my Lord, but I cannot be of assistance on that particular matter."

or

"I do apologise, my Lord, but I am not familiar with that particular case. As a result I am unable to answer this particular question."

Once you have said something along these lines, you have effectively put the ball in the judge's court. As a result, you should then wait politely for the judge to tell you to resume your submissions. Do not just carry straight on with your submissions, as though your inability to answer is perfectly normal.

6.2.8 Try to use authority

Your answers to judicial questions will seem far more impressive if, as with your actual submissions, you can make reference to legal authority. You will already have used, or will be about to use, cases and other authorities in your submissions. If you can think quickly on your feet and find a way to use these authorities in answer to judicial questions, the judges will be impressed. Remember that mooting is not about giving your opinions, it is about using the law to put submissions before the court. Judges will be looking for an authoritative answer to their questions, not simply an answer that appears to be off the top of your head. Whilst the judges are asking you questions you should, therefore, if you are well prepared, be thinking of ways to reconcile the question with the legal knowledge and authorities at your disposal.

6.2.9 Do not be afraid of the judges! Where possible, stick to your submissions!

One of the tendencies of the new, inexperienced mooter is to be too much in awe of the judge(s). This can particularly manifest itself during exchanges with the bench. Of course, you need to be aware that the judges in your moot will be either lecturers or practitioners or judges. As such, they will undoubtedly bring a great deal of expertise to the moot and should be treated with respect.

However, this is certainly not to say that the moment a judge looks unconvinced by your submissions, that you should abandon your line of argument. You need to have the courage of your convictions and the courage to stick to the submissions that you are making, wherever possible. The only foolproof way of having the confidence to do this is by making sure that you prepare properly. If you have properly prepared your submissions, they will be based on sound legal authority and logic. If this is the case, then you should have the confidence to stick to your guns, safe in the knowledge that there is some substance behind what you are saying.

One of the most impressive aspects of a mooter's performance, from the judge's perspective, can be that a mooter has the ability to stand up to rigorous questioning and to back up their answers with reference to the law. Judges will sense if you have this ability and will ask you more questions as a result. Judges tend to ask fewer questions when they perceive that a mooter is weak and will not be able to offer much in the way of satisfactory answers. If you know your submissions well, and have prepared yourself for judicial questions, this should not be a problem for you.

One point to bear in mind, if you do come to clash with the judges on issues arising from judicial questions, is that you must remain courteous at all times. The fact that you are disagreeing and that you have some good authority to back you up should not be regarded as a green light to address the judges in a discourteous manner. Even if you feel that the judge is wrong and you think you can demonstrate it, you should never let the mask of courtesy slip. There are many ways of disagreeing with a person and, moreover, a judge, without being unpleasant about it.

Example

"My Lord, I am grateful for that suggestion. However, my submission is that the situation in this case is quite the contrary. I would submit that ..."

or

"My Lord, I would submit that the case to which your Lordship refers, whilst analogous to this case in some ways, is nevertheless distinguishable from it. My reasons for submitting this are ..."

Whilst it is clearly important for mooters, and advocates alike, to stick to their submissions, the above should not be taken as an absolute rule which should be followed in all circumstances. If it becomes apparent, during the course of judicial questions, that one of your submissions is untenable, there will come a point where you will have to concede the point. The judges will not be impressed by a pig-headed refusal to admit that you are wrong, when all the evidence points to that fact. This is far less likely to happen, of course, if you are well prepared for the moot. Good preparation also gives you the ability to recognise more readily when one of your submissions has become untenable. Some mooters plough on with a poor submission, despite that fact that the judge has clearly demonstrated, through questioning, that it is untenable.

6.2.10   Preparing in advance for judicial questions

It was noted in chapter 5 that there is a lot that you can do, prior to the moot, to prepare yourself for your opponent's submissions and your response to them. The same can also be said of judicial questions. Unlike with your opponent, the judge(s) will obviously not disclose the cases that they intend to refer to before the moot. However, you will have the moot problem. The information provided in this can be a huge help in assisting you in your preparations so that you can insulate yourself against judicial questions.

A) The moot problem

As with the medical evidence in *R v Owen Owens*, the moot problem may provide you with facts that are open to dispute. If you are going to be submitting that one version of those facts should be accepted by the court, there is a fair chance that the judges might question on that very point.

B) The findings of the lower court, and the cases referred to by the judge(s)

These are also likely to be the subject of judicial questions. If, for example, you are leading counsel for the appellant in *R v Owen Owens*, you will be required to argue that Evans HHJ got it wrong on the issue of intention, and that he misused the cases he referred to in the process. The judges, as a result, may well ask you exactly why Evans HHJ was wrong and whether you can point to passages in the judgments that back this up. The judges may also point to passages in the judgments that seem to contradict you, and ask you for your response.

C) The grounds of appeal

The grounds of appeal provided in the moot problem are also an excellent source of information for the mooter who is trying to antic- ipate the judges' questions. One can never be certain on these mat- ters, but the vast majority of judicial questions will be on matters that the judges will regard as directly relevant to the grounds of appeal. Generally, judges are not terribly interested in matters that are not determinative of the case. It is, therefore, normally a safe bet that the judges will ask you questions on the matters that the court is sitting to decide, namely the grounds of appeal. For more on this, see section **6.2.13** below.

D) The list of authorities used by your opponent

The judges will certainly be interested in your responses to what the other side have said, and they may wish to tease this out of you with questions. This is especially likely if the judges feel that you have not directly commented on points or authorities referred to by the other side.

6.2.11   Preparing during the moot for judicial questions

There is a limit to what can be done at this late stage, but there are some indicators that will at least give you more time to get a feel for what the judges might ask you, and how they might ask it. This is par- ticularly the case if your place in the order of speakers is such that you get the chance to hear your opponent speak before you rise to address the court. According to most speaking orders, this would be of benefit to those appearing for the respondents. If you get the chance to hear your opponent speak, you will also get the chance to hear what questions the judges ask them.

Whilst there is no certainty that the judge will ask you similar ques- tions to those he or she asked your opponent, careful attention to the questioning of the other side may provide you with valuable clues as to the issues and authorities that the judges regard as important.

Additionally, if a judge, in questioning your opponent, constantly refers to certain case law which you are going to refer to yourself, it may give you added confidence in your own submissions. It may also give you the chance to refer back to the point the judge made in answer to a question put to you on the same issue.

Example

"In response to that question I would refer back to the point that your Ladyship rightly made in a question put to my learned friend during her submissions. I would submit that your Ladyship was correct in asserting that the *Nedrick/Woollin* direction only applies where ..."

Listening to your opponent being questioned by the judge(s) will also give you an idea of the courtroom persona of the judge(s). Some judges can be quite abrupt. If you know about this beforehand, you will be able to brace yourself for the ordeal and consider how you will respond. For more on courtesy in court, see later in this chapter.

6.2.12 What if a judge asks a question that is outside the grounds of appeal?

For reasons discussed in the previous section, this is unlikely to happen too often. However, some judges may have a different view from you as to what is relevant to the grounds of appeal. Others may simply want to ask you some more general questions, to test how sound you are on the law surrounding the moot problem.

How best to respond in this situation really depends on whether you know the answer to the question put. If you do know the answer, simply answer the question as best you can. If you do not know the answer to the question, as noted previously, it is best to admit this, rather than attempting to waffle your way out of a difficult situation. If you feel quite confident that the question relates to issues that are not relevant to the grounds of appeal, it is fine to say this, as it provides a reason for why you are unable to answer the question. Nevertheless, it should be pointed out that this is no more than an exercise in damage limitation.

If you cannot answer the question, you should adopt an apologetic stance, even if you think that the question is not directly relevant to the appeal. If you appear to be blaming the judges for asking you a question that you think is irrelevant, you will create a bad impression. It may well be, of course, that the question is actually more relevant than you think, but, due to poor preparation, you do not spot this at the time.

6.2.13   Do not ask the judges questions

Whilst the judges can ask you questions, they are not there to make submissions themselves. They are not representing either side in the moot and should be neutral. The participants in the moot, on the other hand, are there to make submissions and, consequently, be asked questions about those submissions.

As a result, asking the judges questions during exchanges with them should be avoided (subject to the exceptions listed in **6.2.15** below). It can be tempting, when the judges ask you a question, to fire back with a question of your own, as you would if you were having a discussion or argument with someone in an everyday situation. This is generally inappropriate for a mooter or for an advocate. It can also look very impertinent during an exchange with the bench. If you do this, the chances are that the judge will refuse to answer the question and explain that, as a judge, they are not there to answer questions.

Example

Consider the following scenario set within the context of *R v Owen Owens*.

Question from the judge to senior counsel for the respondent:

"Mr Smith, is this not a fairly straightforward case of a misdirection to the jury on the issue of oblique intention?"

Answer from senior counsel for the respondent:

"Well, my Lord, if that's the case, why did you ask my learned friend all those questions about how 'highly probable' means the same thing as 'virtually certain'?"

This is clearly an inappropriate response. It is the type of thing you might say to someone you were arguing with in a public house. It is not the way that you should be speaking to a judge in the Court of Appeal or House of Lords. It sounds combative, and as though the judge's authority and right to ask questions is being challenged. As noted previously, you are trying to impress the judges and persuade them to adopt your submissions, not to become fractious with them.

6.2.14 Acceptable questions to ask the judge

In spite of the above, there are some limited situations where it might be appropriate to ask a judge a question. Below is a list of commonly asked questions that are perfectly acceptable in a moot:

1)   If, during an exchange with a judge, you do not fully understand what they are asking you, there is nothing wrong with politely **asking the judge for clarification** or for them to put the question to you again.

2)   When you are **ending one submission and beginning the next**, it is customary to ask the judges if you may do so.

3)   When you come to the end of your answer to a judicial question, you might ask the judges **if you may continue your submissions**. This is not only polite, but also makes it clear to the judges that the answer to the question is complete, and that you are now returning to your submissions.

4)   If you are referring to a case during the course of your submissions, it is normal practice to **ask the judges if they require a brief summary of the facts** of the case.

5)   When referring to cases and other materials in the moot, it is advisable to check, either with a question or by simply looking, whether the judge(s) have the relevant page and paragraph etc.

6)   At the end of your submissions, it is good practice to **ask the judges if they have any further questions for you**.

6.3   Be courteous to the judges at all times

The issue of courtesy has already been touched upon several times in this chapter, in a number of contexts related to questions from and to the judges. However, it is worthy of a mention in its own right in terms of your dealings with the judges generally. It is very easy to lose your courteous demeanour, especially when you are concentrating hard or where you are under pressure or nervous.

A particular problem with the requirement for courtesy, which often comes out after moots, is that not all judges regard themselves as bound by the same constraints. Often, mooters will complain that the judge was rude or abrupt or patronising. They will then use this as justification for the fact that they also assumed a prickly demeanour during the moot. Try to avoid this at all costs. It may

seem unfair, but the relationship between the judge and the participants in a moot is not a relationship of equals. This is the same in
practice, with judges, barristers and solicitors. In moots, as well as in
the real courts, judges often conduct themselves in a way that would
be unacceptable in a social context. Do not be put off by this. It is all
part and parcel of the experience of being in court, and you should
learn to enjoy it rather than let it upset you.

As a result, although it can be very difficult, you must maintain
your composure and be courteous throughout the moot, even if the
judges do not follow suit. The judges are judging and assessing you,
not the other way around. They do not have to impress anyone or
prove anything. When you get into practice, you will have to accept
this as a fact of everyday life.

A small part of your preparations for any moot should be to ready
yourself for the possibility that the judge may not be especially
friendly. If you can maintain a courteous manner in the face of
judicial abruptness, your professionalism should be reflected when
the moot is judged or assessed. Some judges, of course, will be perfectly polite, and will present none of these difficulties. Rudeness is
certainly not a necessary qualification for becoming a moot judge.

6.4 Eye contact with the judges

The importance of eye contact is dealt with in detail in chapter **3**.
However, it is worth mentioning some of the problems with eye contact that can arise, depending on the judges in your moot. Some
judges will have habits that make it difficult for you to maintain eye
contact; some judges will appear to have their head constantly buried
in a book; others will be constantly writing notes; and a small number
have even been known to close their eyes. Whatever the habits of the
judge(s), do not let yourself be distracted and allow your discipline to
waver. It is tempting, in such circumstances, to give up with eye contact and concentrate on your notes. The reality is that virtually all
judges will notice if you are not engaging them with eye contact, even
if they do not seem to be looking at you very much. The disadvantages
of appearing to be reading have also been considered in chapter **3**.

6.5 Modes of address

The correct ways to refer to the judges in your moot are considered
in chapter **3**. Getting this right is vital if you want to impress the
judges and actually look something like a real lawyer as, during your

submissions, you will be referring to the judges and things they have said many times. For some, it takes considerable practice to get used to referring to judges in the formal manner required. For others, this is a more straightforward task. As a result, if you get this wrong, it will be a defect that the judges will be constantly reminded of. It will also be something that you will feel awkward about during the moot. Faults such as this can be fairly easily avoided. It is simply not worth allowing something such as modes of address to be a blow to your confidence. You should, therefore, make sure that you are comfortable with basic matters such as this before you ever walk into a moot court.

Chapter 7

Use of legal authorities

7.1 Introduction

It has already been noted several times that mooting is not about expressing your own opinions, but making submissions based on the law. In chapter **4**, it was suggested that individual submissions should always be backed up with reference to legal authority or, at the very least, some recognisable legal principle.

As well as making sure that you back up your submissions with authorities, it is also important that, when you do so, you refer to authorities in the correct way. Like all courtroom speech, referring to authorities is done in a formal manner that is governed by tradition and convention. In order to impress the judges and actually look like a lawyer, you need to be able to assume an appropriate courtroom manner. This is particularly the case when you are referring to authorities.

Despite the importance of referring to authorities in moots, many mooters score badly in this respect. Some of the defects are the result of poor knowledge of the legal system. Some students, for example, will not seem to appreciate the difference between the *ratio decidendi* of a case and comments made *obiter dicta*. Others will be weak in terms of spotting whether they are using a majority or a dissenting judgment.

Weaknesses of this sort can be difficult to put right as, on most law courses, the basic principles of the relevant legal system are studied at the beginning of the course. Some students, unfortunately, will go through their entire course of study with a far from perfect grasp of the basics. The only remedy, if you find yourself in this situation, is to go back to these basic principles and study them again before you start mooting. This is undoubtedly time-consuming but, if you want to be a successful mooter and practise law as a career, it is essential.

Other students struggle with referring to authorities for reasons that are much more straightforward to remedy. It is surprising how many students, who are otherwise quite well prepared, make a mess of referring to authorities and make basic mistakes such as getting page numbers mixed up when referring to law reports.

This chapter considers a range of issues that you need to be aware of when you attempt to back up your submissions with authority.

7.2   How many authorities to use in a moot

Most mooting competitions or assessments place a limit on how many authorities each participant can use in the moot. Students often approach tutors to ask how many authorities they should use. Unfortunately, there is no right or wrong answer to the question. The number of authorities that you include, subject to any upper limit imposed, is entirely dependent on what is appropriate for the submissions you wish to make. It can be perfectly acceptable to only include a small number of cases, if that is all that your submissions require. In other moots, you may find that the nature of your submissions demand that you refer to many more authorities.

The most common problem is that students who are not well prepared will be somewhat threadbare in terms of how many authorities they include in their submissions. This can mean that it is hard to usefully fill the allotted time with meaningful submissions. This, however, is easily remedied by greater preparation.

7.3   Referring to too many authorities

A less common problem is that some mooters, no doubt eager to impress the judges with their legal erudition, will include too much reference to authority. If this happens, your submissions can lose their structure. The bigger picture can be obscured by the fact that there is too much small print. Most judges will be able to recall mooters who constantly seemed to be reading from cases, at the expense of actually giving their own submissions. The other, obvious danger is that you will have too much material and run out of time.

In chapter **4**, a structure for individual submissions is suggested, whereby mooters should provide reference to the law, but should then give their own commentary or submissions on the basis of the law that they have read out. If your submissions are overloaded with references to the law, the danger is that there will be no room for anything else, and that your submissions will come across as little more than a list of readings from various cases and other materials. You will lose time for the vital ingredient that makes sense of the legal authorities you refer to, namely your actual submissions on why those authorities help your case.

Having too many authorities will also obviously have implications in terms of timekeeping. If you include too many references to cases etc, your submissions can be rushed and you can appear breathless and somewhat unconvincing as a result. Whilst you do want to fill the time allocated for your submissions, you do not want to have to speak with a machine-gun voice because you have tried to include too much. As a result, you need to exercise some restraint when deciding which authorities to refer to, and how much you will refer to them. The aim is to have just enough material to fill your time slot, but to still be able to speak in an unhurried, relaxed manner.

7.4   Referring to case law

For those who appear in moots, case law is the source of authority most extensively referred to. Judges of moots, who are involved in providing feedback to mooters, often have to comment that mooters have made errors in their references to case law. This can ruin the flow of your submissions and cause all sorts of embarrassing and awkward moments, which can significantly detract from the overall impression that you make. The following sections are designed to help you avoid the many errors that are commonly made.

Normally, during the moot, you will have your own copies of the cases you wish to refer to and read from. You will also provide the judges with their own copies, so that they can follow what you are reading as you go along. The copies will either be paper copies or will be law report volumes from the institution where you are mooting. Most universities and institutions where students moot have an arrangement with their law libraries, whereby students involved in mooting can, unusually, take volumes from the law library. You need to ask at the institution where you are studying about this. If you are mooting in a competition where you have to travel to the venue, you may be required to take paper copies with you, unless your institution is prepared to let you take them away.

NB: The use of bundles will be considered at the end of this chapter, as a simple method of providing the court with all of your authorities.

7.4.1   Asking the judges if they want the facts of a case you are referring to

In the previous chapter, this question was listed as one of the perfectly acceptable and proper questions to ask the judge. If you are referring to a case, it is only polite to double check that the judges are familiar with it by asking whether they would like a brief summary of the facts. More often than not, the judges will decline and indicate that they are familiar with the case. Occasionally, however, especially if you are referring to a very recent case, the judges may take you up on your offer.

One pitfall to be aware of is that judges will sometimes test whether you are bluffing when you ask them if they want a summary of the facts. Some students assume that their invitation will be declined and do not bother to prepare a summary of the facts. They are, therefore, slightly lost when the judges indicate that they wants the facts. Try to avoid this by making sure that you have a brief summary of the facts of each case upon which you intend to rely ready in advance.

Another pitfall associated with asking if the judges want the facts of a case is that the question might have already been asked by one of the mooters who spoke before you. If you are senior counsel for the appellant, this is not something that need worry you, as you will ordinarily speak first. For the other participants in the moot, however, this can be an issue. If the question has already been asked by another participant, it follows that you should not ask the question again. Unfortunately, many mooters do this. Some judges will find this irritating, as it demonstrates that the person concerned has not been listening properly. In chapter **3**, it was suggested that the best mooters are those who are aware of what is going on around them in the courtroom. This includes the ability to listen to what has been said and to respond appropriately.

7.4.2   How to cite a case verbally when you intend to read from the judgments

With the majority of cases that you mention during your submissions, you will be doing so because you intend to read from the judgments in order to support your case. If you go to court and watch real advocates at work, you will see that there is a particular style in which you should verbally cite a case. The key is that you need to give the judges all the information they need to find what you are referring to. As noted previously, in most moots, the participants provide the judges with either photocopies of cases (usually in a bundle) or volumes from the law reports for the cases they are going to refer to. If there are four participants in your moot, this could mean that the judges have a large number of cases in front of them on the bench. They might even have more than one participant referring to the same case, but from different law reports.

It is surprising how many mooters make a mess of citing cases verbally. However, there is really no great mystery to it and, with a little practice, students should be able to master this skill without much difficulty.

Examples

What follows are two case examples, one a criminal case, the other civil:

1) Written form = R v Venna [1976] 3 WLR 737
This case should be referred to verbally along the following lines:

> "My Lords, the next case I will refer to is that of the Crown and Venna, which is to be found in volume three of the Weekly Law Reports for 1976, at page 737. Would your Lordships like a brief summary of the facts of this case?"

> "Could your Lordships turn to page 740, paragraph B and the judgment of ..."

2) Written form = Knightley v Johns [1982] 1 All ER 851
This case should be referred to verbally along the following lines:

> "My Lords, could I now draw your attention to my next case, which is Knightley and Johns, 1981, volume one of the All England Reports for that year, reported at page 851?"

> "As my learned friend Miss Smith has already supplied your Lordships with the facts of this case, could I direct your Lordships to page 860, in particular, paragraph D and the speech of ...?"

Where a judgment was delivered on or after the 11th January 2001, it is probably best to give the judges the neutral citation first and then the traditional citation from the law report you are using in the manner suggested above. For more on this, see section 7.8.

Many students make basic errors when referring judges to cases. As a result, thinking ahead and employing some basic organisational skill is often profitable.

7.4.2.1 Checklist to follow when you are referring the judges to a case

If you are presenting your cases to the judges in bundle form, please read section 7.7 of this chapter in conjunction with this checklist.

A) Make sure you refer to the right set of law reports

With many cases that you refer to, you will find that they are reported in a number of different law reports. As a result, a case can appear in the All England Reports, the Appeal Cases, the Weekly Law Reports, and many others at the same time. It might be that other mooters are using the same case as you, but have used a different set of law reports. Because of this, all the pages and paragraph numbers that they refer to will be different to yours.

As was noted earlier in this section, many universities and institutions will allow you to take reports out of the library when you are mooting. Often you will meet the other participants in the library beforehand, where you will get a trolley and load it up with all the cases needed. If this is the case, make sure, if you are using some of the same cases as others in the moot, that the actual volume that you will be using ends up in the courtroom. It is common for mooters to become very flustered, and shoot angry glances at their opponent or partner, when they refer to an All England Reports version of a case, only to find that the judges only have the Appeal Cases version. In this situation, the judges will not be able to follow what you are reading from. It is **your responsibility** to ensure that the judges can do this, so do not delegate it to somebody else. If they let you down, it is you who will look and feel foolish.

B) Make sure you have the correct dates and volume numbers for your case

Another source of awkwardness or embarrassment, when mooters are referring to cases, can be simple mistakes about volume numbers and dates of cases. There is no reason why such mistakes should be made, apart from the fact that some students do not adequately prepare for their moots. As a result of this, they are disorganised when it comes to small matters. Unfortunately, such small matters can come back to haunt them in the moot and cause wholly avoidable friction with the judges. All too often, mooters refer judges to the wrong volume or the wrong set of law reports. Such mistakes get on the nerves of the judges. They also make you look unprofessional and disorganised, as well as being damaging to your confidence and your composure. You can, if you are not careful, end up spending much of the time allocated for your submissions with the judges frantically trying to find the report you are hoping to read from. In this chaos, your submissions get completely lost. All of this can be avoided by making sure of these points before you go into the moot.

C) Give the judges the correct page and paragraph numbers

Some mooters will plunge in and read from a case without telling the judges which page they should be looking at, or which specific paragraph they are referring to. The judges will then have to stop the mooter to get this information. If this happens to you, the fact that the judges have even had to ask is bad enough. This will interfere with the flow of your submissions and will make you look and feel somewhat lacking in efficiency. It is essential that you look in control of your own submissions. Being efficient with this sort of thing, when you are referring to cases, is one way of giving the right impression. This is one of the main ways in which some mooters will make it very evident to the judges that they are not properly prepared for the moot.

Unfortunately, some mooters look blank when asked which page number and paragraph they are referring to. Often they are not even in a position to look at their own copy of the case and tell you, as some mooters, regrettably, only keep the parts of a case that they intend to read from in front of them during the moot, without the references to where it is in the judgment. It is essential that, if possible, you have the whole case in front of you in the same format that the judges have, so that such problems will not arise. An additional problem, which stems from the above, is that most judges will question you on the cases you refer to. In order to do this, they may read out a quote from elsewhere in the judgments. In this situation, you will clearly be at a great disadvantage if you do not have the relevant passages in front of you.

Some law reports will not have letters next to the paragraphs. If this is the situation with a case you are referring to, the next best thing is to guide the judges along the following lines:

> "My Lords, if you would turn to page 173 and the speech of Lord Griffiths. About half way down the page, at the bottom of the second paragraph, on the line that begins 'It appears', his Lordship says …"

D) Make sure that you get names and pronunciations right

It may seem an obvious fault to avoid, but some mooters are sloppy when it comes to giving the correct names of the parties to cases and the judges they refer to in the judgments. As a result of sloppy preparation and reading of cases, Lord Hailsham can, for example, become "Lord Halisham", or Lord Slynn can become "Lord Slyme". When this happens, it sounds pretty awful as well as potentially disrespectful. It is also the sort of thing that a competent advocate would easily avoid.

E) Using bookmarks/slips of paper to help the judges

Many mooters adopt the helpful practice of putting slips of paper (or something of the sort) into the appropriate page of the volume of the law reports that they intend to read from. They will then write the relevant information – who the judge is, the page number, which paragraph etc – on the slips of paper. This will therefore accompany what the mooter is saying when he refers to the case, and makes it easier for the judges to find the place in the judgment that they are being referred to. It also has the advantage of looking both efficient and considerate.

F) Wait for the judges

It has been noted previously, particularly in chapter **3**, that the best advocates are comfortable in court and are aware of their surroundings. When you refer judges to cases, you need to be aware that finding the appropriate page and paragraph will take them a bit of time. Many students, probably due to adrenalin, forget this and begin reading from the judgments without waiting to see whether the judges have found the relevant passage. As a result, it can often be the case that, by the time the judge has found the relevant passage, the mooter has practically finished with it and is moving on to something else. If you are reading from a judgment and the judges are not listening because they are still trying to find the appropriate page, you might as well not have bothered with the passage in the first place. It will have no persuasive effect on the judges.

It is important, therefore, that you are careful to wait for the judges when you are referring to cases. Look at the judges when you are giving them the citations for the case, and do not begin reading from judgments until you are satisfied that they have found the relevant passage. This way, they can properly follow your submissions and, hopefully, be persuaded by them. The judges will be grateful for this. The added advantage is that it gives you a bit of breathing space, and prevents your submissions from being too fast and appearing breathless.

G) Meticulously write down all the information that you need when referring to a case

It is not uncommon for mooters to fail to do some, or all, of the things mentioned above when referring to a case. It is advised, therefore, that you write down all the relevant information, in the form in which you wish to say it (if needed), for all the case references that you intend to make. As you become more experienced at referring to cases, you will need to write less and less, as the correct format will become second nature.

7.4.3 How to cite a case verbally when you do not intend to read from the judgments

There may be some rare occasions where you will wish to refer to a case in passing, whilst not intending to read from the actual judgments. In *R v Owen Owens*, for example, you may wish to briefly refer to the uncontroversial and widely accepted statement from *R v Cunningham* [1982] that the *mens rea* for murder is intention to kill or do serious bodily harm. As this is an uncontroversial and well-known point, and not an integral part of any likely submissions, you may wonder whether it would be possible to refer to the case without reading from the judgments. As will be discussed later in this chapter, the general rule is that you should also back up your references to cases by reading from the relevant passages of the judgment.

There are slightly differing schools of thought in this situation, and a lot will depend on the attitudes of the judges in your moot. One possible approach is to introduce the case along the following lines:

"My Lords, it is well established, and uncontroversial that the *mens rea* of murder is intention to kill or do serious bodily harm. A relatively recent statement of this principle can be found in the Crown and Cunningham [1982]."

In this situation, some judges may not begrudge the fact that you have not provided them with proper citations for the case or read from the actual judgments.

However, some judges are much stricter on such matters. As a result, a safer option is probably to say something along the following lines:

> "My Lords, it is well established, and uncontroversial that the mens rea of murder is intention to kill or do serious bodily harm. A relatively recent statement of this principle can be found in the Crown and Cunningham [1982]. I will not be referring to this case any further, but it can be found in the 1982 volume of the Appeal Cases at page 566."

If you choose this option, it is also advisable to make sure that a copy is available in court, so that you can give the judges the relevant passages if asked, and that the case is on your list of authorities.

The last two options, it should be stressed, are based on the assumption that the judges will give you a bit of latitude in not demanding that you read from the judgments. As noted previously, judges differ greatly on matters such as this. Some judges are real sticklers, and will require you to read from the judgments, even if you are making the most well known and uncontroversial of points *en passant*.

As a result of the above, it is important that you do not make a habit of referring to cases in this way, if you do it at all.

7.4.4 Referring the judges to a case that you have already referred to earlier in your submissions

Whilst you should generally give full citations when you initially refer to a case, this does not apply to any subsequent references to the same case. You may, for example, refer the judges to a passage in a case, and then make some submissions of your own on how that passage impacts on the moot case. Later on in your submissions, you may return to the same case in order to refer to some other passages. In this type of situation, it can sound repetitive and clumsy to keep on giving full citations for the case. It is generally far simpler, and more elegant, to confine yourself to saying something like:

"My Lords, may I refer back to the Crown and Woollin, in particular page …?"

If the judges need the full citations again, they will ask you to remind them. Alternatively, you could just ask the judges if they want to hear the citations again.

A similar situation can arise where you are referring to the same case as another participant in the moot who has already spoken, and you are referring to the same set of law reports. In this situation, as more time will have elapsed since the judges heard the citations, it is probably sensible to say something like:

"My Lords, for my second submission I would like to refer to the Crown and Woollin. This case has already been referred to by my learned friend Miss Jones, but the citations are the same. They are …"

Here, you will be acknowledging that another mooter has already referred to the case, which shows you were listening when others were speaking, as well as reminding the judges of the citations, as they may no longer have the volume to hand. The judges are also not robots. The chances are that they will not have remembered the citations of the case if they heard them some time ago.

7.5 General tips for referring to cases

As well as making omissions and mistakes when citing cases verbally, some mooters struggle when referring to cases for other reasons. Most of these are to do with poor knowledge of the legal system. This section looks at some of the more common problems which judges frequently notice.

7.5.1   Use of the headnote

The headnote is at the beginning of a law report. It contains a summary of the facts and includes a section starting with "Held". The headnote is **written by the law reporter**, not the judges Whilst the headnote is undoubtedly a valuable source of quick reference, it is certainly **not part of the judgment**. It is not written by any of the judges in the case and, as a result, does not technically form part of the precedent.

Nevertheless, some mooters read from the headnote as though it has some authority, and look surprised when the judges stop them. There are two possible reasons why this is a common error, both of them equally unimpressive.

The **first** is laziness. If you are a mooter who does not relish the hard work required to prepare properly, reading from the headnote can seem far more attractive than reading lengthy judgments. The headnote is normally very short and gives you a quick, and easy to understand, summary of the majority judgments. Mooting is about really engaging with the law in depth. You cannot do this by simply reading one paragraph.

Secondly, some students genuinely seem to be unaware of the status of the headnote. This is surprising, as a cursory look at most textbooks on the English legal system will provide this information.

You should not, therefore, be using the headnote for anything other than your own reference or research purposes. It is a useful tool during your preparation for moots, as it will help you to quickly decide whether a case is any use to you, without you having to read the whole judgment. If you actually want to refer to cases in the moot, however, you need to carefully read the judgments and use in your submissions what the judges in the case have actually said.

7.5.2   Mentioning cases in your submissions and then not referring to the judgments

The situations where it might be acceptable to do this were mentioned in section 7.4.3 above. It was also noted in that section, however, that when you refer to a case and give the judges the full citations, it is usually the prelude to you actually referring to the judgments. Some mooters, however, will provide the judges with a copy of a case, refer to that case with full citations, and then move on. The judges, in the meantime, will have found the volume, located the relevant page and will be waiting expectantly for the mooter to read passages from the judgment. It can create a very strange impression if you do this. The judges are left wondering why you have taken the trouble to provide a copy of the case and give full citations, and then not refer to the judgments.

The most likely reason for students making this mistake is probably that they do not actually know what the judgment says, and have only read about the case in an undergraduate textbook. Most textbooks only give a small amount of commentary on individual cases. As a result, reading about a case in a textbook is only the starting point when you are preparing for a moot. On its own, a textbook will not provide you with enough information to use a case competently in a moot. Additionally, what is said in a textbook is not the law. It is the law through the lens of the author. The author might interpret the case in a way that is not consistent with your submissions or which is plain wrong.

Unfortunately, there is no substitute for hard work. It is not enough to refer to a case in a moot and then simply quote from a textbook. You need to read cases thoroughly before the moot and refer to them in detail during the moot.

7.5.3   Double check that the case you are referring to has not been appealed to a higher court

It is not uncommon for mooters to be gleefully referring to a Court of Appeal case which suits their submissions perfectly, only to be told that the matter has since been appealed to the House of Lords, and that the Court of Appeal decision was overruled. Not surprisingly, if this happens to you, it can be a most unpleasant experience, as it can completely pull the rug from under your feet in terms of your submissions. Services such as Westlaw and Lawtel make it fairly easy to check such matters, and you should familiarise yourself with how such services can be of use to you.

7.5.4   Read the cases you refer to carefully

This sounds obvious, but it is surprising how many mooters place great reliance on a certain case, without actually checking certain basic points about what they are referring to. If your knowledge of cases you are referring to is threadbare, the judges will easily be able to pick up on this, especially if they ask you some questions on them. You do not necessarily have to read every word of every case that you refer to, but you should have a good working knowledge of the whole judgment, not just the little bits that you intend to rely on. The temptation is to cut corners in this respect, especially if you have other work to do as well as preparing for the moot. Such temptation should, wherever possible, be resisted. If you get yourself into bad habits like this as a law student, you will find it hard to change later.

Things you should know about cases you refer to

All of the points below are matters that could easily come up in the context of a judicial question or a submission from the other side. If you do not know such matters, the judges will almost certainly draw negative inferences.

1) *Who are the judges in the case?*
This does not just apply to the judges that you are quoting from. You also need to know which other judges gave judgments in the case.

2) *What is the history of the case?*
For example, if you are referring to a case in the Court of Appeal (Criminal Division), which court(s) has that case been heard in prior to that?

3) *Which judges are in the majority and which are dissenters?*
A classic mistake made by many mooters is to read from a dissenting judgment. As was noted in chapter **2**, dissenting judgments do not form part of the precedent and can, therefore, be no more than persuasive, at best. Students who make this mistake are normally those who have not read the judgments carefully. Often, such students will have read a textbook, which will have given them a reference to a case and something that a judge said in that case. The danger is that you can get carried away when you think you have found a decent submission and you do not check it properly before using it in the moot. You certainly can, where appropriate, read from dissenting judgments, but you must be aware of the status of what you are reading out.

4) *Check whether the judges who are in the majority really are completely unanimous*
Judges who are in the majority in cases are not always in total agreement on all matters related to the case. As a result, whilst judges may agree that an appeal should be allowed or dismissed, they may reach their conclusion for very different reasons. An

example of a case like this, which is mentioned in *R v Owen Owens*, is the decision of the Court of Appeal in *Re A (Children)* [2001].

If the above situation applies with a case that you are referring to, it goes without saying that, ideally, you need to know about it. There are two main reasons for this.

First, there is every chance that this sort of issue could be the subject of a judicial question. A good advocate would not refer to what a judge has said in a case without some idea of the potential hazards involved.

Secondly, three judges might all agree that an appeal should be allowed. If one of the judges, the judge that you are referring to, concludes that the appeal should be allowed for reason A, and the other two judges conclude that the appeal should be allowed for reason B, it is hard to know what the true reason for deciding the case is. If you are attempting to submit that *your* judge's pronouncements represent the *ratio decidendi* of the case, you are likely to encounter opposition in the form of judicial questions or submissions from your opponent. If you do not even know about what the other judges have said, you are in a poor position to deal with this.

5) *Check which comments are the ratio decidendi and which are merely obiter dicta*

In the situation in point 4 above, it is highly arguable that the comments of the judge being referred to by the mooter would be regarded as *obiter* comments. The reason for this is that there are two judges who have stated that the appeal should be allowed for a different reason to that particular judge. With some cases, it might be more straightforward to determine which comments are the *ratio decidendi*. Nevertheless, you need to be sure of the status of passages that you are putting before the moot court. This is where reputable textbooks can be helpful, if used properly. They can help you to make decisions about which are the key pronouncements in a particular judgment. As noted previously, however, reading textbooks, no matter how reputable, should not be a substitute for reading the primary source.

6) *Reading from a part of a judgment where the judge is quoting from another judge in another case*

Occasionally, you might want to refer to a passage in a judgment where the judge you are quoting from is, in turn, quoting from another judge in a previous case. Whilst there is certainly nothing wrong with this, it hopefully goes without saying that you need to have read the case carefully enough to know who said what in the passages you are using.

Some weaker mooters, who are poorly prepared, will not even know that the judge they think they are referring to is actually quoting from someone or somewhere else. In some unfortunate cases, the judge will quote from another judge, not because he agrees with those comments, but in order to explain why he disagrees with them. The mooter who is ignorant of this looks not only unprepared but also foolish.

7.5.5   Making submissions about the distinguishing and overruling of cases

These were mentioned in detail in chapter 2, but are worth mentioning again in this particular context. As noted previously, the ability to suggest that a case be distinguished or overruled is an important part of the mooter's armoury. You will probably find cases that do not suit the submissions that you need to make. As a result, you will need to provide the court with arguments that enable them to avoid following such cases.

As a result of the above, arguments about distinguishing, use of the *Practice Statement* [1966], and overruling are common in moots. You should avail yourself of these opportunities, particularly if the law does not favour you in a moot. The judges may not agree with everything you say, but they will appreciate the use of sophisticated arguments on distinguishing and overruling, as long as they are within realistic parameters. Most judges will also recognise the courage required to be creative in using such arguments. You will, of course, need to be prepared to respond to such arguments from your opponents in respect of cases that you put before the court.

7.5.6   How many references to make from a case which suits your submissions

This chapter has already considered the dangers of overloading your submissions with too many references to cases and other authorities. This section, however, is concerned with how many references you should make to individual cases. There will be some cases that are particularly helpful to you, in that the judgments say things that suit the submissions that you need to make.

For example in *R v Owen Owens*, senior counsel for the appellant, in particular, would doubtless wish to make extensive reference to *R v Woollin* and *R v Nedrick*. Both of these cases will provide many passages that would be useful to help the argument that the appeal should be allowed.

It is because some cases will have so many passages that are potentially useful to you that you must exercise some discernment and selectivity in deciding which references to include in your submissions. It is tempting to include every passage that is helpful to your submissions, but the problem with this is that you risk turning your submission into a list of quotations from decided cases, and running out of time.

It was noted in chapter **4** that each individual or miniature submission that you make should include reference to the law, as well as your own commentary or submissions on why those legal references help your case. If you include too many quotations from a case, your submissions are at risk of losing this key element. In some judgments, the same point can be made again and again, albeit with different words, either by the same judge or by the various judges who heard the case. If you look at the judgments in *R v Woollin*, for example, there are many passages which could be used by the appellants to support the submission that the appeal in *R v Owen Owens* should be allowed. As a result, unless the case you are referring to provides you with virtually all your submissions, you may have to be highly selective in deciding what to include.

7.5.7   Length of quotations from cases

A common occurrence in moots is that participants, who are quite rightly referring to cases, will sometimes choose quotations that are far too long. As a result, the judges can be subjected to a prolonged period where a mooter is simply reading from a judgment. This can make your submissions seem rather tedious and can lead to the judges switching off. Whilst the judges will certainly be looking for you to be referring to authority, they do not want to sit and listen to mooters reading endless passages from a judgment.

If you are planning to use a quotation that is very long, there are ways of getting round boring the judges with lengthy spells of reading. The most obvious is to give serious thought to whether the passage, in its entirety, is really necessary to your submissions. If you do decide that all or most of the relevant passage should be included in your submissions, there are **two** easy ways of avoiding the aforementioned problem.

The **first way** is by not reading out the whole quotation, but cutting out bits of what the judge has said.

Example

One way of doing this is to refer the judges in the normal way to the passage that you wish them to consider. When you have done this, you will then begin reading from the judgment. At some point in the lengthy quotation, you may come to some lines that do not add much to your submissions. At this point, you can break away from the text, miss the lines that you do not wish to refer to, and then resume the quotation from where you think is appropriate.

After having read from a passage, something along the following lines would be appropriate:

> "My Lords, further down the page, at the beginning of paragraph D, her Ladyship goes on to say ..."

As a result of the above, you are not wasting time by reading bits of judgments that do not help you, or testing the patience of the judges in the process.

Another way of dealing with this situation with the minimum of fuss is to break up an excessively long quotation with your own commentary. This way, you can read a few lines from a passage, then provide some of your own submissions on why the passage helps your case, before continuing to read from the judgment. This is a good way of dealing with this situation, as it has the advantage of you giving submissions on passages from the judgment as soon as you have read them out. As a result, the passages will be fresh in the minds of the judges when you come to comment on them. It also achieves the desired objective of breaking up a quotation that would have been too long.

Example

After reading a paragraph from a judgment, you might appropriately say something along the following lines:

> "My Lords, I would submit that it is reasonable to interpret Lord Diplock in paragraph B as saying ... Further down the page, at paragraph F, his Lordship goes on to say ..."

7.5.8 Do not only use recent cases

The importance of being, and appearing to be, up to date in the law cannot be ignored. However, there is a tendency amongst some mooters, and practitioners, to concentrate on the latest cases, rather than those that are necessarily the most significant. By definition, a landmark case will be followed by later cases. The judges in the later cases may take several pages explaining why they are sticking with the old authority. Despite the length of some such judgments, cases that do this will sometimes add very little to the law as it was laid down in the landmark case. As a result, such cases can sometimes represent no more than a modern restatement of the law.

Because of the above, you are advised not to be so blinded by modernity to the extent that you will always choose a new case over an old one. Many very old cases are still good law. You should not let their relative antiquity put you off.

Example

One recent landmark case in criminal law, that was also referred to in chapter **2**, is that of *Attorney General for Jersey v Holley* [2005]. This is a Privy Council case that made significant pronouncements on the law on provocation, with the court providing extensive analysis as to why they reached the conclusions they did. In *R v James and Karimi* [2006], the Court of Appeal decided that the *Holley* decision represented the law on provocation in England and Wales, and should be followed instead of the House of Lords decision in *R v Smith (Morgan)* [2000].

If you were appearing in a moot where provocation was an issue, and looking for cases to use, you would probably find that, although *James and Karimi* is a more recent decision, *Holley* provides a more comprehensive judgment on provocation law. The reason for this is that the main focus in *James and Karimi* was on the separate issue of which authority should be followed, rather than a detailed examination of the law on provocation.

One way of looking as though you know the really significant aspects of the law in an area, at the same time as appearing up to date, is to try and use both landmark cases and more modern, but perhaps less significant, cases in tandem. If one of your submissions requires extensive reference to a well-established legal principle, or to a principle that was laid down in a landmark judgment, you should use that judgment as the central plank of the relevant submission. The more modern cases can then be used to hammer the more established point home, as they will emphasise the significance of the landmark judgment. You are effectively trying to have your cake and eat it, by referring the judges to a familiar principle and, at the same time, making it look cutting-edge. If the case law suits your submissions, then you may well have the opportunity to impress the judges in this way.

7.5.9   Referring to lines of authority

There tend to be few revolutionary changes brought about by case law. Instead, it is often the case that the courts will, through a line of cases, develop the law gradually and incrementally. Good submissions in moots will often reflect that the individual mooter appreciates this fact. For example, in *R v Owen Owens*, there may be some benefit to senior counsel for both sides making submissions on the case law which has developed over the years on the meaning of oblique intention. The reason why this type of submission can be valuable is that it is sometimes hard to understand the current law without some knowledge of the steps that led to it. If you appreciate why the law has changed over the years in a certain area, you will probably understand the current state of the law much better.

As a result, you may sometimes wish to give the judges some historical background on an aspect of the law, particularly if you are submitting that they should interpret the law in a certain way. Putting your submissions into a historical context may make it easier for the judges to understand them, and more likely that the judges will accept them.

One possible problem with using lines of case law, and introducing a historical context into your submissions, is that you can sometimes go too far. If you do, your submissions can lose their focus and sound more like a lecture on legal history than a set of submissions with a specific, persuasive aim in mind. Try to avoid this problem and remember that mooting is not lecturing; you are not trying to educate the judges, but to get them to adopt your line of argument, in accordance with your fictitious client's case.

At the beginning of a law report, usually just after the headnote, there will be a list of cases that were referred to in the judgment. This will often include some information on how those cases were regarded by the judges. For example, the list will often include cases that were overruled, approved, distinguished or merely considered.

These lists can be very helpful to you in your research, as they will provide you with other sources to look at and other potential avenues for your submissions.

7.5.10   Do not be afraid to refer to cases from other jurisdictions

The key with foreign cases is that you must understand the status of what you are referring to. In the English and Welsh courts, foreign case law has no binding effect, but it can certainly be persuasive. As a result, it is worth being courageous, and cautious at the same time, when considering whether to use foreign cases. It may be that there are no, or very few, domestic authorities on a particular subject. Alternatively, you may be appearing in the House of Lords and asking for the *Practice Statement* [1966] to be used in respect of a very unsatisfactory precedent. In both these instances, being able to point to a foreign case, where the point in question has been dealt with well, will provide you with a highly persuasive avenue of argument. Obviously, if you have domestic authorities available to you, you will use them first. Nevertheless, even where there are domestic authorities available, your submissions can be bolstered greatly by use of a good foreign case. Additionally, foreign cases can add a touch of exoticism to your submissions, as well as showing that you have the courage and research acumen to cast the net a bit wider than most.

In England and Wales, the most common example of foreign precedents will be those set by the Judicial Committee of the Privy Council. Because the judges who sit on the Judicial Committee of the Privy Council are the Law Lords sitting in a different context, the judgments of this court are particularly persuasive in the English and Welsh courts. Decisions of the European Court of Justice are not classed as foreign for these purposes, as the English courts regard themselves as bound by its decisions on matters of European law.

Because of the above, as long as you make it clear to the judges that you understand that foreign cases are not binding on domestic courts, you should be prepared to use foreign cases if they assist you.

Example

"My Lords, could I ask you to refer to the Privy Council decision of …? Whilst I have to concede that this decision is not strictly binding on this court, I would submit that the case nevertheless be treated as highly persuasive."

7.5.11   Referring to judges other than the judges in your moot

In most moots, during the course of your submissions, it is likely that you will have to refer to judges other than those in your moot. The two most frequent instances where this will be the case are as follows.

A) When you refer to a judgment in order to back up your submissions

As noted previously, in these circumstances you will be required to give the judges all the information they need to be able to follow the passages you are referring to. As a result, you will need to give them the name of the judge in question.

B) When you refer to the judges in the moot problem

Virtually all mooters, whether they appear for the appellant or the respondent, will refer to the findings of the judge(s) in the lower court. In *R v Owen Owens*, for example, it is unlikely that you would make submissions without referring to Evans HHJ. His summing up to the jury/pronouncements on the law are the reason why the appeal is taking place. Much of the Court of Appeal's attention is therefore going to be focused on whether Evans HHJ got the law right or wrong.

In spite of the fact that referring to other judges is a frequent requirement for mooters, many still make mistakes in this respect or appear to be uncertain. The key thing to remember is that the way that a judge is referred to in the law report is not quite the same as the way you refer to them in court. The law report will give you an abbreviated version: for example, Evans HHJ or Evans LJ.

The **table below** gives you the way in which a judge's name would be written down in the law reports and, alongside it, the way in which you should refer to that judge orally during the moot.

Written form	Spoken form
Evans HHJ	"His/Her Honour Judge Evans"
Evans J	"Mr/Mrs Justice Evans"
Evans LJ	"Lord/Lady Justice Evans"
Evans CJ	"Lord/Lady Evans, the Lord Chief Justice"
Sir Leonard Evans MR	"Sir Leonard Evans, the Master of the Rolls"
Lord Evans MR	"Lord Evans, the Master of the Rolls"
Lord Evans of Dover	"Lord Evans"

The above table will, of course, only apply to your initial reference to the judge in question. If you were to keep on saying "Lord Evans, the Master of the Rolls" every time you referred to him, it would start to look a little clumsy. As a result, when you do make further references to a judge, after having introduced them in the manner suggested above, it will suffice to say something along the following lines:

"At the bottom of page 673, his Lordship goes on to say ..."

or

"At the bottom of page 234, the learned judge develops this theme by stating that ..."

7.6   Referring to other sources

Cases are undoubtedly the most common source referred to by mooters, but they are certainly not the only source. This section briefly considers some of the other sources that you may wish to refer to when you are appearing in a moot. As with case law, the key is to understand the nature and status of the sources that you are referring to. If you understand this, it is much more likely that any submissions you make, which are based on other sources, will be within realistic parameters.

7.6.1   Statutes

Statutes are a highly significant source of English law. Because of this, it is quite possible that you will want to refer to statutes at some point in a moot. Whilst referring to statutes is not as fraught with difficulties as referring to cases, there are still a number of matters that you have to be careful to get right. The essence of referring to an authority is, of course, giving the judges all the information that they need to find what you are referring to. If the judges can do this, they are much more likely to understand your submissions and are in a better position, as a result, to question you on them.

When you refer the judges to a statute, you should normally **refer to it by its short title**. This is the title by which the statute is generally known, for example, the Fraud Act 2006, or the European Communities Act 1972.

As with case law, you should make sure that you know your way around a statute before you refer to it in court. If you only have knowledge of the section that you intend to refer to, this can create problems. Many statutes will have sections that put flesh on the bones of earlier sections. For example, in the Theft Act 1968, section 1 defines the offence of theft. However, you cannot fully understand the definition in section 1 unless you read sections 2 to 6. These sections provide some explanation for the terms contained in the section 1 definition. These sections are, of course, further supplemented by case law.

Other pieces of legislation will have interpretation sections that are often tucked away at the back of the Act, a long way from the section that you are referring to. The same can be said of schedules, which are also at the end of statutes, and which can contain passages that help you to interpret or understand sections from the Act.

After referring to the short title of the Act, you will want to refer the judges to the particular part of the statute that you are making submissions on. Do not simply tell the judges to turn to a certain page of a photocopy or a volume; give the judges the relevant sections, subsections and paragraphs.

Example

"My Lords, for my next submission, I would like to draw the court's attention to the Theft Act 1968, copies of which are before your Lordships. Could I refer your Lordships, in particular, to section 2(1)(a), which states ..."

If you simply give the judges the section number and nothing else, they will find it harder to follow you. As noted previously, a key aspect of referring to authorities is that the judges should be able to follow you every step of the way.

It therefore goes without saying that you should read legislation carefully before introducing it into your submissions. You should also take steps to ascertain that the Act that you wish to use is still in force or, if it is a new piece of legislation, that the Act is already in force.

When you are using statutes in your submissions, you also need to try to see matters from the viewpoint of the judges. As a result, you should familiarise yourself with the approaches to statutory interpretation and the various presumptions that can apply. Additionally, you will need to know what aids to interpretation the judges are permitted to use. If you are weak on such issues, it is possible that you will make submissions that are unrealistic. For a much more detailed examination of statutory interpretation issues, see section 2.7.

7.6.2   Textbooks

The use of textbooks as a secondary source of law was also dealt with in chapter **2**. Whilst you should certainly exercise caution when considering using textbooks, there is certainly no rule against it. The key is to make it clear to the judges that you understand the status of the source you are using.

When you do refer to such sources, you must, as with all other legal sources, provide the judges with all the information they need to keep up with you and to appreciate what the source actually is. As a result, you need to give the judges the following information:

1) The author(s) of the book.

2) The full title of the book.

3) The number of the edition you are referring to.

4) The publisher and the year of publication.

5) The particular page(s) you are referring to.

Example

"My Lords, could I now refer the court to Jonathan Herring's textbook 'Criminal law: Text, Cases and Materials'? The edition in front of your Lordships is the third edition, published by Oxford in 2008. I would be grateful if your Lordships could turn to page 225 where, at the beginning of the second paragraph, it says ..."

7.6.3   Articles from learned journals

Again, the use of articles in learned journals as a secondary source of law was mentioned in chapter **2**. The use of such sources, although they are not binding, can be beneficial to your submissions in many ways. Judges in the appellate courts are often prepared to consider the views of leading academics in the relevant area. As a general rule, you will be on safer ground with the more eminent sources and academics. A certain amount of discretion is therefore required in this respect.

When you do decide to refer to an article in a moot, the judges should be given the following information:

1) The title of the article.

2)   The author(s) of the article.

3)   The title of the article.

4)   The name of the journal where the article is to be found.

4)   The date of the article.

5)   The page number.

Example

"Could I now draw your Lordships' attention to the article 'The Duty of Care in Gross Negligence Manslaughter' by Jonathan Herring? The article is to be found in the January edition of the Criminal Law Review, at pages 24 to 40. I have provided your Lordships with copies of the relevant passages."

7.6.4   Reports from government and other agencies

During your research for moots, you may come across the reports of Royal Commissions and government departments, as well as reports from agencies such as the Law Commission. Such reports will often be recommending changes or additions to the law. These can provide you with fruitful avenues for your submissions, especially if they are on an area of law where there are few authorities, or where you are arguing, in a moot in the House of Lords, that the Practice Statement should be applied.

One slight cautionary note, which was mentioned in chapter **2**, is that, if you are proposing major changes to the law based on such a report, the court may respond that such major changes are a matter for Parliament and not the courts. Obviously, you need to be ready to counter this argument, and to persuade the court that it would not be too great a step for them to implement the changes you are suggesting.

When you are referring to reports, be careful to provide the judges with the following information:

1)   The name of the report.

2)   The name of the body or department that wrote the report, including the names of the author(s), if the author's name is closely associated with the report.

3)   The number of the report (if applicable). For example the Law Commission usually gives a number to each of its reports.

4)   The date that the report was published.

5)   The relevant pages/paragraphs/sections of the report that you wish to refer to.

6)   Using bundles looks more slick and efficient.

7.7 The use of bundles

It is not essential that you bring volumes of law reports, statutes etc from your law library into the moot court. One alternative is to provide the judges with a bundle (or bundles) of the authorities you wish to rely on. Some moots will insist on the use of bundles, and others will leave the choice to you.

There are a number of **advantages** to using bundles:

1)   If you do your research using services like Westlaw or Lawtel, you can simply print off two (or more, if appropriate) copies of the authorities you wish to rely on. As a result, you do not have to go to the law library and use the volumes, which may be being used by someone else at the time.

2)   You can present your bundle well, by clearly separating the cases and placing them in the order in which you wish to deal with them in the moot.

3)   The judges will then have a neat pile of all the authorities you will use, and will not have to mess around finding the correct volumes on a trolley. Everything they need to follow your submissions will be in front of them in the bundle.

4)   You can have exactly the same bundle in front of you in the moot, so that there is less chance of you having a different version of the case to the judges.

5)   There is no need to do all your legal research in a law library. Instead, it can be done anywhere where there is a computer.

6)   Having a bundle saves the time in the moot that would otherwise be taken up with the judges trying to find the relevant volumes.

The main potential **disadvantages** of bundles are as follows:

1)   It requires lots of printing and is a bit of a waste of paper and money. Unfortunately, you cannot just print off the paragraph from a case that you want to use. The judges will really expect the whole case

as, when they question you, they might want to refer to other parts of the judgment.

2)   You still have to give the citations for the particular version of the case that you are using. If you use services like Westlaw or Lawtel, they will give you the option of which version of the law reports to use. Even though everything is in a bundle, you still need to give full citations for the case. It is not enough to simply say "I got this off Westlaw".

3)   Those who are not very proficient with services like Westlaw or Lawtel may accidentally print off different versions of cases for themselves and the judges.

7.8   Referring to cases where judgment was delivered after the 11th January 2001

For all cases, where judgment was delivered after the 11th January 2001, a new system of "neutral citations" has been introduced by way of Practice Direction. The reasons for this are to conform to international practice and to facilitate the publication of judgments on the World Wide Web. The system means that, where you see citations for any case in the High Court or above decided after that date, for example in the table of cases in a textbook, you will see the neutral citation as well as the traditional citations that relate to specific series of law reports.

For example, *R v Hasan (Aytach)* [2005] would have the following neutral citation: *R v Hasan* [2005] UKHL 22. This means that the case was heard in the United Kingdom House of Lords, and was the twenty-second case where judgment was delivered in 2005.

A more traditional citation for the same case would be [2005] 2 AC 467. This, of course, means that the case can be found in volume two of the Appeal Cases of 2005, at page 467. All law reports will contain the official transcript, which is what the judges actually said in their judgments, but will differ in the bits that are written by their own reporters, for example, headnotes and case history etc. Services like Westlaw and Lawtel will provide you with the official transcript, as well as all the reports of the case provided by the leading series of law reports.

Some judges may not want the neutral citation, but if in doubt, give the neutral citation first and then the specific citations for the law report that you are using. If you are just using the official transcript, then the neutral citation alone will suffice.

Chapter 8

Analysis of online moot demonstrations

8.1 Resources on the web to accompany this chapter

If you go to www.palgrave.com/law/hill, you will find the following web resources:

1) Sample moot performance (first recording) of *R v Owen Owens* **(senior counsel only)**.

2) Eight "highlight" clips of the above.

3) Seven "lowlight" clips from a performance of *R v Owen Owens* that was recorded to illustrate examples of bad mooting practice (second recording).

8.2 The structure of this chapter

The **first,** and largest, part of this chapter is dedicated to commentary on, and analysis of, the sample moot performance of *R v Owen Owens*. This commentary follows the same order as chapters **3** to **7** and, accordingly, focuses on the assessment and scoring criteria referred to in those chapters. As a result, it provides practical illustrations of many of the points referred to in those chapters. As well as giving a full commentary on the whole performance by senior counsel in *R v Owen Owens*, this section also provides references to the shorter "highlight" clips of the same performance that are available.

The **second** part of the chapter provides commentary on the short "lowlight" clips that are available, to provide illustrations of some common examples of bad mooting practice.

8.2.1 Guidance for reading this chapter and watching the accompanying web resources

A) When you visit www.palgrave.com/law/hill, you should be able to watch the following:

i) Full performance of *R v Owen Owens* (senior counsel only). The submissions of Ms Fairclough and Mr Cooper in full, including Ms Fairclough's right of reply.

ii) Eight "highlight" clips of the above.

iii) Seven "highlight" or "lowlight" clips of the second recording of *R v Owen Owens* to illustrate bad practice.

B) The web resources, it follows, only deal with the first ground of appeal which are covered by senior counsel for both sides. The second and third grounds of the appeal, which would have been dealt with by junior counsel, are not covered on the available clips.

C) The time limit on submissions for this moot was **20 minutes**, with a further **five minutes** given to senior counsel for the appellant for the right of reply.

D) The **eight** highlight clips of the moot will be referenced as and when appropriate throughout the commentary on the full performance. This is both for ease of reference and also to save you having to keep watching the full performance in its entirety.

E) The commentary in **part one** of this chapter, as noted previously, is presented in line with the structure of chapters **3** to **7**. It is, therefore, advisable that you consult the relevant chapters as you read the commentary and watch the film. The comments on each mooter's performance are, therefore, presented in the following order:

i) Style and presentation (see also chapter **3**).

ii) Structure and content of legal argument (see also chapter **4**).

iii) Responding to opponents (see also chapter **5**).

iv) Dealing with the judges in a moot (see also chapter **6**).

v) Use of authorities (see also chapter **7**).

F) Where the intention is to draw your attention to specific examples, the **approximate** relevant time from the film appears in brackets next to the description of the comment, for ease of reference. Where more general comments are made, no such time indications are given.

G) If your moot is assessed, you will probably receive written feedback on your performance. It is unlikely, however, that the feedback will be anywhere near the length of the commentary in this chapter. What follows is feedback of a type that most judges or tutors would like to give, if they had the time. For more on dealing with the feedback you receive, see chapter **9**.

H) There are a few instances in the commentary that follows where some points are dealt with more than once, albeit in different contexts. This is deliberate, and stems from the fact that there is a degree of overlap between the assessment and judging criteria for mooting. For example, a point that is relevant to style and presentation may also be relevant to structure.

I) **Part two** of this chapter provides commentary on the seven "lowlight" clips from the second recording of *R v Owen Owens*. Whilst some of the errors made may seem a little humorous, it should be noted that they are based on mistakes made by real mooters in real moots. Indeed, some of the mistakes are surprisingly common.

8.3 Commentary on first recording of *R v Owen Owens* (senior counsel)

8.4 Performance by senior counsel for the appellant (Mrs Fairclough)

Ms Fairclough's submissions are now considered in light of the above guidance.

8.4.1 Style and presentation

This part of the commentary could usefully be read in conjunction with chapter **3**.

Introduces herself and her opponent (00:03)

Ms Fairclough, right at the beginning of her submissions, makes a point of saying who she is and which side she appears for. She also does the same for her opponent. This is not only courteous and professional sounding, but allows you to start your submissions on a straightforward and simple note. If your submissions start brightly and confidently, it can set you up nicely for a good performance. If you go to the appellate courts to watch, counsel will invariably begin in this way. A chief difficulty for most new mooters is that of adopting an appropriate courtroom manner and speaking like a lawyer. The way in which introductions are done is an example of this.

As Ms Fairclough does, you should also make sure that you remind the judges of which ground(s) of appeal you are dealing with. The judges will, of course, already be aware of this, but it will make your opening comments sound comprehensive if you briefly refer to the grounds you are covering.

Use of a script (12:56)

One of the things that is slightly noticeable during these submissions is that, at times, Ms Fairclough appears to be reading from a script. This is certainly not an extreme case of a mooter being too reliant on a script, but it is nevertheless apparent at some points during the submissions.

As a result, the submissions suffer from some of the problems mentioned in chapter **3**. Sometimes (for example, at 01:00), the expressiveness of the delivery could be improved. Most mooters, when they are reading, struggle to vary the intonation of the voice as much as they would if they were speaking without having to constantly look down and read.

The pace of the submissions can also be adversely affected by reading, as many mooters tend to speak more quickly when they are reading from notes. This is perhaps noticeable occasionally here, for example during the reference to *R v Nedrick* (09:18), although it is not generally a particular problem with these submissions.

Occasionally, throughout the submissions the delivery is not quite as lucid and natural as it would have been had Ms Fairclough not been so reliant on notes. This aspect of Ms Fairclough's submissions improves later on, as she seems to become more relaxed. You are advised to adopt bullet points as early as you can in your mooting career. This is especially the case if, as with Ms Fairclough, you have some potential as a speaker.

Nerves (00:44)

There are a few occasions during the moot where Ms Fairclough looks a little nervous. As noted in chapter **3**, nerves are perfectly normal and, in some ways, essential to the mooter. As a result, whilst there is some evidence of nerves during these submissions, this could certainly not be described as a highly nervous performance. Any nerves were well controlled and, generally, fairly well concealed. After a few minutes, Ms Fairclough seems to settle down and become more relaxed. This is particularly the case with her second submission, which was delivered with more poise and aplomb than the first. Such a phenomenon is not uncommon, with many mooters initially struggling with nerves and relaxation in the early part of their submissions.

Asks for the appeal to be allowed early on (00:46)

Mooting is all about using the law to be persuasive. It is, therefore, imperative that you never lose sight during your submissions of what it is that you are asking the judges to do. Additionally, you must not let the judges lose sight of what you are asking of them. As a result, it is a good idea to provide little prompts at key points in your submissions. After covering the ground of appeal that she will be dealing with, Ms Fairclough clearly makes the point that it is on that basis that she will be submitting that the appeal should be allowed. This point is also relevant in terms of structuring submissions, and is returned to in section **8.4.2** below.

Outlining the two main submissions (00:52)

A relevant point for style purposes (as well as for structure) is that you must make it clear to the judges where your submissions are going and, as a result, what you are asking them to do. Ms Fairclough clearly states from the outset what her two main submissions are going to be. The benefits of setting your stall out in this way are that the judges can visualise your submissions in advance. This is important if the judges are going to be persuaded by them. It is not in your interests to keep the judges in suspense. If they can see where your submissions are going, they can truly address their minds to how persuasive and logical your arguments are. Judges will not enjoy being kept guessing about the direction of your arguments. They will want to feel that they are able to follow your arguments every step of the way, and to know in advance roughly what you are going to say.

Volume and clarity of submissions

There were no problems here. Anyone of average hearing would find that the submissions were loud enough to be easily heard. This was augmented by the fact that the speech was generally very clear. Occasionally, the speech was a little fast, but this did not affect Ms Fairclough's ability to be heard and understood. At the same time, the submissions were never too loud. (See also highlight clip 3.)

Pace of submissions

This has already been considered previously. One or two parts of the submissions were slightly fast (for example, at 16:10), but these submissions were generally delivered at an appropriate speed. As far as the fast parts are concerned, Ms Fairclough could easily remedy this slight defect by a more judicious use of pauses during submissions and by a slight decrease in pace of delivery. (See also highlight clip 3.)

Some mooters' submissions, however, are obviously too fast, and this is painfully evident when they watch a recording of themselves. That is not the case here. Any improvements to be made, as far as pace are concerned, are only minor ones.

Eye contact

Although there was some evidence of reading during these submissions, Ms Fairclough nevertheless maintained good levels of eye contact with the judges. This was certainly not a case where the mooter's head was down, clearly reading from a script. As a result, although the submissions could have been a bit more natural and lucid, they were still fairly engaging from the judges' perspective.

Good eye contact normally commands the attention of an audience. If there is little eye contact, it makes the mooter look insular and remote. It also makes it very difficult for the mooter to develop any sort of rapport with the judges and to be persuasive. You do not have to be looking at the judges all the time. There is nothing wrong with looking down from time to time, as long as you do maintain eye contact.

Asks for permission to start first submission (02:40)

This is another point that will be considered in terms of structure in the next section, but which is also relevant to style and presentation. If you ask for permission to begin your first submission, or announce that you are coming on to it, you are signalling the end of your opening comments and the beginning of your detailed submissions. This is not only good style, but is also courteous to the judges, and shows that you care about whether they are following what you are saying.

It is also good if you develop a little bit of rapport with the judges as a result of brief exchanges such as these. It will make you, and the judges, feel more at ease. This can also have the effect of making it less daunting when the judges start to ask you some questions. Another advantage is that it provides a natural pause for you to breathe more easily and for the judges to perhaps use the moment to ask you a question. This is far better than being interrupted in mid-sentence.

Announces the end of the first submission and the beginning of the second (07:07)

The same points apply here as in the previous section. See also highlight clip 2.

Announces that the judgments in *R v Nedrick* and *R v Woollin* will be referred to shortly (08:15)

This is good practice, from both a style and a structure point of view. The judges here were put on notice that Ms Fairclough would soon be referring to these sources. If the judges know where you are going with the points you are making, it is much less likely that they will lose their patience with you or that their attention will drift.

The importance of so-called signposts has been emphasised elsewhere in this book. If you introduce regular signposts into your submissions, you are showing consideration for the judges and helping them to understand what you are saying. The more they understand you, the more likely they are to be persuaded by what you say.

Improvement in confidence, relaxation and expressiveness (09:15 approximately)

Only an approximate time is given above for this point, because it is difficult to say when exactly this aspect of Ms Fairclough's submissions improved. Nevertheless, if you rewind the clip to the beginning, you should be able to note how much more relaxed the delivery is. As a result of this, the delivery is more expressive, engaging and persuasive. As noted previously, improvements of this sort as submissions progress are not uncommon.

More use of signposts (17:57), (17:59)

Signposting is used to good effect on these two occasions. On the first occasion (17:57), Ms Fairclough makes it clear that she is concluding her second submission. This again tells the judges where she is up to in her submissions, and gives them the opportunity to consider whether they want to ask any questions at that point.

On the second occasion (17:59), Ms Fairclough states that, "before concluding", she will briefly deal with the case of *R v Hancock and Shankland*. There are a number of benefits to this in terms of a number of the assessment/judging criteria. In terms of style and presentation, however, it looks competent to mop up and deal with a case that is not a central part of your submissions, but which is mentioned by the judge in the lower court. It gives the submissions an appearance of completeness.

Another benefit of this signpost is in terms of timekeeping. As noted in chapter 1, mooting submissions are timed, and these time limits are normally adhered to quite strictly. The chances are that most mooters will, as they reach the end of their submissions, not know exactly how much time they have left. By using the words "before concluding", Ms Fairclough is sending out the signal to the judges that she is close to finishing her submissions. Her concluding remarks, it follows, are imminent. This is important for the judges if they are conscious that a mooter is running out of time. If they are told that the end is nigh, they are more likely to be a bit more generous with the clock, if necessary.

A final benefit of this sort of signpost is that it might have the effect of making a judge postpone a question for a few moments. If a judge can see that a more suitable moment for a question will arise soon, he or she may decline to interrupt. It is far better if you can exercise some control over when questions will be asked. Use of signposts is one way in which you can try to influence this.

Conclusion to the submissions (19:24)

This is a reasonably good attempt at a conclusion. The key points are that you briefly reiterate your submissions and state how they all point in one direction, in terms of what the court should do. Ms Fairclough attempts to finish strongly by stating that the conviction is unsafe and that it should be quashed. She also asks for the appeal to be allowed. As noted previously, it is surprising how many mooters fail to make these basic points. When you sit down at the end of your submissions, what you want the judges to do, and why you submit they should do it, should be ringing loud and clear in their ears. Your concluding remarks should achieve this objective. Do not leave the judges to work these basic points out for themselves. Advocacy is the art of persuasion, not the art of giving the judges a puzzle to work out. Ms Fairclough largely succeeded in this respect.

Politeness and respect

Ms Fairclough's demeanour throughout her submissions is respectful towards the judges, without being sycophantic. The judge is in charge, and Ms Fairclough seems to appreciate this. Questions were always answered politely and in an appropriate way. (For more on modes of address and appropriate language, see later in this section.)

Body language

There were no glaring examples of inappropriate or distracting body language during these submissions. Ms Fairclough generally remained fairly still throughout. There were some hand gestures, but they were generally within acceptable parameters for courtroom speaking.

By way of a contrast to this, have a look at the answer to the last judicial question (20:13). Arguably, a slightly informal manner is adopted here, coupled with some slightly over-the-top and inappropriate hand gestures.

Posture during these submissions is not a problem. There is no slouching, nor, on the other hand, does Ms Fairclough appear to be too rigid. Her notes are kept on the lectern in front of her, at a height where they can easily be consulted without too much movement. It was noted in chapter **3** that some mooters hold their notes or cards in front of them whilst they are speaking. This creates a defensive demeanour, which is displeasing to the eye. This was certainly not a problem here. (See highlight clip 3.)

Awareness of surroundings

In chapter **3**, it was noted that the best advocates are at ease in the court environment and, as such, have a good awareness of their surroundings. This can manifest itself in many ways, but one of the most important of these is in an advocate's dealings with others in court. In this respect, Ms Fairclough fared reasonably well, and seemed to have a sense of self-awareness and awareness for those around her.

Such awareness is illustrated by the reference to the case of *Nedrick* where, after giving the citations for the case, Ms Fairclough clearly waits for the judges to find the volume, page and passage she is referring to. Poorer mooters find this skill hard and often plough on, head down, with little awareness of their audience.

Another illustration of this is when the judge asks questions. If you watch Ms Fairclough, she appears to be ready for, and almost anticipating, the questions when they are asked. At no point do the judges have to forcefully interrupt her. If you are aware of the judges whilst you are speaking, their manner and body language will often tell you that a question or interruption is coming. Good eye contact is obviously essential to awareness of surroundings.

Dress

There were no problems with dress. The clothing worn demonstrated a degree of effort and respect for the proceedings, and were certainly not inappropriate for a moot.

Modes of address and appropriate language

Apart from on a few occasions, which will be referred to in a moment, the language was generally what one would expect of an advocate in the appellate courts. The language used was not excitable or theatrical, but was moderate and forceful. As a result, the submissions sounded like a lawyer arguing a case in court, rather than, for example, a political speech. Ms Fairclough correctly used phrases like "in my submission" or "I would submit" instead of "I think", "I believe" or "in my opinion". When addressing the judges, the correct forms of address were used throughout, for example, "my Lord(s)" or "your Lordship(s)". When referring to judges from the law reports or when referring to Evans HHJ, Ms Fairclough did this correctly, for example "His Honour Judge Evans" or "the learned trial judge".

One example of slightly inappropriate language was the use of "OK" (04:02). Whilst this is not a major fault, and was barely noticeable, it was nevertheless inappropriate. It is very easy to slip into informal speech when you are in a moot, and to use expression like "OK", "you know" and "yeah". In these submissions, this was not a big problem, but with some mooters it can be highly noticeable and detract quite badly from the impression they give to the judges.

On the whole, it would be fair to say that Ms Fairclough was comfortable with the courtroom way of speaking, and was able to adopt it without sounding pompous or too strained. (See also highlight clip 3.)

Use of humour and wit

This was not a performance where any great attempt was made to use humour to enhance the submissions. Nevertheless, the submissions did have an element of personality about them, and did not come across as bland or boring.

8.4.2   Structure and content

This part of the commentary could usefully be read in conjunction with chapter **4**.

Actual criminal law content

A detailed discussion of the criminal law issues in the moot is outside the scope of this book. Nevertheless, you should realise that how well you appear to know the relevant law, and how well you use it to make your submissions, will be a big part of the assessment/judging process. A few brief comments will, therefore, be made on this aspect of the performance.

Ms Fairclough certainly came across as reasonably confident on most of the legal issues raised in her submissions, as well as pretty well organised. It was clear that there was a reasonable understanding of the two types of intention (direct and oblique) and how they impacted on the moot case. Ms Fairclough also seemed to be familiar with the judgments that she used in her submissions. On the whole, when she was asked questions by the judge, Ms Fairclough seemed to be fairly comfortable, indicating a degree of preparedness. One exception to this (at 12:20) was when she seemed either surprised or confused by the supplementary question from the judge about *R v Nedrick*.

Both submissions, on direct and oblique intention, could possibly have been more detailed, with more on the issue of accepted medical practice in the former, and more on some of the finer aspects of the *Woollin* direction in the latter. However, in spite of this and, bearing in mind the time constraints, a likely counter-argument is that it would have been hard to include very much more in these submissions. Overall, the impression was of a mooter who was comfortable with this area of the law and who did not struggle with it.

Timing of the submissions (21:27)

The maximum time for submissions was 20 minutes. Bearing in mind that the judicial questioning took perhaps three to three and a half minutes, it is arguable that there was a little more time available for these submissions. Nevertheless, especially when the clock is stopped for judicial questions, it is very hard to be absolutely precise on timing. Ms Fairclough used the vast majority of the time available to her, and filled it with meaningful submissions. This was certainly not a case of a mooter who was short on material. The impression given was of a mooter who had prepared well, so that her submissions would be very close to the maximum time allotted, without going over time.

Overall/macro structure of the submissions

These submissions clearly had a beginning, a middle and an end, in that Ms Fairclough very clearly told the judges, when she was making her opening remarks, that she had two main submissions. Ms Fairclough also made it clear when her main submissions actually began and when she was concluding. As a result, her overall/macro structure was very clear and easy to follow.

As noted in chapter **4**, your opening remarks should give the judges a clear idea of what you will cover and in what order. The main body of your submissions should explain in detail what your submissions are, and how they help your case. Your closing remarks should then mirror both of the above, and hammer home to the judges that you have done what you said you were going to do at the beginning.

These submissions clearly achieved these three structural objectives. Extensive use was made of signposting and mirroring, so that the judges were in no doubt what the structure actually was, and where Ms Fairclough was up to in it. If the judges know where you are up to and where you will be going with your submissions, they are more likely to be persuaded by what you say.

The order of the submissions

This aspect of Ms Fairclough's overall structure was also fairly straightforward, as there were only two submissions to be made. It was noted in chapter 4 that, when considering the order of the submissions you wish to make, it is worth thinking about the most persuasive arrangement of them. If, however, you only have a very small number of submissions, ordering may be fairly easy. Ms Fairclough, therefore, simply adopted the same order as to be found in the moot problem with Evans HHJ's findings and relevant ground of the appeal. Indeed, Ms Fairclough even admitted that her first submission was perhaps outside the scope of the ground of appeal, but that she nevertheless wanted to cover it, for the sake of completeness.

The second submission, rightly or wrongly, was dealt with at much greater length than the first. Ms Fairclough clearly felt that her most persuasive points were in respect of this second ground, and that these were the points she wanted to be uppermost in the judges' minds when she sat down.

The reference to *Hancock and Shankland* (17:57) could have been an example of finishing submissions on an inappropriately low ebb. However, that was not the case here as, even though *Hancock and Shankland* was not a case Ms Fairclough was relying on, she still managed to make a good point out of it (17:57), namely that the law had moved on considerably since that case.

As a result of the above, the overall/macro structure of these submissions was easy to follow and persuasively ordered.

Mirroring and signposting

These techniques have been referred to already in this section, but are worthy of a mention in their own right. The points raised in Ms Fairclough's opening remarks were all dealt with in detail in her submissions, and these, in turn, were all returned to in her conclusion. As a result, the key elements of the submissions all mirrored one another, giving the submissions a degree of continuity and consistency. This made them easier to follow.

Signposts were also used at regular intervals, to remind the judges either of where Ms Fairclough was up to in her submissions, or to inform them of what was coming next. As a result, the judges should have been in no doubt as to where Ms Fairclough was up to in her submissions. It was also very obvious when one point or submission was ending and another beginning. (See highlight clip 2.)

Structuring and content of individual points/micro structure

In chapter **4**, it was noted that each individual point or submission you make should, ideally, have four elements to it. Both of Ms Fairclough's main submissions had all four elements in them, although not always in the precise order suggested. This is not a problem, as long as the submission still has a logical structure and is persuasive.

When Ms Fairclough deals with her second submission on oblique intention (07:05), she does the following:

1) Tells the court what the submission is.

2) Refers to the law on it in some detail (for example *Nedrick* and *Woollin*). (See highlight clip 3.)

3) Gives her own commentary or submissions on the passages she has read out. (See highlight clip 3.)

4) States that, because of this, Evans HHJ had wrongly directed the jury, meaning that the appeal should be allowed and the conviction quashed.

As a result, the judges should have no doubts as to what Ms Fairclough's submission is, what law is being used to back it up, and what she is asking them to do.

Overloading of submissions

This was not a problem here. Ms Fairclough used the majority of the time allotted to her, and filled it with mostly meaningful submissions. Only two main submissions were made and only a small number of cases referred to. Many mooters feel that they should pack their submissions with many references to lots of different cases. This is not necessary. Only use cases if they really make points that help your case. If two cases say the same or similar things, you may need to consider whether you need to refer to both.

8.4.3   Ability to respond to opponent's submissions

This part of the commentary could usefully be read in conjunction with chapter 5.

In order to follow this part of the commentary, you must go to Ms Fairclough's right of reply, which is to be found towards the end of the full recording of the moot (44:05).

Timing of the reply

Ms Fairclough's right of reply took just under four minutes in total. She was allocated a maximum of five minutes. It is fair to say that, whilst not all the allocated time was used, Ms Fairclough certainly made a decent attempt to respond to Mr Cooper's submissions. Some mooters, when they are poorly prepared, or when they have not properly listened to their opponent's submissions, find that their right to reply (or response, if they are a respondent) is very brief indeed. This was not the case here. Ms Fairclough had clearly been listening to Mr Cooper's submissions and had a number of meaningful points to make.

Overall structure of the reply

This could arguably have been made a bit more obvious, especially when one bears in mind the fact that Ms Fairclough could have spoken for another minute or so. As a result, a few comments setting out her stall for the reply would certainly not have gone amiss. For example, Ms Fairclough could have briefly explained how many points she wished to make in reply, which of Mr Cooper's submissions they related to, and what they were. Instead, the reply began with Ms Fairclough explaining that she had "a number" of points to make. This is a small point, but it would have given the reply a more polished look.

On the more positive side, Ms Fairclough simply structured her reply according to the order in which Mr Cooper had dealt with points in his submissions. As a result, the first point in reply was on the disputed medical evidence. The second and third points were on Mr Cooper's first and second submissions respectively.

During the reply, Ms Fairclough continued to make good use of signposts to explain which submission of Mr Cooper's she was referring to. It is essential when you are replying that the judges understand exactly which submissions of the other side you are dealing with. This was not a problem here.

Structure of individual points/micro structure in the reply

In chapter **5**, it was suggested that each individual point you make in response to a submission of your opponent should contain certain basic points. As far as these were concerned, Ms Fairclough scored fairly well. Each point she made was clearly linked to a submission that had been made by Mr Cooper. Ms Fairclough was also very clear as to what her responses were. As a result, the reply was certainly easy to understand.

Where appropriate, for example with the points on the cases of *Bolitho* and *Woollin*, Ms Fairclough also made use of authority to back her points up. She could have done this more directly, in the sense of referring to passages from the judgments, with *Bolitho*, but did better with *Woollin*, with a direct reference to Lord Steyn.

Many poorer mooters struggle with this, as they find it hard to organise their thoughts well enough, before they reply, to use authorities. As a result, many judges will be looking at whether you can incorporate use of authorities into your right of reply or response. As a result, it was good to see Ms Fairclough attempt to do this.

Style of presentation for the reply

In parts, the delivery seemed more lucid than parts of the main submissions, with Ms Fairclough appearing to be less reliant on a script. In other parts, however, there was some stammering and tripping over words. This is a common problem with mooters who are a bit heavily scripted in their main submissions. The lack of a script during the reply can make them feel uncomfortable and exposed. Eye contact was certainly well maintained during the reply, as it was during the main submissions, and the general style of speech was, once again, appropriate to the occasion. Ms Fairclough, happily, did not slip into the trap of addressing her opponent instead of the judges during her reply. Indeed, a courteous manner was retained throughout, with her opponent correctly being referred to as "my learned friend Mr Cooper".

Were the main submissions just repeated?

On the whole, the answer to this question has to be no! Virtually everything that Ms Fairclough said in her reply was in direct response to points that Mr Cooper had specifically made in his submissions. As noted in chapter **5**, there is something of a temptation to simply repeat the submissions you have already made. This is especially the case where you are short on material for your response or where you do not have the flexibility and knowledge to respond well.

This was not the case here. There was evidence that Ms Fairclough was well prepared for the moot and that she must have been listening carefully when Mr Cooper was speaking.

Responding to a poor/strong opponent

Mr Cooper's submissions were audible and structured and, as a result, pretty easy to follow. Whilst many mooters may pray for a poor opponent, it can hopefully be seen from the video that, if what your opponent says is clear and well structured, it actually gives you far more in terms of good points to make in your response. It was largely because of the fact that what Mr Cooper said made sense that Ms Fairclough was able to make a few decent points by way of reply.

8.4.4   Dealings with the judges

This part of the commentary could usefully be read in conjunction with chapter **6**.

Allowing the judges to interrupt

When judicial questions came, they usually came at pretty convenient moments, when there was a pause in the submissions. Some judges, as noted previously, will not be so courteous and will just interrupt you. Whilst Ms Fairclough did not have to deal with this difficulty, she did not seem surprised by questions. She seemed aware of when questions were coming and was calm when they did. As a result, there was none of the awkwardness that can result when the judge and the mooter find themselves talking at the same time.

Listening to and answering judicial questions

The video suggests that Ms Fairclough was generally listening well to judicial questions, and was able to understand most of what was said to her. In spite of this, the effectiveness of the answers did vary somewhat. The first question (05:45) was answered in a slightly unconvincing manner, with Ms Fairclough seeming slightly unnerved by this first serious interaction with a judge.

The second question (11:02) was a fairly long question, which meant that there was a lot for Ms Fairclough to take on board. Nevertheless this question was dealt with pretty competently, with Ms Fairclough making light work of a potential clash with the judge. Additionally, there was some evidence here of Ms Fairclough being able to think on her feet. The supplementary question (12:20) seemed to confuse Ms Fairclough, however, and her response to it was far from convincing.

The third question, on the case of *Woollin* (14:53), was also dealt with fairly confidently, with the answer being backed up by a reference to the judgments.

The last question came at the end of Ms Fairclough's submissions (20:13) and was, once again, a fairly long question. Ms Fairclough demonstrated good listening skills and made a decent attempt at answering the question. However, at this late stage she did adopt slightly informal speech and distracting hand gestures. (See also highlight clip 4.)

Avoid annoyance or impatience with the judges

There were no problems in this respect. Ms Fairclough was, at all times in the moot, courteous and respectful. There were times, particularly at the beginning of her submissions, when she seemed nervous, but this did not translate itself into rudeness or awkwardness with the judges.

What questions were asked?

As noted in chapter **6**, in most moots, the questions that will be asked are usually fairly straightforward to predict by anybody with a strong knowledge of the subject area and who has read the moot problem. None of the judicial questions here were particularly surprising, nor were they outside the parameters delineated by the grounds of appeal.

When were the questions asked?

As noted in chapter **6**, judges will vary enormously as to how many questions they will ask and when they will ask them. Here, Ms Fairclough was certainly not bombarded with questions, but was asked a few. As far as timing was concerned, the questions seemed to come at fairly regular intervals throughout the submissions, usually at fairly convenient points. There were no questions during the right of reply, but this will not always be the case.

Not knowing the answer to judicial questions

In chapter **6**, some alternative methods were considered for when a mooter does not know the answer to a judicial question. Generally, Ms Fairclough seemed fairly well prepared on the law, and appeared to understand what was being said, in her exchanges with the bench.

There was, however, one awkward moment (12:20) when the judge asked a supplementary question about the case of *Nedrick*. It is very difficult to read a mooter's mind in these situations, but Ms

Fairclough's answer looked decidedly uncertain and even had some of the hallmarks of a guess about it. On this occasion, the judge did not follow the matter up, but it is sound advice never to guess when answering judicial questions. If you do not know the answer, it is far safer, and more commendable, to simply admit that you cannot answer the question. The judges will often sense that you are guessing. The situation will become even worse if the judge probes a bit further and catches you out. (See also highlight clip 4.)

Use of authorities when answering questions

Ms Fairclough, as noted previously, appeared well prepared on the relevant law. Because of this, she was able, when answering questions, to refer to case law and to certain passages from judgments. One good example of this was the reference to the judgments in *Nedrick* during her answer to the question on that case (11:02). Being able to refer to authorities in this way when answering questions is impressive, as it shows that you know the relevant law well and in some detail. It also shows that you can think on your feet and that you have the flexibility to use your knowledge in response to events during the moot. (See also highlight clip 4.)

Do not be afraid of the judges. Stick to your submissions whenever possible

There were no particular problems here. The questioning here was fairly genteel and certainly not the most ferocious that you will come across. Ms Fairclough was not unduly cowed by judicial questions and interventions. Where required, she was prepared to stick to her submissions and not be led too much by suggestions from the judge. It will be noted that this was generally done in a polite way, for example with the answer to the question on *Woollin* (14:53).

Evidence of preparation for judicial questions

On the whole, Ms Fairclough seemed to be well organised and prepared on the law that was relevant to the moot. The questions were generally answered fairly well, which suggested that some attempt had been made to use the moot problem, and the information it contained, to prepare for judicial questions.

Modes of address

There were no major problems here. The judges in the moot were referred to appropriately throughout, as were the judges referred to from the moot problem and from the cases that Ms Fairclough referred to. A good example of a reference to Evans HHJ was when, in her conclusion, Ms Fairclough referred to the material misdirection of "the learned judge". Elsewhere, use of "my Lord(s)" and "your Lordship(s)" were entirely appropriate.

Eye contact

As noted previously, eye contact was maintained throughout the submissions, despite there being some evidence of the submissions being slightly over-scripted. The eye contact was particularly good whilst Ms Fairclough was answering judicial questions (when there was no reliance on a script) and during her concluding remarks (19:22).

8.4.5 Use of authorities

This part of the commentary could usefully be read in conjunction with chapter 7.

How many authorities should be referred to?

Whilst Ms Fairclough referred extensively to authority throughout the moot, you will notice that she only in fact referred to a small number of cases. From a criminal law viewpoint, there are one or two other cases that could have been referred to in this moot by senior counsel for the appellant. There was also a little bit of extra time that could have been used by Ms Fairclough for this purpose. The maximum allowance for this moot was ten authorities but, bearing in mind the time constraints, the number of authorities referred to was appropriate. Ms Fairclough certainly referred extensively to the most significant cases of *Nedrick* and *Woollin*, and did not overload her submissions with too many references to too many cases. As noted in chapter 7, your submissions should be backed up by law at all times, but at the same time, you need to be conscious of not turning them into a mere list of cases. In terms of achieving this balance, Ms Fairclough was successful, subject to the slight qualification mentioned above.

Asking judges if they want the facts of cases referred to

If the case has not yet been referred to in the moot, you should always give the judges the option of hearing the facts of the case. Ms Fairclough did this with all the cases that she referred to during her submissions. On each occasion, the judge declined to hear the facts. Please bear in mind that this will not always happen, and that some judges will want the facts of some of the cases you refer to. (See highlight clip 3.)

The verbal citing of cases

As noted in chapter 7, many mooters struggle in terms of basic organisation on this issue. Ms Fairclough was well organised, however, and there were no particular problems with citations. The key is to give the judges all the information that they need to follow what you are saying about an authority. With each of the cases mentioned, Ms Fairclough provided the judges with the name of the case, the law report she was referring to, the volume number and year, as well as the name of the judge and the page and paragraph numbers that she wished to refer to.

As a result, there was no confusion arising from problems such as the judges having the wrong volumes in front of them or not having the right page numbers. As noted in chapter 7, the key here is to have all the information you need in front of you every time you wish to refer the judges to a case.

In spite of the above, there are a couple of areas where small improvements could have been made. The first relates to the style in which Ms Fairclough referred to cases, and in particular the reference to the case of *Bolam*. Whilst all the required information was conveyed to the judges, Ms Fairclough's manner could have been more confident and less hesitant-looking. The way she referred to this case made it look as though the whole thing was a bit of a struggle and as though it could easily have somehow gone wrong.

Secondly, there could perhaps have been a more obvious pause between Ms Fairclough providing the references for cases and her asking the judges if they were familiar with the facts of the case. As noted previously, the judges need time to locate the report and the pages you have referred them to. It looks professional if you show that you are aware of the judges and whether they need more time. The judges are not in camera at the relevant times, but it is arguable that more time would have been beneficial. Having said this, it should be noted that Ms Fairclough was, at this time, maintaining eye contact with the judges. The judges certainly did not indicate that they needed more time, so this may not have been too much of a problem. (See highlight clip 3.)

Referring to cases and then not reading from the judgments

As mentioned in chapter 7, there may be some rare situations where you wish to refer to cases *en passant*, without actually referring the judges to particular passages from the judgment. Ms Fairclough did this correctly when referring to the case of *Cunningham* (01:56), by explaining that she did not wish to refer to the judgments, but giving the judges the citations in case they wanted them. The reason why it was arguably appropriate not to refer to the judgments in this instance is that *Cunningham* was being referred to to make a point of criminal law that is widely known and completely uncontroversial.

As noted in chapter 7, this is a course of action that should only be adopted in very rare circumstances. As a result, it is probably a safe bet to have the case handy, so that you can refer briefly to the judgments if necessary. If the judges insist that they want you to read from the judgments, and you have unilaterally decided that this is unnecessary, this could cause awkwardness between you and the judges. (See highlight clip 1.)

Reference to cases that had already been referred to

Sometimes, you will refer to a case more than once during your submissions. One question that needs to be considered in this situation is the extent to which you should provide the court with full citations when you have already done it once. Obviously, you will need to tell the judge which judgment you are now referring to, and which page and paragraph you are reading from. It might not, however, be necessary to give the full name of the case again, together with the year, the series of law reports and the volume number. To do this every time you refer to a particular case will be both cumbersome and repetitive.

The judges, however, may well have put the relevant volume to one side or may not remember the citations you originally gave them. If you just plunge in and start referring to the judgments they will, as a result, be lost. One example of where this was a potential issue for Ms Fairclough was during her right of reply when she referred to the case of *Woollin* again. On this occasion, the full citations were provided again, without any indication from the judges that they needed them.

Probably the best policy in this situation is to simply ask the judges if they require the citations for the case again. If the judges need them, they will say they want them; if they do not, you can simply refer to the next part of the case that you wish to refer to, making sure that you provide the additional information needed for the judges to find where you are reading from.

Knowledge of cases referred to during submissions

If you are going to refer to cases in your submissions, you need to know a lot about them. These issues are dealt with in detail in chapter 7. Mooters sometimes struggle when they are referring to a judgment which, in turn, refers to what a judge has said in another case. This was a slight issue with Ms Fairclough when she was referring to the judgment of Lane LCJ in *R v Nedrick*. In his judgment, Lane LCJ referred to what Lord Bridge had said in *R v Moloney*. When Ms Fairclough had read out this passage, the judge had to intervene to clarify who had said what (10:34). When asked, Ms Fairclough easily clarified the issue, so no harm was done on this particular occasion. Some students in this situation would not have known who had said what.

How many quotations should be used from a particular case?

As noted in chapter 7, much will depend on the material you have for your submissions. Your submissions, as with Ms Fairclough, may be highly dependent on one or two very important cases. If that is so, then extensive reference to those cases will obviously form the backbone of your submissions. Having said that, you need to be careful not to read too extensively from the cases you rely on. Your submissions should also clearly include your own commentary on what you have read out. This was not a problem with Ms Fairclough. Whilst she certainly did read extensively from the judgments in *Nedrick* and *Woollin*, it would not be fair to say that she did this too much. She also attempted to explain, in her own words, why the passages that were read out helped her case.

As far as the length of any references were concerned, these were not too long, and were often broken up with Ms Fairclough's own commentary. For an example of this, see the references to *Woollin* (12:40). The key here, as noted in chapter 7, is to avoid reading for too long from a judgment without a break, as the judges will soon become bored with you if you do this.

Use of sources other than cases

The only sources referred to by Ms Fairclough were cases.

Use of bundles

Ms Fairclough did not use a bundle to present the authorities upon which she intended to rely. Instead, the more "old-fashioned" approach was adopted, whereby all the authorities were brought to the moot in their respective volumes of the law reports. Whilst this approach may not seems as slick as the use of bundles, it can work well if, as here, the mooters are well organised.

8.5   Performance by senior counsel for the respondent (Mr Cooper)

Mr Cooper's submissions are now considered in accordance with the guidance in section **8.3** above.

8.5.1   Style and presentation

This part of the commentary could be useful when read in conjunction with chapter **3**.

Introductions

Ms Fairclough had already introduced both herself and Mr Cooper at the beginning of her submissions. However, there was nothing wrong with Mr Cooper briefly introducing himself at the beginning of his submissions, even though the judge clearly knew who he was. Moreover, Mr Cooper's introduction of himself struck a good note from the outset, striking an appropriate balance of formality and easiness of manner. One of the keys to becoming a good advocate or mooter is the adoption of an appropriate courtroom manner. Many struggle with this and are either too informal or too rigid and pompous as a result. This was not a problem here. (See highlight clip 5.)

Use of notes/script

There were some parts of the submissions that seemed as though they might have been slightly scripted (for example, at 21:58). However, it is also fair to say that, if these submissions were very scripted, it did not adversely affect the style and presentation of the submissions to any great extent. On the whole, the submissions were delivered whilst maintaining good eye contact, and with a degree of lucidity that one would expect from a mooter who was not heavily reliant on a script. Some mooters are able to refer extensively to notes without making it obvious that they are doing so and without losing out in terms of style. The only potential problem for such mooters is that they still need the flexibility to juggle with their structure if the judges make them deal with an issue out of their planned order.

Eye contact

A sure sign that a mooter is over-reliant on a script is a lack of eye contact with the judges. Such mooters will not be able to risk losing their place by looking up at the judges. Mr Cooper maintained a perfectly acceptable level of eye contact with the judges and, whilst he did regularly look down at his notes, he also regularly looked up at the judges. As a result, it is possible that Mr Cooper was referring to bullet points that enabled him to look up and down without difficulty. (See also highlight clip 6.)

The beginning of the submissions (21:50)

Mr Cooper started in appropriate style, by submitting very early on that the conviction was safe and that the appeal should be dismissed. As noted in chapters **3** and **4**, it is important, if you wish to be persuasive, to leave the judges in little doubt as to what you are asking for and why. This should be done as soon as possible during the submissions, and at regular intervals thereafter.

Outlines the three submissions he will make

As well as asking the judges to dismiss the appeal, Mr Cooper also states that he has three submissions to make and, briefly, what they will be (21:56). This is good practice, not only in terms of style, but also in terms of structure. The judges are effectively given a signpost to let them know in advance what they are going to be listening to.

Indicates early on that he will respond to Ms Fairclough's submission

This will be dealt with in more detail later on, in the section dealing with Mr Cooper's response, but it is worth dealing with now as a separate style point. Right from the start (22:26), Mr Cooper sends out a clear signal to the judges that he is going to respond to his opponent's submissions. This is another form of signposting, and is effectively telling the judges "I am going to deal with my opponent's case, therefore you can give me good marks for doing so".

You should note that many judges are painfully aware of the lack of a response from many mooters. The judges will be looking for clear evidence of you having satisfied the assessment/judging criteria. Clear signals such as this help to dispel such negative thoughts from the minds of judges early on. This signpost was reinforced throughout Mr Cooper's submissions, with frequent references to "my learned friend Ms Fairclough". (See also highlight clip 6.)

Pace of delivery

No problems here. The submissions were delivered at an appropriate pace, being neither too fast nor too slow, and were always easy to follow. As was noted in chapter **3**, the use of pauses can be highly beneficial to a mooter's performance if they are used appropriately. Throughout the submissions, the feeling was that Mr Cooper was

taking his time and was in control of what he was doing and saying.
Pauses were used on a number of occasions to good effect (29:34),
(31:51). The benefits of these pauses were that they gave Mr Cooper
time to think and also time to breathe properly and maintain composure. They also demonstrated that Mr Cooper has the confidence to
not say anything for a few seconds while he gathered his thoughts.
Less confident advocates often feel that they have to make a constant
noise whilst they are on their feet. As noted in chapter **3**, it is important that pauses do not go on too long. This was not a problem here.

Volume

As with pace, volume was fine, bearing in mind the size of the room
where the moot was held. Nobody of ordinary hearing would have
had any difficulty hearing Mr Cooper's submissions.

Intonation

Mr Cooper was able to speak expressively by varying the tone, pace
and volume of his voice. This was even the case with those parts of
the submissions where Mr Cooper was arguably a bit too reliant on a
script. As a result of this, the way that Mr Cooper spoke was engaging and persuasive.

Politeness and respect in dealing with the judges

As with Ms Fairclough, Mr Cooper was perfectly proper and polite
in his dealings with the judges. At no point did he appear particularly
flustered or uncomfortable. This was especially the case when judicial questions were asked. On these occasions, Mr Cooper seemed
very relaxed, and listened to the questions politely before giving his
answers (30:16), (37:22), (40:00), (42:41). Obviously, it is far easier
to keep calm in the face of judicial questions if you are well prepared
and feel confident that you will be able to answer properly.

Mr Cooper used correct modes of address throughout, and did not
show the signs of irritation or nerves that can adversely affect the
performance of some mooters. If you are trying to persuade a judge
of something, it is generally a good idea to keep him or her on your
side. Mr Cooper certainly succeeded in this respect. (See also highlight clip 8.)

Body language

Again, as with Ms Fairclough, there were no problems here.
However, there are a few points that are worthy of mention. This first
is that Mr Cooper's posture was largely dictated by where he had his

notes. You will notice that they are on the lectern in front of him, high enough for him to refer to them without having to shift his position too much. As a result, he is able to look at his notes easily whilst retaining a relaxed posture.

The second point is that there is very little in the way of unnecessary movement. Hand gestures are minimal and there is only a small amount of foot movement. There is nothing wrong with this. Occasionally, during your submissions, you may wish to rock back on your heels slightly or change your stance for reasons of comfort.

On the whole, Mr Cooper's body language was appropriate to the setting, not distracting, and indicative of a degree of respect for the court.

Awareness of surroundings

As noted previously, the best advocates are those who are at ease in the courtroom and who are able to use their senses to appreciate what is going on around them.

Mr Cooper demonstrated this ability on a few occasions during the course of the moot. When referring to the *Bolam* case (26:32), Mr Cooper acknowledged that the case had already been referred to by Ms Fairclough. He also explained to the judges that he was referring to the same passage as his opponent, but that he was going to read some additional lines out that had not yet been referred to. This is to be commended, because it shows that Mr Cooper was listening carefully to what Ms Fairclough was saying, and because he was able to make use, under pressure, of the information he had acquired.

The reference to the case of *Nedrick* was also done well, in the sense of awareness. Mr Cooper gives some brief commentary of his own on *Nedrick* before providing the court with the citations. When he provides the citations, he makes it clear that he is aware that the citations have been provided earlier by Ms Fairclough. Nevertheless, Mr Cooper shows awareness that the judges may well not have the volume in front of them and may, as a result, want the citations again.

Many mooters during moots retreat into their own personal mooting bubble, where they are largely unaware of what is going on around them in the courtroom, because they are so busy concentrating on what they are going to say. This was certainly not a problem with Mr Cooper's performance.

Mr Cooper also seemed to be aware of the judges whilst he was speaking. When referring to authorities, he seemed aware that the judges needed time to find the correct volume, page etc. Pauses were therefore successfully employed to give the judges time. See, for example, the reference to *Bolam* (26:32).

Another example of awareness that is worth mentioning is in relation to the pace of submissions. If an advocate is aware of the needs of the judges, he or she will conduct their submissions at a pace that allows the judges to take notes and to digest the information being put before them. Mr Cooper was successful in this respect.

With the exception of the first judicial question (30:16), Mr Cooper did not have to be interrupted by the judges. Even on this occasion, the interruption did not seem to be a problem and composure was maintained. As noted previously, advocates who are aware of their surroundings will generally not be interrupted too peremptorily by the judges, because they will sense when the judge is going to ask a question. This contrasts favourably with the advocate who is reading from a script and not maintaining eye contact with the judges. (See also highlight clip 8.)

One final situation where Mr Cooper showed that he was listening well throughout the moot was when dealing with the case of *Nedrick*, when he referred the judge back to a question he had earlier asked of Ms Fairclough (32:57). Not only is Mr Cooper proving that he has been listening here, but he is actually using to his own advantage a point that the judge has raised in a question. As noted in previous chapters, if you listen carefully to the judicial questions put to your opponents, it can be of great value to you in a number of ways. This is just one example of that.

Style and reference to authorities

As discussed later in the chapter, Mr Cooper referred correctly to authorities throughout his submissions. As well as this, however, he also referred to authorities with a certain degree of style and easiness of manner. For an example of this, see again the reference to *Bolam* (26:32). This case was referred to in a manner which was wholly consistent with what would be appropriate in the higher courts, and in a manner which was formal without being pompous.

Closing the submissions

The conclusion to these submissions was not the strongest thing about them. Whilst Mr Cooper did make it clear that he was beginning his conclusion (a useful signpost for the judges), the concluding remarks did not last very long. As a result, the submissions did not finish on a very comprehensive, high or engaging note. As noted previously, the key with your concluding remarks is to really impress upon the judges what you are asking for and why. As a result, when you sit down, the judges will have your strongest argument(s) ringing in their ears. The opportunity for a really strong finish was, arguably, missed here. More could have been done in terms of reiterating the submissions already made, with the emphasis on the stronger points. On this basis, Mr Cooper could *then* have closed his submissions by saying that the appeal should be dismissed and that the conviction was safe.

Dress

There were no issues here. Mr Cooper was attired in a manner befitting an appearance in court.

Modes of address and appropriate language

As with Ms Fairclough, Mr Cooper addressed the judges in the moot correctly, with phrases like "my Lords" and "your Lordships" being used extensively. Judges referred to from law reports were also referred to in an appropriate manner.

On the whole, Mr Cooper's manner and use of language was convincing and appropriate to a courtroom setting, in the sense that you could genuinely imagine a performance like this in the Court of Appeal. Correct use was made throughout of phrases like "in my submission" or "I would submit". There was none of the inappropriate "I think" or "I believe" comments that blight some performances. Another elegant phrase that was used was "it is not the Crown's contention" (24:16), and there were many similar phrases throughout that gave this performance a convincing, articulate and professional feel. (See also highlight clips 6 and 8.)

There were, however, a couple of instances where slightly inappropriate language was used. First, there were a couple of occasions where Mr Cooper said "You know" (30:57), and during the answer to the question on *Woollin* (42:41). As noted in chapter **3**, use of phrases like this is not suitable for an advocate in court. Similar phrases that are inappropriate include "Yeah" and "OK". Such phrases are too informal, and rarely add anything to what a person is trying to say. As noted in chapter **3**, it is far better to pause for a second or two regularly during your submissions, rather than to fill in time with phrases such as these. (See also highlight clip 8.)

One final use of inappropriate language was again during the answer to the question on *Woollin* (42:41), when Mr Cooper said "if I were a betting man". This may not be a major breach of courtroom etiquette, but it is, nevertheless, an example of being over-familiar with the judges. It is the sort of thing one would say in a pub. It is also an example of an advocate giving his own personal opinions, rather than submissions based on the law.

Nerves

Mr Cooper did not appear to be afflicted by nerves during this performance. He probably did feel nervous, as this is a performance where there was evidence of a certain amount of adrenalin. However, nerves certainly did not have a negative effect on the submissions. On the whole, Mr Cooper appeared to be confident and in control of what was happening.

8.5.2 Structure and content

This part of the chapter could usefully be read in conjunction with chapter 4.

Actual criminal law content

As noted in the commentary on Ms Fairclough's submissions, a detailed commentary on the criminal law issues is outside the scope of this book. Some comments on legal content can, however, be made.

Mr Cooper seemed to have a fairly good grasp of the principles of criminal law raised in the moot. This was despite the fact that, certainly on the issue of a possible misdirection on oblique intention, Mr Cooper had a more difficult argument to put than Ms Fairclough. Nevertheless, he did a reasonably good job with the resources he had at his disposal.

According to the cases, there probably was a misdirection on oblique intention. However, there was room for the argument employed by Mr Cooper, that any misdirection was not a "material misdirection" and that, as a result, the conviction was safe. This argument was a lifeline for Mr Cooper, and perhaps it could have been developed further by reference to case law.

Mr Cooper had clearly read the judgments in cases like *Nedrick*, as he spotted the point that the reason highlighted for the misdirection in *Nedrick* was not that the trial judge had used the phrase "highly probable". The reason, rather, was that the judge in that case had suggested that the *Nedrick* direction was a definition of oblique intention rather than an evidential rule on it. This is quite a subtle point, and requires some knowledge in order to explain it properly.

There was, however, room for improvement in some areas. Mr Cooper was representing the Crown and arguing that a murder conviction should be upheld. His chief argument on the issue of oblique intention was that there was nothing in the judgments in *Nedrick* or *Woollin* that specifically disapproved of the phrase "highly probable". As a result, these submissions somewhat ducked the key issue of whether "virtually certain" and "highly probable" mean two different things. This may be because there is little in the judgments that really helps the submission that Mr Cooper had to make. Nevertheless this is an aspect of the performance, in terms of content, that could have been improved.

Timing of submissions

Mr Cooper's submissions took around 23½ minutes, including judicial questions. It is likely that the judicial questions took something in the region of three and a half minutes. Mr Cooper, therefore, used his full allocation of time. In fact, he may even have been given a degree of latitude by the judges, bearing in mind that he made it clear that he was coming to the end of his submissions. This is one of the reasons why signposts can be so important for both you and the judges.

As noted in chapter **4**, it is important that mooters make good use of their allotted time. Mr Cooper certainly succeeded in this respect, but it is worth noting that, bearing in mind the comments in the preceding section, some of the time might have been better spent developing certain points. Nevertheless, the impression was that Mr Cooper was certainly not short of material for his submissions.

Overall/macro structure of the submissions

As with Ms Fairclough, these submissions clearly had a beginning, a middle and an end. It was clear at all times what Mr Cooper's structure was and where he was up to in it. The overall/macro structure was simple and easy to follow, as it consisted of opening remarks, three submissions and a conclusion.

Mr Cooper made use of signposts in his opening remarks to indicate that he would make three submissions (21:56), and also to indicate that he was finishing his opening remarks and moving on to his first submission. The other two submissions were also similarly signposted, so that it was clear when one submission ended and another began (24:44), (31:55). Mirroring was also used to ensure that the points raised in the opening remarks were covered in the main body of the submissions. As noted in the previous section, however, Mr Cooper might have benefited from briefly reiterating his main submissions in his concluding remarks. The fact that the judges would have found this structure clear, straightforward and well signposted would have made it easier for the judges to be per-suaded by what Mr Cooper said within that structure.

The order of the submissions

Mr Cooper began by announcing that he had three submissions to make and that, in terms of order and content, they mirrored the sub-missions made by Ms Fairclough. Whether this order was planned in advance, or whether Mr Cooper thought that it would be a good way to present his case and respond to Ms Fairclough's at the last minute, is open to debate. In any event, structuring his submissions in the same order as Ms Fairclough had the happy effect of making his structure very easy to follow. The judges had already heard submis-sions in a particular order from Ms Fairclough, and now they heard the same again, but this time from the respondents. As with Ms Fairclough, the ordering of the points made was perfectly logical, in that it mirrored the issues raised by the moot problem and by the findings of Evans HHJ. Sometimes the findings of the lower court, as in this moot problem, will provide you with a running order for your submissions. Both Ms Fairclough and Mr Cooper took advantage of this here.

As a result of the above, Mr Cooper's overall or macro structure was very easy to follow.

Mirroring and signposting

Mr Cooper made extensive use of these techniques. As a result, his submissions had a clear structure and were delivered in an appropri-ate and persuasive style.

The first example of signposting was where Mr Cooper announced that he had three submissions which mirrored, in terms of content, the submissions which had been made by Ms Fairclough (22:00). Assuming the judges had been listening carefully to Ms Fairclough's submissions, they would instantly have been given a very clear idea of where Mr Cooper's submissions were going. As noted in chapter 4, one the key issues that you should consider, when thinking about structure, is making sure that the judges understand you and are with you every step of the way. Only then are they likely to be persuaded by what you say.

Mr Cooper also used signposts frequently throughout his submis-sions, for example to announce the end of one submission and the beginning of another. As a result, the judges should have been in no doubt as to where Mr Cooper was up to in the structure announced at the start of the submissions. One example of this was at the end of the first submission and beginning of the second (24:44). However, on this occasion Mr Cooper arguably could have paused slightly, to give emphasis to this signpost and to give the judges time to digest the submission or to ask questions.

A variation on mirroring was used when Mr Cooper announced that his submissions would mirror those of Ms Fairclough. Here, Mr Cooper was effectively using his opponent's structure to make his own structure stand out more clearly in the minds of the judges. There is nothing wrong with this if you appear as counsel for the respondent, especially as it will also enhance the judges' perception of your ability to respond. (See also highlight clips 6 and 7.)

One more example of mirroring was the way in which Mr Cooper asked, at the beginning and end of his submissions, for the appeal to be dismissed and the conviction upheld. As noted previously, there is nothing wrong with frequent references to your central point or request. This is particularly true at key moments in the submissions, such as the beginning and the end. Such use of mirroring and sign-posting also ensures that the submissions have a degree of symmetry and neatness about them.

It has already been noted that Mr Cooper could perhaps have done more to ensure that his conclusion mirrored both his opening remarks and the main body of his submissions. This could have made the conclusion more emphatic, and made the submissions as a whole more neat and tidy.

Structuring and content of individual submissions (Micro structure)

On the whole, Mr Cooper developed his individual submissions well and with the type of content and structure necessary to make them persuasive in a courtroom.

For example, Mr Cooper's second submission (24:44) contained the following:

1) An announcement of what the submission is, including reference to how this involves a response to the appellant's submissions.

2) Detailed reference to the law on that submission, namely the references to the cases of *Bolam* and *Bolitho*.

3) Actual commentary on the passages referred to and how they are relevant to the respondent's case.

4) Why the submission means that the conviction should be upheld and the appeal dismissed.

It is not essential that each individual submission has to be in the precise order stated above. Mr Cooper demonstrates this with his reference to *Nedrick* (33:02), where he actually provides some commentary on the case before he has referred to the judgments. This reverse type of approach can work, as the judges are told what you are submitting first and then the icing on the cake is provided by reading from the judgments. All of this of course assumes that what you read out from the judgments confirms what you have said in your commentary.

Overloading of submissions

As noted previously, the danger can be that, because of overloading, submissions can lose their structure and become rather tedious and hard to follow. Mr Cooper made three main submissions and only referred to a relatively small number of cases throughout. As a result, despite the fact that the full allocation of time was used, it could not be said that there were too many submissions, or too many references to too many authorities.

One method for avoiding the appearance of overloading was adopted by Mr Cooper with, for example, his second submission on direct intention. Within this submission, Mr Cooper made a number of points, but still presented them as being within the umbrella of the second submission. One tendency amongst some mooters is to unnecessarily sub-divide their submissions, so that they have too many. As a result, the structure becomes complicated or apparently non-existent, and the submissions lose their shape and prestige. One can end up with the situation where one is saying "My Lords, if I could now deal with my thirteenth submission". None of this, however, was a problem with Mr Cooper's submissions.

8.5.3 Ability to respond to opponent's submissions

This part of the commentary could usefully be read in conjunction with chapter 5.

No right of reply for Mr Cooper

As Mr Cooper was counsel for the respondent, this meant that he had no extra time for a right of reply, as he had already heard Ms Fairclough's submissions when he rose to speak. As a result, Mr Cooper had to include a response to Ms Fairclough's case in his actual submissions.

As noted in chapter 6, it is imperative that mooters demonstrate that they have the flexibility to respond to the other side's submissions.

If you are a respondent, you have to make it very clear to the judges that you are addressing the other side's case. (See also highlight clip 6.)

Use of signposts to highlight that a response was being made

Mr Cooper was very prolific in referring to Ms Fairclough and her submissions, so that the judges were left in no doubt that he was responding to the appellant's case. Much of this can, of course, be planned in advance, if you are well prepared for the moot and have formed a good idea of what the other side will argue.

Mr Cooper responded to Ms Fairclough's submissions in a very direct manner, and even adopted a structure that mirrored hers. He therefore dealt with the same ground as Ms Fairclough in his three submissions, and responded to points made by her as he went along. Furthermore, Mr Cooper clearly announced that this was what he was going to do (22:26), (22:37).

With each submission that was then made, Mr Cooper made a point of couching his submissions not just in terms of his own case but also in terms of responding to what Ms Fairclough had said on those issues. The start of Mr Cooper's first submission provides an example of this (22:35). As a result of this use of a signpost, it was clear that Mr Cooper was not just making his own points, but was also responding to Ms Fairclough's submissions. (See also highlight clips 6 and 7.)

As a result of the above, listening to Mr Cooper speak, it was impossible for the judges to miss the fact that he was overtly responding to the other side's submissions. Many mooters, unfortunately, fail to make it clear that this is what they are doing. As a result, the judges can be left with the impression that a mooter's submissions contained little or no response to the other side, with the mooter themselves often thinking the exact opposite. Signposting and mirroring are crucial tools to help you ensure that you do not fall into this trap.

Structure and content of response points

As noted in chapter **5**, when you do respond to a submission or point made by your opponent, you should make sure you include certain points in order to do so convincingly.

These are:

A)   Which particular point or submission of your opponent you are responding to.

B)   What your response to it actually is.

C)   The reason why you are responding in that particular way. This will often include some reference to authority.

Mr Cooper was largely successful in including these things in his response points. In his first submission (22:35), he responded to Ms Fairclough's submissions on the factual issues in the case. Mr Cooper, in doing this, clearly indicated which comments of Ms Fairclough's he was taking issue with. He also made it clear what his submissions were in respect of those issues, and referred to the moot problem in order to explain why he was adopting that line of argument.

Similar observations can also be made with respect to Mr Cooper's second and third submissions (24:44) and (31:57) respectively. In introducing both of these submissions, Mr Cooper refers very early on to Ms Fairclough's submissions and how he is responding to what she had to say. As a result of these signposts, the judges are reminded regularly throughout Mr Cooper's submissions that he has not lost sight of the need to respond to his opponent.

Politeness issues

Mr Cooper did not fall into the trap of responding to his opponent in a rude or unpleasant way. Ms Fairclough's submissions were tackled head on, but Mr Cooper always referred to her in a respectful and courteous manner. As noted previously, some mooters, in the heat of the moment, end up referring to their opponents inappropriately as "him" or "her", or "he" or "she". This was not a problem here.

Mr Cooper also addressed the judges at all times, and did not make the mistake of directing his response points to Ms Fairclough.

Dealing with a strong/weak opponent

Both Ms Fairclough and Mr Cooper had the benefit of dealing with an opponent whose submissions made sense and were easy to hear and understand. As noted in chapter 5, having a reasonably strong opponent will usually, if you are well prepared, provide you with much more material for your response. The quality of the moot will be higher and you will benefit from this. Mr Cooper clearly understood what Ms Fairclough had said in her submissions and was able to reply to all of the submissions she made. The only possible problem with having a stronger opponent is that they can intimidate you, if you are a bit nervous or lacking in confidence. There was no evidence of that here with either mooter.

8.5.4   Dealings with the judges

This part of the commentary could usefully be read in conjunction with chapter **6**.

Allowing the judges to interrupt

The first question put to Mr Cooper (30:14) was an occasion where Mr Cooper's flow was interrupted slightly by the judge. Nevertheless, Mr Cooper dealt with this interruption in a professional and courteous manner and in a way that showed that he was perfectly at ease with being asked a question. (See also highlight clip 8.)

It has been noted previously that the best advocates are aware of their surroundings, particularly the reactions of judges. On this occasion, Mr Cooper anticipates the interruption and spots that a question is on the way before the judge even speaks. If your submissions are too reliant on a script, you will not be able to react in this way, and the judge will probably have to cut across you whilst you are speaking. The first question to Mr Cooper came after he had been speaking for around nine minutes. As a result, Mr Cooper had ample time to fall into a false sense of security and to concentrate on his notes rather than on the judges. Happily, this did not happen.

A similar point can be made with the second judicial question on the case of *Nedrick*. Often in moots, participants find it hard to allow the judges to interrupt them. As noted previously, the moment the judge starts to ask a question, you should fall silent. There should not be an awkward period where you and the judge are speaking at the same time, competing for air-time. Mooting is not about a battle of wills between you and the judges. It is about you persuading the judges that your submissions should be followed. If the judges ask you questions, the most persuasive thing you can do is to answer them. Mr Cooper succeeded in this respect.

Avoid signs of annoyance or impatience

There were no problems here. Mr Cooper was clearly co-operating with the judges, and his dealings with them were respectful and professional.

What questions were asked?

The questions related directly to the ground of appeal and to the points raised by Evans HHJ in relation to direct and oblique intention. As a result, the questions put were all questions that could have been foreseen by a well-prepared mooter who had read the moot problem and researched the law properly.

How well were the questions answered?

As noted previously, extensive discussion of criminal law issues is beyond the scope of this book. However, it is necessary to discuss the issues briefly here in order to address the issue of how well Mr Cooper answered the questions put to him.

The **first** question (30:14) was answered pretty competently. Mr Cooper kept calm and did his best to address directly the issues that the question raised. Mr Cooper answered at some length and, in doing so, demonstrated good knowledge of the case of *Bolitho* and the facts of the moot problem. When the judge asked a supplementary question, which arguably required a succinct answer, Mr Cooper gave that without any hesitation. This suggested a certain degree of confidence on Mr Cooper's part that he understood the material he was using. (See also highlight clip 8.)

The **second** question put to Mr Cooper (37:20) was on his second submission and, in particular, the case of *Nedrick*. Whilst Mr Cooper maintains his composure and demonstrates some knowledge of the judgments in *Nedrick*, there are a few points in relation to this answer that may invite negative comment from some judges. First, Mr Cooper makes reference to a judge not being an "ass" if he fails to use the phrase "virtual certainty" in his direction. This is probably not appropriate in a moot court. It would have been preferable to say that a judge who failed to use these words would not necessarily be in error.

Secondly, Mr Cooper fails to answer this question in a really positive matter. Generally, it is not all that persuasive for an advocate to answer a judicial question by simply saying that it is a matter for the court. This is to some extent what Mr Cooper does here. As a result, he is arguably abdicating responsibility over the issue. The judges know that the matter is for them to decide. What they are looking for is the advocates to make persuasive submissions which help them come to a decision. It is not terribly persuasive to simply remind them that the decision is theirs.

Thirdly, Mr Cooper describes the issue at stake on oblique intention as "a game of semantics". Whilst this may be consistent with Mr Cooper's submission that the direction on oblique intention is not a material misdirection, Mr Cooper still could have done more to explain why the alleged misdirection was no more than a quibbling and semantic one. It should be noted, however, that, on the issue of oblique intention, Mr Cooper had a hard argument to put before the court. In general terms, he did pretty well, despite the obvious difficulties he faced.

The **third** question put to Mr Cooper (40:00) was on the issue of putting some kind of percentage figure to the phrases "highly probable" and "virtually certain". With this question, Mr Cooper rightly does not take the bait and get drawn into a debate about what range of percentages can be equated with the two terms mentioned. In doing this, Mr Cooper demonstrated a certain ability to think on his feet. He also demonstrated his knowledge of the relevant judgments, as he was able to say that there is nothing in them that equated the terms mentioned with percentages. Furthermore, Mr Cooper also showed that he understands the role of an advocate, by declining to give his own personal opinion on the matter.

As a result, this third question was answered well. If the judge asks you a question that you simply cannot answer in an authoritative manner, you can decline to do so. Before you adopt this line, however, you need to be sure of your ground. This requires hard work before the moot.

The **final** question put to Mr Cooper (42:41) was on the case of *Woollin*. This question was less well answered than some. The judge was clearly trying to give Mr Cooper another chance to address the difference between "high probability" and "virtual certainty". Unfortunately, here Mr Cooper gave pretty much the same answer about percentages that he gave to the previous question. As a result, some judges might have felt that he was somewhat abdicating responsibility over the issue.

In reality, the difference between the two terms was vital to the determination of the appeal. Simply saying that it is a matter for the court to decide the issue, and that the case law offered no explanation as to the meaning of the two terms, did not go far enough to answer the question. Possibly, therefore, Mr Cooper could have prepared for this aspect of the moot more thoroughly. On the other hand, Mr Cooper largely kept his composure and did his best to answer the question put, even though he clearly struggled with this line of questioning.

When were the questions asked?

Mr Cooper was allowed some time (nearly 10 minutes) before the first judicial question to develop his submissions. After that, the questions came at fairly regular intervals, usually at fairly convenient pauses during the submissions. Some judges may not give you this initial time to develop your submissions, and may try to ask questions from the outset, potentially disrupting your flow in the process.

Questions for which Mr Cooper did not know the answer

There were no questions here where Mr Cooper was completely stuck for an answer. He may have struggled to answer a couple of the questions to the full satisfaction of the judge, but it was clear that Mr Cooper understood the questions and why he had a difficult legal argument to advance.

Use of authorities when answering questions

Most of the questions asked were in relation to points or authorities that Mr Cooper had already made. In answering the questions, Mr Cooper demonstrates a good knowledge of the moot problem and of the cases he is using. However, there could have perhaps been more direct reference to the judgments to back up the answers. On the whole, Mr Cooper largely confined himself to saying things like "there is nothing in the judgments on this". As a result, the answers are couched in slightly negative terms. One explanation for this is that, as noted previously, the authorities on the issue of oblique intention did not particularly suit what Mr Cooper was obliged to argue.

Stick to your submissions

Mr Cooper did not allow judicial questioning to deflect him from what he was trying to argue. This was in spite of the fact that, legally, his submissions were based on rather shaky foundations. One example of this was the answer to the question on the case of *Nedrick*, where Mr Cooper refused to be drawn into the debate about percentages. It clearly did not suit his submissions to be drawn on this issue and, moreover, there was no authority that he could usefully use to back up any submissions that he may have made on the issue.

Courtesy, eye contact and modes of address

These are all referred to elsewhere in the chapter. Mr Cooper had no problems in this respect, apart from the occasional use of informal expression such as "you know" and "if I were a betting man".

8.5.5   Use of authorities

This part of the commentary could usefully be read in conjunction with chapter **7**.

How many authorities were used?

Mr Cooper only referred directly to a relatively small number of authorities. However, it was not possible to say that Mr Cooper's submissions were not backed up by reference to legal authorities. As noted previously, the law, particularly on oblique intention, did not favour the respondents in this moot. Nevertheless, Mr Cooper did make fairly good use of the authorities that were available in order to cobble together an argument.

Mr Cooper also avoided the temptation to make too many references to too many authorities. As a result, his submissions were not overloaded and retained a clear structure, with plenty of submissions of Mr Cooper's own punctuating the references to authority.

Asking the judges if they wanted the facts of cases referred to

Mr Cooper often referred to cases that had already been referred to by Ms Fairclough. As a result, it was not necessary for him to ask the judges if they wanted the facts of those cases, as Ms Fairclough had already done so. As noted in chapter 7, some mooters demonstrate that they are not really concentrating on what is going on around them, by asking this question when it has already been asked.

When it was required, as with the case of *Bolitho*, Mr Cooper did put the question to the judges. This demonstrates a clear awareness of which cases Ms Fairclough had referred to earlier.

Verbal citation of cases

Mr Cooper's citation of cases was generally of a high standard. All the information that was needed by the judges to locate the volumes, pages and paragraphs that they were being referred to was given. As noted in chapter 7, this is one area where many mooters get themselves in a complete mess, quite unnecessarily. In Mr Cooper's case, however, the references to cases were well organised, confident and assured. A good example of this is the reference to the case of *Bolam* (26:31). Note with this reference how Mr Cooper gives the judges appropriate time to find the report that he is referring to before reading from the judgments.

As noted previously, awareness of the judges is a key tool for mooters. Mr Cooper also shows good awareness of his opponent's submissions when he refers to *Bolam*, and acknowledges the fact that he is referring to substantially the same passage as Ms Fairclough, with the exception of the last line. This is the sort of precision that is required if you are going to get to grips with your opponent's case.

Lastly, Mr Cooper shows awareness of the judges with his reference to *Nedrick* (33:40). As Mr Cooper had already given some commentary on *Nedrick* before referring to the judgments, and as the volume had not been required for some time in the moot, Mr Cooper rightly felt that he needed to give the judges the citations again. Many mooters would forget this sort of thing and start reading from a judgment when the judges no longer had it in front of them.

Referring to the judges and others mentioned in the law reports

As well as knowing how to refer to the judges in your moot, you will need to know how to refer to the judges in the cases that you refer to in the law reports. One example of an appropriate reference is in Mr Cooper's reference to the case of *Nedrick* (33:30), before reading from the judgment of Lane CJ.

Both Mr Cooper and Ms Fairclough could have possibly explained who Mr Fox-Andrews was when they read from the case of *Bolam*. The passages that both read out referred to this person, yet who he is was never explained.

Length of quotations from cases

Generally, the length of readings from cases was appropriate, in the sense of not being too long. In any event, Mr Cooper generally punctuated his readings from cases with submissions or commentary of his own.

Choice of cases to use

Mr Cooper resisted the temptation to use too many cases and also the temptation to only refer to the most recent cases. The few cases referred to were all cases of a certain status and prominence. As noted previously, referring to recent cases can be highly desirable, but the significance of the judgment, in terms of the precedent set by it, also has to be given its due weight when considering which cases to use. Criminal lawyers will spot one or two cases that Mr Cooper could have referred to additionally, for example *R v Mathews and Alleyne* [2003], but generally the big cases that needed to be included in these submissions were there.

Making submissions before reading from the judgments

With both *Nedrick* and *Woollin*, Mr Cooper gives some commentary on why the cases help his submissions before he reads from the judgment. As noted in the section on Mr Cooper's structure, this is fine. The alternative, of course, is to read from the judgments first, before making any submissions as to why the passages help you. Either approach can be effective, if done properly.

Use of authorities

Cases were the only authorities referred to by Mr Cooper.

Use of bundles

As with Ms Fairclough, Mr Cooper did not use a bundle of authorities. As with Ms Fairclough, Mr Cooper's performance certainly did not suffer from the lack of a bundle.

8.6　Commentary on highlights, or lowlights, from the second recording of *R v Owen Owens*

The following commentary is on the seven "lowlight" clips from the second recording of *R v Owen Owens*. You will, once again, be able to view aspects of the submissions of both Ms Fairclough and Mr Cooper. Please refer to guidance letter I in section **8.3** above. This commentary, as with the longer commentary on the first recording of this moot, could also be read usefully in conjunction with chapters **3** to **7**.

8.6.1　Clip 1

In this clip, you can see some of Ms Fairclough's opening remarks from the second filming of the moot. The main issues for consideration from this clip are to do with style and presentation.

The first thing you should notice here is the complete reliance on a prepared and seemingly verbatim script. The result of this is that the delivery is flat, monotonous and completely lacking in the power to engage, let alone persuade, the judges. Because Ms Fairclough is reading the submissions, the levels of eye contact are very poor. Judges watching submissions like these would certainly feel very little in the way of rapport with Ms Fairclough.

As with many mooters who merely read out their submissions, the delivery here is also too fast, with Ms Fairclough rattling through some sections at great speed. In other sections, the delivery is hesitant, with Ms Fairclough tripping over her words on occasions. Again, this is a common fault with mooters who are too reliant on a script. If you do attempt to look up and establish some eye contact, you can lose your place. When your eyes return to the script, it is all too easy to read from the wrong line.

Body language is also a problem here, with Ms Fairclough holding her notes out in front of her. This reinforces the impression of over-reliance on notes, and makes it look as though Ms Fairclough is clinging on to the notes for dear life.

Ms Fairclough also makes a mistake in terms of modes of address, referring to the trial judge as "his worship". This is actually the correct mode of address for a lay magistrate. When asked where the case of *R v Owen Owens* started, Ms Fairclough shows every sign of guessing, suggesting a poor knowledge of the moot problem. Hesitancy, on a very basic question such as this, suggests poor preparation.

The references to cases were similarly disorganised. With *R v Cunningham*, Ms Fairclough refers to the "Appeal Courts" when, in fact, she should have referred to the "Appeal Cases". This is the sort of mistake that is easy to avoid with a little bit of basic preparation, such as reading the cover of the volume you are using.

Similarly, with the reference to the case of *Bolam*, the page number is confused with the volume number. This, again, is the result of poor preparation and over-reliance on a script. Many weaker mooters seem not to know the various types of law reports that can be found in a law library. As a result, it may seem quite plausible to refer to "volume 582 of the 1957 Weekly Law Reports". To a mooter who knows the various sets of law reports well, such a mistake is highly unlikely.

In this clip, Ms Fairclough appears to be finding the whole process of referring to cases a great strain. Mooters who have not really prepared thoroughly often find they struggle with matters like this. Before the moot, they can seem minor; during the moot itself, their importance becomes magnified.

Some inappropriate language was also used in this clip. Ms Fairclough uses the expression "in my opinion", which is not the done thing in a courtroom. An advocate's opinion is completely irrelevant to court proceedings. What matters is the submissions that the advocate is making.

In apologising for her mistake with the *Bolam* reference, Ms Fairclough refers to the judge as "your Lord". This is clearly incorrect and ungrammatical. Aspects of Ms Fairclough's manner in this clip are also too informal for a moot, such as when she says "the two points I'm making today". A preferable form of words would be something like "the two submissions which I am putting before the court on the first ground of appeal".

8.6.2   Clip 2

This clip relates to a simple point on the issue of style and presentation, namely body language. If you watch this footage carefully, you will see that Ms Fairclough is swaying from side to side, almost in time with her speech. This may not be massively noticeable to all judges, but is an example of body language that can distract the judges and look inappropriate in a courtroom. As noted previously, you do not have to keep completely still during a moot, but you certainly should not be moving around too much in a nervous and fidgety manner.

8.6.3   Clip 3

As noted previously, it is essential that you conclude your submissions strongly, as opposed to simply stopping speaking. In this clip, Ms Fairclough's submissions end with such a whimper that the judge is unsure whether they have actually ended or not. The judges should be in no doubt about when your submissions have come to an end, and should, ideally, have the strongest aspects of your submissions ringing in their ears as you sit down. Here, Ms Fairclough simply looks at the judges as though it is their job to bring her submissions to a close. Whilst the judge is certainly in control of the court, you must retain as much control over your own submissions as possible, within the parameters of court etiquette.

8.6.4   Clip 4

In this clip, Mr Cooper exhibits a number of faults which can be common amongst mooters. The first problem which jumps out at one is that of body language. Whilst it has been noted that you do not have to stand to attention like a soldier, there are still acceptable parameters for body language that you must stay within. Mr Cooper is simply moving around too much and changing his position too often and too dramatically. As a result, this is likely to be a distraction to the judges.

Additionally, some of the postures that are adopted are inappropriate. Some of the time, Mr Cooper is actually not facing the judges at all and is standing sideways on. It is almost as though somebody other than the judges is being addressed. It also has the effect of making it look as though Mr Cooper could not care less about the impression he is giving the judges. As a general rule, you should be facing the judges and trying to maintain eye contact with them, not facing in another direction. In this clip, the eye contact is also generally very poor.

Another body language fault that is exhibited here is that of slouching on the lectern. This sort of posture is clearly too relaxed to be appropriate and, as a result, demonstrates a potential lack of respect for the court. It looks more like a drunk person leaning on a bar in a public house, than an advocate appearing in the Court of Appeal.

Mr Cooper is also clearly reading verbatim from his notes, and holding those notes up in front of his face in a manner that is not terribly attractive for an advocate. As is often the case with mooters who read from a script, Mr Cooper also reads too fast. The style adopted also suggests impatience, and that Mr Cooper has more pressing calls on his time.

In fact, the whole clip is suggestive of over-confidence and arrogance. Certainly, confidence is generally a good thing for an advocate or a mooter. However, it is surprising how many mooters feel that it is good advocacy to adopt a highly pompous and self-important manner. It is very rare for such mooters to build a good rapport with the judges, or to be particularly persuasive. The effect is often, as in this clip, of a mooter who is in a world of his own and completely lacking in self-awareness. Some mooters also suffer from over-confidence, which can lead to the same results.

The reference to the case of *Bolam* was bungled, with the wrong volume having been given to the judges. It is surprising how many mooters struggle to grasp that they alone are responsible to see that the judges have a correct copy of any authorities that they wish to read from. If the wrong volume is in court, or if the judges have a different version of a case to the one you are reading from, this is your fault and nobody else's. In this clip, Mr Cooper appears completely unapologetic about this. As a result, his response to the judge's query is highly inappropriate.

Mr Cooper also uses some inappropriate phrases such as "in my opinion". As noted previously, lawyers make submissions in court, rather than treating the judges to their own personal opinions.

Finally in this clip, when questioned by the judge on the case of *Bolam*, Mr Cooper is unable to back up his assertions with proper authority. Additionally, Mr Cooper seems rather unconcerned about his inability to do this and attempts a rather lame reference to Lord Denning. As noted previously, if you are making legal submissions, they should be backed up by reference to legal authority. Otherwise, the submission is worthless, as it simply represents your own personal opinion, which has no authority in a court of law.

The reference to Lord Denning is also relevant to the issue of humour in moots. As noted previously, you should only attempt humour with the judges after exercising extreme caution. One type of humour that is certain to fall flat is attempting to get the judges to laugh at how bad you are. This type of humour makes it look as though you are simply trying to debase the proceedings, because you are poorly prepared, and to get a few cheap laughs out of your own incompetence.

8.6.5 Clip 5

This clip is a little bit tongue-in-cheek, but mobile phones and other gadgets have been known to go off in moots and in real courtrooms. Make sure that yours is turned off before you go into the moot court. Some judges will not be at all amused if this happens, and even the most benevolent of judges will not like it. It should go without saying, but a moot should be far higher up your list of priorities than your friend texting you about social arrangements for the weekend.

8.6.6 Clip 6

The purpose of this clip is to highlight the acceptable parameters of hand gestures. Here, Mr Cooper's gestures are borderline inappropriate, as they are arguably too expansive. This is particularly the case with the windmill-style gesture at the beginning of the clip.

8.6.7 Clip 7

This clip deals primarily with faults to do with the answering of judicial questions, although there are other issues across the board which will also be dealt with. Here, Mr Cooper is asked the question about the possible difference between the phrases "virtually certain consequence" and "highly probable consequence".

The first fault is that Mr Cooper admits that he does not understand the question. In itself, this might not be too bad, but it is in the manner in which it is done that the problem lies. Mr Cooper gives the impression that any problems in terms of understanding are not his responsibility. The reality is that the question asked was perfectly straightforward, bearing in mind the moot problem. There is no reason why a well-prepared mooter should have had difficulty understanding the question put. The general rule is that, if you do not understand a judicial question, you must resist the temptation, if there is one, to blame it on the judge. Judges will expect you to be well prepared. If you do not understand the judge, you should at least have the decency to look apologetic about it.

When Mr Cooper does attempt an answer to the question, he makes the cardinal errors of guessing the answer and not using authorities to back up what he is saying. As a result, the statements he makes about percentages are quickly shown up by the judge to be illogical and no more than Mr Cooper's opinions.

Despite the fact that his answer to the question takes a hammering from the judge, Mr Cooper appears to be blissfully unaware of the fact. At this stage, as at others in the clip, Mr Cooper's manner is too informal and disrespectful to the court. The use of expansive hand gestures also gives the impression of a used-car salesman, rather than an advocate in the Court of Appeal.

Part 3

Miscellaneous issues

Chapter 9

The provision of feedback and how to deal with it

9.1 Introduction

Whether you are mooting as part of a formal assessment or in a mooting competition, the likelihood is that you will receive some feedback on your performance at some stage. This feedback can come from the judges or from tutors, if they are not the same people. Feedback can, of course, also be given informally by other participants in a moot, or by members of the audience. This chapter is primarily concerned with feedback of a more formal type given by judges and tutors, although feedback from other sources can still be of value.

For a number of reasons, feedback in moots is often a more sensitive issue than it is in other situations where students receive comments on their work. For example, most students who are getting a piece of coursework back from their university tutors will receive it with a certain degree of acceptance. The likelihood, in most cases, is that the student will not question either the mark or the comments that have been made. Mooting feedback, on the other hand, is more frequently received negatively by students. Indeed, a small minority of mooters are far more litigious when it comes to arguing about their marks and feedback than they ever were during the moot itself.

It is important, therefore, that you prepare yourself to receive feedback and respond to it in a positive way. One of the aims of this chapter is to help you to do this. For many students, dealing with feedback is not a problem. Students with a positive attitude to feedback benefit far more from the feedback they receive. An acceptance of the fact that you are receiving feedback in order to help you is vital to the learning experience that mooting offers.

The first thing to remember, when you get feedback, is why you are doing mooting in the first place. Mooting is a form of legal education. Its main aim is to help you develop your knowledge of the law, court procedure and etiquette. It is also an opportunity for you to develop as an advocate and as a person. Of course, your aim will also be to progress in competitions, or to score well in assessments. However, you need to look further than these limited aims if you really want to develop into a good advocate. If you are only concerned with the "here and now", it is unlikely that you will give yourself a chance to improve. Getting a good mark, or getting to the next round of a competition, will become the end you are trying to achieve, rather than learning about the law and advocacy. Most people who moot wish to become lawyers. Mooting, therefore, represents the first steps in what may become the basis of your future career, so you need to take a long-term approach to mooting, as becoming a good advocate, for many, involves a steep and long learning curve.

9.1.1   Accepting feedback

One of the reasons why some mooters find feedback harder to accept than in other situations is the highly personal nature of mooting. Standing up in front of any audience and speaking is something that you have to put a lot of yourself into. If what you do is criticised, it can feel like a rejection of you as a person. Because of this, it is easy to see why feedback in moots can sometimes be a sensitive matter. Such personal reactions to feedback are relatively uncommon with written work, where students, rightly or wrongly, feel much more detached from the comments they receive. Any temptation to become defensive or negative about feedback should be strenuously resisted.

There are a number of reasons why you should open yourself up to feedback:

1)   Feedback, of course, will not always be negative. Most judges will try to encourage you, if possible, and to give you some positive feedback on your performance. If you can accept the good things that are said about you, you should be able to deal with the bad things as well.

2)   It might not cheer you up, if you receive bad feedback, but the reality is that learning from your mistakes is a key part of developing any skill. Mooting is no exception to this. If you learn to accept what has been said about your performance, you are less likely to become attached to bad habits. The alternative is to be so stung by bad feedback that you actually resolve to do the opposite of what you are told.

3)   Virtually all feedback will have some truth in it. Judges and tutors will tell you it as they see it. They are generally not biased and will not have a grudge against you. As a result, unless there is some pressing reason not to, you must accept the authority and knowledge of those providing you with feedback. Most moot judges will be experts in the field of law involved, and will also have a good idea of what mooting and advocacy are about.

4)   For better or for worse, having a thick skin and not being too sensitive are characteristics that are required for life as an advocate. The English legal system, along with others throughout the world, is adversarial. Even legal systems that are not adversarial are still characterised by a certain amount of "rough and tumble". Virtually all legal systems conduct their proceedings with the appearance of civility. Nevertheless, under the surface, life can be tough for lawyers.

As a result, if you get into practice, you will come up against opponents who will not spare your feelings, together with judges who will not suffer fools gladly. Having your arguments rejected, and not necessarily in a very pleasant way, is part of everyday life for the advocate. You need to get used to it if you are serious about pursuing a career as an advocate. Learning as a lawyer can be something of a school of hard knocks. Being judged, and receiving feedback in moots, may be your first introduction to this type of situation. It may be hard at first, but it is essential that you learn from your experiences and do not take too personally what is said to you.

5)   Do not be too proud to learn. Even the greatest of advocates were beginners at one stage and had to learn like everyone else. Quite apart from being hurt by criticism, some mooters will not learn from feedback because they are too proud to take on board what judges and tutors say.

Taking pride in your advocacy, and your performances, is essential if you are going to develop your skills. The mooter who takes pride in their performance is much more likely to have the motivation to prepare well and to learn from others and from their own mistakes.

However, despite the above, do not allow yourself to become afflicted by the sort of pride that makes it impossible for you to take criticism. As noted previously, mooting is something that you will put a lot of your personality into. If you have worked hard preparing, and feel comfortable with some of the habits that you have formed, you may become so attached to what you are doing that you are unwilling to change. Many moot judges will have had the experience of dealing with mooters who seem disinclined to accept their advice.

If you do receive some negative comments, think about them, and try to put them right in the next moot. Do not become wedded to poor ways of doing things, simply because they are your own ways. There may be some comments which, after serious thought, you still do not agree with. There are some aspects of mooting where reasonable and knowledgeable observers could find themselves in disagreement. Some things are more subjective than others, such as issues to do with style. If you give serious thought to negative comments, at least you will not be disagreeing with them lightly. You will also be aware that you are doing something in moots which some people would take issue with. This is far better than just rejecting the advice.

Where there is room for disagreement on an aspect of your performance, you should be prepared to approach the matter with an open mind, so that you are open to all reasonable viewpoints. If you are simply predisposed to agree with yourself all the time, you will fail to develop as an advocate.

6)   All of the above still applies if the feedback is given in a slightly abrupt, or even rude, manner. As noted in chapter **6**, some judges or tutors will address you during and after a moot in a way that you may not like. Do not let this put you off or allow you to become negative. The most successful lawyers are usually those who, in their early years particularly, are receptive, in the sense that they use their experiences to help them learn. They are like sponges, who soak up the useful things that are put in front of them. As a result, you should adopt a slightly selfish approach, to the extent that you use your experiences for your own benefit, instead of letting those experiences defeat you.

7)   A cautionary note should be sounded about setting yourself up in disagreement with those who give you feedback. As noted previously, most feedback will have some truth in it. Although judges can have differences of opinion on issues to do with a mooter's performance, they will generally be pretty unanimous on things that they see as really bad.

The more difficult issue is where mooters feel that the judges did not give enough credit for something positive, or came down too hard on something that was negative. At the end of the day, you have to take a reasonably laid-back approach. You are there to moot, and the judges are there to judge. Sometimes you will not like what they say, and sometimes you will.

9.2   The different forms that feedback can take

There are three principal ways in which the modern mooter may receive feedback from the judges or from their tutors. They are:

1)   Orally.

2)   In writing.

3)   A recording of the moot.

With all three of the above, you can expect something different from the judges. Additionally, all three have their own advantages and limitations. These issues are considered in more detail in the following three sections.

9.2.1   Verbal feedback

At the end of a moot which is part of a competition, it is normal for the judges to provide some feedback on the performance of the participants. If the moot is part of a formal assessment, the judges may decline to give feedback at this point. There are two main reasons for this. The first is that the judges will have to give a mark for this type of moot and write up a feedback sheet. Normally, they will want to confer and agree the mark and comments before giving the participants any information. The second is that other students may be doing the same assessment, and therefore the same moot problem. If the judges make comments about what was good and bad about a performance, those who have not yet done the moot may come to hear of them, thus contaminating the assessment process. It is also for this reason that judges in assessed moots will often decline to give a judgment on the law.

If your moot is part of a mooting competition, comments and feedback from the judge are far more likely. However, it is also likely that the comments made will be relatively brief, although judges can vary in this respect. When judging in a competition moot, some judges will temper their comments with mercy, particularly their comments about the losers. Some judges, however, may not be so kind and will not spare your blushes. As a result, it can sometimes feel as though salt is being rubbed into your wounds, when you lose a moot and then receive negative feedback from the judge.

In general, judges in competitions will offer a few words of guidance, perhaps picking up on a few things that you did well or badly, but little more than that. They will, of course, also announce who the winner of the moot is, and will often provide some reasons to back up their decision. It goes without saying that you should take this information on board, as it may give you several clues as to why you won or lost. It is easy, if the judge has already announced the winner, either in the euphoria of victory or the despondency of defeat, to stop listening and switch off at this point.

9.2.2   Written feedback

Written feedback, in general, is only given after moots that are assessed. As such, it is likely that the feedback will be written by one of your tutors, who will also probably have been one of the judges in the moot. The aim of the judges/tutors who write up your feedback will be to deal with each element of the assessment criteria. As noted previously, the assessment criteria may vary, either in their content or in the weighting to be given to each criterion. Nevertheless, despite some differences, most moots are assessed according to roughly similar criteria, and what is a good moot performance in one institution will probably also be regarded in the same way at another. The feedback sheet will normally include your mark for the moot and, depending on the institution involved, perhaps a breakdown of the marks that you were given for each assessment criterion.

Generally, the feedback will be fairly short as, unless the form that an institution uses is very large, there will only be a small place to deal with each assessment criterion. As a result, it is often the case that students are left wanting more information. To counter this, many judges will offer the chance to come and see them for further feedback or clarification. You are advised to take this opportunity if it is offered to you, as a five-minute consultation with the judge can often be better than many pages of written feedback. This is because you will get the chance to ask questions, and the judge/tutor will get the chance to flesh out and develop their comments.

Most moot performances will have some good and some bad in them, and very few performances will be wholly good or bad. As a result, judges will try to reflect this in their feedback, the aim being to provide the mooter with a realistic impression of how their performance came across. Whilst most judges will want to be encouraging, they will also want to avoid giving you a more positive impression than your performance merits. As a result, some feedback can seem more negative than the mark suggests it should be. This can be because the judges want to use the space available to them on the feedback sheet to deal with the bad aspects of your performance. That way, you will learn for the next moot.

If the judge simply takes up all the available space eulogising about your performance, the negatives will become lost. The feedback can look pretty positive, but the mark seems as though it does not fit with what has been written.

As noted previously, it is vital that you adopt a positive approach to feedback. Try to learn from it, not argue with it. It is not always easy to make it so that the mark for the moot is precisely mirrored in the feedback. The judges/tutors are trying to help you to learn, and would much rather award high marks and give good feedback than vice versa.

9.2.3   Recordings of the moot

Most institutions offering mooting now have the facilities to record their moots. As a result, some institutions are now providing copies of moots to students as an aid to learning, usually in video or DVD form. This is undoubtedly a huge advantage and, if you have the opportunity to watch yourself, is an opportunity that should not be missed. It is often a somewhat agonising experience to watch yourself in a moot. Perhaps a good explanation for this is that many people tend to judge their own performance with more of a critical eye than they would other people's. When you do watch yourself, you should make allowances for this, so that you do not draw too negative a conclusion about your own performance.

Being able to watch your own performance in a moot is beneficial for the following reasons:

1)   It often comes as a surprise to see how you look and sound to others. However, the self-awareness that can come from this is very valuable to the budding mooter. If you are trying to be persuasive, it is very important that you are aware of how you come across to your audience.

2)   As was noted in chapter **3**, some mooters have nervous habits, such as hand gestures or other bodily movements, that can be either distracting or irritating to the judges. Either way, such habits can certainly detract from a mooter's performance, as they give the impression of a person who is not in complete control of what they are doing. Many mooters are surprised when they see themselves in a recording and the little habits that they have. If you are aware of these habits, you can take steps to get rid of them or, at least, to mitigate the damage done.

3)   Having a copy of your moot provides a good way of assessing the feedback given to you by the judges. It goes without saying that you should always read your feedback sheet in conjunction with watching any recording of the moot. The introduction of recordings has done much to reduce the incidence of mooters complaining about their feedback and marks. If you can see with your own eyes what the judge is talking about, you are much more likely to accept the point being made.

4)   In your early days as a mooter, you will be trying to develop your own style and courtroom personality. You may have gone to court, watched real advocates and tried to copy aspects of their style. Watching a recording of yourself will tell you if your style is working. You will, of course, already have an idea of this from the response of the judges, but watching a recording will give you a more concrete impression of how well you are doing.

5)   It may be the case that your institution does not just give you a recording of your submissions, but a recording of the whole moot. If this is the case, you will have the opportunity to watch the performances of the other participants again. This can also be instructive, as you will watch these performances with a more objective eye than you will your own. As a result, you may be in a better position to spot the good and bad aspects of the performances and to plan your next moot, bearing these points in mind.

Chapter 10

Skeleton arguments

10.1 What are skeleton arguments?

The idea behind skeleton arguments is that advocates or mooters can provide the court with a precise, but persuasive, outline of the submissions that they intend to make orally when they get into court. Skeleton arguments are so called because they should be a skeleton version of your argument, not a verbatim script of what you will say when you make your oral submissions. The skeleton or outline of your argument is, therefore, provided for the judge(s) before you get into court. When you get into court, your oral submissions should put the flesh on the bones of the skeleton.

Judges who are given skeleton arguments will be able to give the submissions that are subsequently made some thought before the hearing or moot. They will also be able to consult the authorities referred to in the skeleton argument, rather than having to assimilate lots of possibly complex information during the hearing. As a result, a judge who has read a well-written skeleton argument will be in a better position to grasp the submissions being made and to ask pertinent questions.

It is hopefully a sermon on the self-evident to say this, but judges will expect you to stick to the submissions raised by your skeleton argument, if they are a requirement in your moot. From a judge's perspective, it is very irritating to take the time and trouble to read a skeleton argument, only to find that a mooter has unilaterally decided to dispense with the submissions or structure laid down in it.

Skeleton arguments should be seen as your first chance to impress the judges. It is perfectly possible that many judges will form an impression of you before you get into the moot court, on the basis of the content and layout of your skeleton argument. If you have provided them with a well-written, persuasive skeleton argument, that appears to demonstrate a soundness of legal knowledge, they will form a much better impression than if they have read some half-hearted, disorganised nonsense.

10.2 How are skeleton arguments used in practice and in a mooting context?

10.2.1 In practice

In recent times, the civil and criminal justice systems have become very much concerned with "case management", with judges increasingly being looked upon as case managers. As a result, judges are expected to reduce the time that court proceedings take and, therefore, to cut the costs of litigation. One of the key aspects of good case management has been the policy to reduce the number of unnecessary adjournments. One of the most important ways of achieving this has been the push towards ensuring that advocates and judges are ready on the day that hearings are listed.

Because of the above, it is now probable, if an advocate is proposing to make extensive legal argument, and is likely to refer extensively to authority, that the judge will ask for a skeleton argument to be sent to him a certain amount of time before the hearing. The reason for this is that the judge will not want to have to adjourn the case because he or she is not familiar enough with the points of law or authorities being raised by an advocate. Asking the parties to provide skeleton arguments insures against this.

10.2.2 In a mooting context

As noted previously, many mooting competitions now require that the participants provide skeleton arguments at some time before the moot hearing. Where mooting is an assessed part of a course of study, skeleton arguments may well also be part of the assessment strategy.

It has been noted a number of times in this book that mooting is generally intended to be a simulation of what happens in practice in the real courts. As a result, it is an introduction to an important aspect of court practice for you to become involved in the preparation and submission of skeleton arguments from an early stage.

Additionally, the preparation of precise and persuasive skeleton arguments is a difficult skill to master. Because of this, many moots, whether they are national or international mooting competitions, or internal, assessed or extra-curricular moots, now give marks for skeleton arguments or written submissions as well as for the more traditional, oral side of mooting. One thing that you should be aware of is that your university may employ different assessment criteria for the skeleton argument or written submission part of mooting, where it is an assessed part of a course of study. You should check with the tutor in charge, or the course materials that you are given.

10.3 A brief checklist for the structure and content of skeleton arguments

The content of your skeleton arguments will obviously vary widely according to the issues you are mooting on. However, it is fairly safe to say that a decent skeleton argument will normally include most, or all, of the information set out in the checklist below. Some of the matters touched upon in the checklist are dealt with in more detail in later sections of this chapter.

10.3.1 A proper heading

Like a letter, there are certain ways in which, it is generally accepted, one should begin a skeleton argument. See later in this chapter for an example of how this should be done.

10.3.2 State early on the nature of your submissions

This means that you should say clearly what it is that you are asking the court to do, such as allow or dismiss the appeal.

10.3.3 Summarise the factual and legal issues that are in dispute or are likely to be in dispute

As far as the facts are concerned, you do not want to waste valuable words, especially if there is a word limit, repeating the facts of the case. The judges can simply look at the moot problem for that. However, if there are potential factual disputes, such as the medical evidence in *R v Owen Owens*, then you should clearly allude to this in your skeleton argument. This is particularly the case if you are going to say a lot about it in your oral submissions.

10.3.4 How many submissions you are going to make and the order in which you will make them

The order of your submissions may, of course, change on the day in light of judicial questions, but your skeleton argument should certainly make it clear that you have a preferred, and logical, running order. In many cases, the running order of your submissions will broadly mirror the order as laid down by the order of the grounds of appeal in the moot problem. Nevertheless, where you wish to make more than one submission on one ground of appeal, you will obviously have to give some thought to how best to logically order those submissions.

10.3.5 The nature of each submission and the authorities (with full citations) that you intend to rely on

Each submission should be explained in brief, simple and unambiguous terms and backed up by authority.

10.3.6 Headings and paragraphs

Creative and logical use should be made of headings, and numbered or lettered paragraphs, in order to break up the text of the skeleton argument and to give it structure.

10.4 Starting your skeleton argument off with an appropriate heading

As noted previously, this is one part of a skeleton argument where there is a traditional, straightforward way of doing things. All you are trying to do here is to set out the names of the parties, say whether they are appellants or respondents, and state the court which the moot is being held in. Something along the lines suggested below would be appropriate:

In the Court of Appeal (Civil Division)

    Martin Smith   Appellant

and

    British Oil PLC   Respondent

Appellant's Skeleton Argument

10.5 Should there be an introduction?

Skeleton arguments in practice will normally have an introduction, which details certain key facts or assertions for the benefit of the judges, such as who the parties are, what the essence of the dispute is, and a reminder of the material facts.

The difference with skeleton arguments in mooting is that the moot organiser will often put a fairly strict limit on how many words can be used, or how long the skeleton argument should be, in terms of number of pages and font size. For example, the Essex Court National Mooting Competition rules state that skeleton arguments should be no more than one side of A4 paper in length. If there is a strict word limit in your moot, you may not wish to waste too much time and space in writing an introduction of any great length. Remember that the judge(s) will, in any event, have the moot problem (unlike a judge in a real court), and that it is a waste to fill your word limit by repeating key facts that are already in the moot problem. If the word limit for your skeleton argument is a generous one, however, you should generally include a short introduction.

10.6 What should each submission look like?

As noted previously, skeleton arguments are not supposed to contain all that you will say in your oral submissions. They are, however, supposed to give the judge(s) the thrust of what each submission actually is and the authorities which will give legitimacy to what is being argued. As a result, for each submission, you should include reference to authority, where appropriate, as well as a short and simple explanation of what the submission actually is.

Example, in the context of *R v Owen Owens*

Ground 1 of the appeal

1. Submission 1
The learned trial judge materially misdirected the jury on oblique intention. The phrase "highly probable" is not the same as the phrase "virtually certain", nor do the two phrases have the same meaning.
R v Nedrick [1986] 3 All ER 1 (at page 7)
R v Woollin [1999] 2 AC 82 (at pages 84 and 86)
R v Mathews and Alleyne [2003] 2 Cr App R 30 (at pages 35 and 36)

2. Submission 2
In so misdirecting the jury, the learned trial judge unacceptably enlarged the scope of the mental element for murder so as to encompass recklessness.
R v Woollin [1999] 2 AC 82 (at page 87)
R v G and R [2004] Crim LR 369 (at page 372)

It is preferable, in terms of structure and for simplicity, to order the points in your skeleton argument in the same way that you will present them orally in the moot. As noted in chapter 4, it is normally best to put your strongest submissions in first, and leave any weaker or make-weight submissions to the end. The aim of your skeleton argument should not just be the convenience of the judge(s), but to be your first contact with the judges where you are going to begin the process of persuading them. If your submissions are ordered in a logical and persuasive way, the judges will find it easier to read and will be more likely to be persuaded by it.

10.7 Use of headings and paragraphs

To make the skeleton argument stand out, you must use headings which will act as signposts for the judge(s). Nothing is more dull than reading pages of unbroken text. Think of the headings that you use as the bones of the skeleton. The flesh on the bones will be provided by your oral submissions. When using headings, you can, if you wish, be more creative than always using headings like "Submission 1" or "Ground 1". Headings such as "The misdirection on oblique intention" or "The lack of an intention to create legal relations" can also be used.

However, it is worth sounding one cautionary note about being too creative with your headings. The judges will want to know how many submissions you are making, what precisely they are, and when one submission is ending and another is beginning. As a result, something along the following lines is appropriate:

Ground 1

1.   Submission 1:

The lack of an intention to create legal relations

There was no intention between the parties to create legal relations because ...

Paragraph numbers (or letters) are also useful as the judge(s) can see which parts of the skeleton argument deals with which points. This also provides the judges with signposts as to your structure, as well as perhaps giving them an idea of how much time you will be spending on each issue. The number of authorities that you list alongside each submission should also give the judges an idea of this.

10.8 Detailed references to authority

At the skeleton argument stage of a moot, you should not be providing the judges with the actual passages that you intend to read out. That is part of the flesh that you will hopefully put on the bones of the skeleton at the oral stage of the moot. However, there is certainly benefit in giving the judges the page numbers and paragraphs that you will be referring to, so that they can look up the relevant passages if they wish to. If you simply give the judge the citations for a case where the judgments are, for example, 100 pages long, then the bits that you wish to rely on could be anywhere in those 100 pages. This is clearly of little use to the judge(s).

10.9 Do not refer directly to the judges as you would in an oral moot

Skeletons arguments are meant to be read by the judges, not listened to. As a result, you should write it with this is mind. It is not unknown for mooters to pack skeleton arguments with phrases such as "If it pleases your Lordships" or "Would your Lordships like a brief summary of the facts?". Obviously, the judges will not be with you when they read your skeleton argument, so will be unable to answer any questions put to them. Also, as they are reading your argument and not listening to it, you are not addressing them directly. As a result, you do not have to address them as "my Lords", or "your Lordships" etc. In fact, you do not have to address the judges at all. You should simply be stating your argument in outline form.

10.10 Make sure that the flesh fits the bones

This is hopefully an obvious point, but it is worth stating that your skeleton argument and your oral submissions should dovetail with one another and work in harmony together. One of the main points of a skeleton argument is that it helps the judge(s) to understand, and be persuaded by, your oral submissions. If there is some discordance between the impression given by your skeleton arguments and that given by your oral submissions, you are likely to look incompetent or disorganised in the moot.

Marrying your skeleton arguments and your oral submissions successfully requires organisational skill and a lot of hard work. If you have taken shortcuts at some stage, or have prepared your skeleton arguments and oral submissions in isolation from each other, you will probably struggle at some point in the moot. On the other hand, if you have prepared the written and oral stages of a moot in a "joined-up" way, this will normally be apparent to the judges and will create a favourable impression.

Chapter 11

Mooting in England, Scotland and Wales

11.1 Introduction

As noted previously, mooting takes place in a number of different contexts and in many different institutions. The moots that you are involved in could be a formal, assessed part of your course of study. You might also be involved in internal mooting competitions, organised by your own institution, or by an external body such as the Essex Court Chambers National Mooting Competition.

As noted in chapter 1, mooting was once at the very heart of English legal education, when it was used by the four Inns of Court to assess a student barrister's suitability for call to the bar. The growth of universities in recent years, and the increase in the number of law students, has led to an awareness of the importance of learning legal skills to accompany the study of substantive law. With these changes, there is evidence that mooting is regaining its place as an integral part of legal education. As a result, it is more likely than at any time in recent history that you will be involved in mooting at some point during your legal studies.

More students being involved in mooting means more students who have a genuine idea about the skills involved in practising as either a barrister or a solicitor. This means that more students can make properly informed choices about their future. Additionally, they are more likely to understand the substantive law subjects that they study, through the application of their knowledge in a mooting context.

If you become an active mooter, you could be involved in many moots, both at your place of study and externally. If you are in this position, you could find yourself subject to many different approaches to mooting, depending on the institutions involved.

One of the aims of this chapter is to help you to appreciate that the way moots are conducted in institutions is often the result of the personal preferences of the organiser(s), or the traditions of the institution concerned. Approaches can differ quite dramatically, and there is no single right or wrong way for a moot to be organised. The main similarity between moots in all institutions is that they will be attempting to approximate fairly closely to what actually happens in an appellate court. Mooting, after all, is a form of legal training. It is therefore important that moots at least come close to reflecting proceedings in the real courts.

This chapter deals with **two** main issues:

1)   The **first** part of the chapter examines the mooting opportunities that are available to students and junior practitioners in England and Wales.

2)   The **second** part of the chapter considers the different ways in which mooting can be approached by institutions. International mooting competitions are dealt with separately in chapter **12**.

11.2 Mooting opportunities in England, Scotland and Wales

The following sections look briefly at how you can become involved in mooting, either at your own institution of study or through some kind of external competition or institution.

11.2.1 Mooting opportunities at your own university or institution

The first thing that you should do, if you are genuinely interested in becoming involved in mooting, is ask the members of staff at your institution who are responsible for mooting about what opportunities are available at that particular institution. Having said that, there are **five** ways in which your institution is likely to be able to involve you in mooting:

1)   Most institutions that offer legal studies at undergraduate level or above recognise the importance of mooting and advocacy, as a means not only of learning the law but also of developing the key skills needed for practice as a lawyer. As a result, many institutions incorporate an element of mooting into the first year of their undergraduate programmes. You should check with the appropriate staff members to see if this is the case where you are studying. This can be done in **two ways**:

a)   A moot may be incorporated into the study of one or more of the substantive legal subjects studied in the first year of a law degree. For example, you might find yourself involved in a moot during your study of a core subject, such as contract or tort.

b)   Most institutions give students courses in legal skills, so that they have the necessary skills to successfully study and apply the law. More and more institutions are now incorporating an element of mooting into their first year, undergraduate courses through this medium. You may, therefore, find that involvement in mooting is a compulsory element in the first year of your legal studies. This is particularly the case if you are an undergraduate student. If you are studying on a course such as the Graduate Diploma in Law, it is less likely that mooting of this sort will be compulsory. This is largely due to time constraints, and the intensive nature of the Graduate Diploma course.

2)   More and more universities are now offering mooting as an optional "subject". As a result, mooting is, for many students, a formal, assessed part of their course. If mooting is an option at your university, it is most likely that it will be late on, probably in the third year of your degree. There are **two reasons** for this:

a)   Mooting as a major, assessed part of a course of study is probably best left until students have acquired the necessary maturity and legal skills to do well at it. This is more likely to be the case later on in your legal studies than when you are a relative novice, in your first year. As noted previously, you may, however, be given the chance to moot earlier on in one of the two ways mentioned above.

b)   Many moot problems will be based on the core subjects or will, at least, require some knowledge of them. If you do not know the basics of, for example, contract law, it is unlikely that you are going to be able to moot successfully in that area without teaching yourself the subject. It is only when you reach the latter stages of your law degree that you will have studied all or most of the core subjects and will, therefore, be able to moot on them. It should be noted that taking such an option, if it is available at your institution, is not a condition of entry into the legal profession. You will have to do advocacy assessments on either the Bar Vocational Course or the Legal Practice Course in any event.

3)   As well as offering mooting in the ways outlined above, many institutions will offer mooting as an extra-curricular activity. If so, it is likely that you will have the chance to become involved in some kind of internal mooting competition at your institution. Because such activities are extra-curricular, they do not form part of the assessment process. You are strongly recommended to engage in such activities, but bear in mind that this will involve you in a great deal of extra work. You must be ready for this if such activities are to be worthwhile. Some of the principal advantages of mooting were mentioned in chapter **1**.

4)   Those involved in organising mooting at your institution will often give you assistance or advice in how to become involved in external mooting competitions, where different institutions send teams of mooters to compete against one another. Some universities are more organised and active than others in this respect. There are many external mooting competitions in England and Wales. For more information on these, see section **11.2.2** below.

5)   Your institution might also enter teams in some of the many international mooting competitions. Chapter **12** provides more information on this.

11.2.2   National mooting competitions in England, Scotland and Wales

There are numerous competitions that you, or your institution, can enter. This section covers some of the most well known mooting competitions, but does not purport to provide an exhaustive list of all external mooting competitions.

Alexander Stone Scottish Intervarsity Moot Court Competition
www.gla.ac.uk/departments/schooloflaw/forallstudents/ studentactivitiesandsocieties/mooting/
This competition is run on a rotating basis by the five traditional Scottish law schools of Edinburgh, Dundee, Glasgow, St Andrews and Strathclyde who each enter a team every year. At the time of writing, the competition is in the hands of the University of Glasgow, hence the web address above.

Essex Court Chambers National Mooting Competition
www.essexcourt.net/mooting/
This is an inter-university mooting competition, with knockout rounds held throughout the country at entrant universities. Essex Court barristers' chambers has been sponsoring this competition for around nine years, but the competition is run by the English-Speaking Union. Readers who are long enough in the tooth will remember this competition as the Observer National Mooting Competition.

Some attractive cash prizes are available for the winners, together with some nice silverware. To be eligible to enter this competition, you must be an undergraduate law student, or a student on the Graduate Diploma in Law. There are two mooters for each team, a senior and junior counsel. More details of the rules can be found on the competition's website. The semi-finals and finals of the competition are held in London, and a formidable panel of judges is used. The competition also provides mooters with a link to Essex Court Chambers, with mini-pupillages being offered to some participants.

Oxford University Press/ BPP Law School National Mooting Competition
www.oup.co.uk/oxfordtextbooks/law/mooting/
This is another prestigious mooting competition. As with the Essex Court competition, to be eligible, students must be undergraduate or Graduate Diploma in Law students. The knockout rounds are held throughout the course of the academic year, and are held at the entrant universities, as dictated by the draw. This requires a certain amount of organisation on the part of the home team, such as the finding of judges and the organisation of rooms and refreshments. The same goes for most inter-university mooting competitions. Teams, as usual, consist of two mooters, a senior and junior counsel. There is, however, according to the rules, some scope for different mooters to be used throughout the various rounds. More information is available on the competition's website.

United Kingdom Environmental Law Association Mooting Competition
www.ukela.org
This actually consists of two competitions. The first is the Lord Slynn of Hadley Mooting Trophy Competition, also known as the "senior competition". To be eligible for this competition, mooters must either be pupil barristers/trainee solicitors or students on the Bar Vocational Course or Legal Practice Course. In essence, this is a mooting competition for those at the vocational stage of legal training.

The second competition is the UKELA Student Prize Moot, also referred to as the "junior competition". To be eligible, you must be a degree student (not necessarily in law) or a student on a course such as the Graduate Diploma in Law. Students studying for graduate degrees, such as an LLM, are also eligible. In essence, this moot is mainly aimed at those who are at the academic stage of legal education or training.

Unlike most mooting competitions, these two consist of the submission of skeleton arguments. The finalists are then selected on the basis of the skeleton arguments. The finalists then engage in an ordinary oral moot. The teams consist of two members, who do not necessarily have to be from the same institution.

Cash prizes and silverware are again available for those who meet with success. More information about the rules etc is available on the competition's website.

Weekly Law Reports Mooting Competition
www.lawreports.co.uk/mooting
To be eligible for this competition, you must be an undergraduate law student or a student on a course such as the Graduate Diploma in Law. Each institution can only enter one team, and teams may not enter until they have provided the organisers with one original moot problem. The winners receive a year's free subscription to the Weekly Law Reports. Teams consist of two members, a senior and junior counsel. More details of this competition are available on the competition's website.

Honourable Society of the Inner Temple Inter Varsity Mooting Competition
www.itmoot.org/#/intervarsity/
This competition is held at the Inner Temple and is organised by them, rather than being held at the entrant universities. It is open to all students from faculties in England, Scotland and Wales. This is rapidly developing into a popular competition, with a high demand for entries each year. It also has the advantage of being held at the Inner Temple, which means that teams do not have any of the headaches associated with being a host team. More information can be found on the website of the Inner Temple's Mooting Society.

Mooting in the Inns of Court
Mooting still takes place and flourishes in the four great Inns of Court. The tradition is that you can engage in two types of moot, junior or senior. A senior moot is usually held in hall after dinner, with an often formidable panel of judges. The junior moots, once known as "bolts", are slightly less formal, in that they are not held in hall after dinner and do not, as a result, generally attract much of an audience. At the time of writing, however, there seems to be a trend away from holding as many moots in hall. As a general rule, internal mooting at the Inns of Court is reserved for those on the Bar Vocational Course or those in pupillage.

11.3 Differences of approach to mooting in England, Scotland and Wales

As noted previously, there are a number of different approaches to mooting which, in turn, mean that different rules are adopted by different institutions and competitions. This is something that you need to be wary of, especially if you are accustomed to the mooting rules of one particular institution. Most good moot organisers will provide you with all the information you need to moot with them, clearly set out. As a result, you should be left in no doubt as to the rules you are operating under. What follows, however, is a guide to what to look out for in terms of variations in rules and traditions.

11.3.1 Skeleton arguments

Most of the leading mooting competitions now require that mooters provide some form of skeleton argument prior to the moot. However, this is not always the case in universities and institutions where mooting is offered either as an assessed part of a course or as an extra-curricular activity. Some institutions will, therefore, not require any form of skeleton argument to be submitted.

Where skeleton arguments are required, there are often rules as to the length permitted and the typeface etc. As with all such variations, the key is not to let yourself inhabit too much of a comfort zone because the vast majority of your mooting is at one institution. If you come to practise as a lawyer, you will see that different courts and regions often have slightly different practices and requirements. The same goes with mooting. This is something that you need to make the effort to embrace, and not be frightened of.

11.3.2 Matters to do with authorities

There are a number of ways in which practices can vary as far as the use of authorities is concerned. They include:

A) Exchange of authorities

Whilst most moots will require exchange of authorities at some time before the moot, this is not universally the case. It is not unknown for some moot organisers to give all participants a list of authorities that they must use, along with the moot problem. Where this is the case, exchange of authorities may not be required, as all the participants in the moot will have been given a list at the outset. As the mooters are not allowed to depart from the list of authorities provided, the exchange process is arguably redundant.

Where exchange is required, the key thing to look out for is the time by which exchange should take place. Some moots may require that exchange takes place seven days before the moot, whilst others may require that exchange takes place only two days before etc. You need to check with the organisers so that you do not get this wrong.

The last thing you want is to either lose marks or alienate the judges before you even get into the moot court because you have not complied with some pretty basic rules.

Another potential pitfall to look out for is when the rules of a moot state that exchange must take place a certain number of "clear days" before the moot. You need to be certain as to what the organisers mean by this. To some, the phrase "clear days" means that the day of the moot and the day when the exchange takes place are not included in the number of relevant days. If you are not careful with this type of rule, it can mean that you end up exchanging your authorities late or, indeed, earlier than you needed to, due to confusion.

B) Limits on numbers of authorities

Some organisers of moots will allow you what seems like a fairly parsimonious maximum number of authorities. Where the maximum number is more generous, you need to be wary of the possibility of overloading your submissions with too many references to too many cases. This is particularly likely to be a problem where the time limits for submissions are not similarly generous. For more on overloading your submissions, see chapter **4**.

The transition can be hard to make for mooters who are used to being allowed to use only a small number of authorities, but who then enter a moot where the maximum number is more generous. Be careful of these pitfalls, and remember that you will not necessarily be expected to use the maximum number of authorities available to you.

C) Copies of the authorities that you intend to use

Most moot organisers will require you to provide the judge(s) with copies of the authorities you intend to rely on. This will either be a photocopy or a copy of the relevant law report etc. If you are unsure of how many copies to bring with you, this can usually be easily answered by the organiser of the moot, who should know well in advance of the moot how many judges there will be.

11.3.3   Time limits for submissions

How long you will have for your submissions is vital in determining what form your submissions will take. Some moots give you as little as ten minutes to make your submissions, whereas others may give as much as 20 minutes. Where the time allocation is at the lower end of the scale, you will find that, if you are well prepared, you have an incredibly short amount of time to properly develop a detailed, comprehensive argument with extensive reference to authority. As a result, you may have to be highly selective and economical when deciding what to include in your submissions. The tendency is to want to include things if you have spent a long time reading them, and think they are relevant. For the well-prepared mooter, who has done extensive research, being selective and economical can, therefore, be very difficult.

One other issue worth mentioning is that, in many competitions, senior counsel will get a bit more time for their submissions than junior counsel. In assessed moots in universities, the time allocations will, however, usually be equal, to ensure parity between students. The obvious exception to this is that counsel for the appellant will still be given the extra time for a right of reply.

11.3.4   Interruptions/questions from the bench and time limits

An important variation is that some moot organisers will stop the clock during the time when the judges are asking questions, and when you are answering them. If this is the case, then it makes life much easier for you as a mooter. You will be much better able to plan your arguments, in terms of timing, and much less likely to have your submissions dominated by lengthy questions from the bench.

If the organisers do not stop the clock during questions and answers, the chances of your submissions turning into a lengthy question and answer session are much greater. This is especially so if you only have a short time allocation for your submissions. In these circumstances, you need to show greater flexibility and to ensure that your answers to judicial questions include the points that you actually wanted to make in your planned submissions. If you answer questions defensively, you will probably not achieve this. As a result, your main submissions may not see the light of day.

If questions and answers are included in the time allocation, the final and most obvious problem is that it is much more difficult for you to plan your submissions in terms of good time-keeping. As a result, preparation and knowledge of what questions might be asked is crucial to you in planning how long your submissions should take.

11.3.5   Rights of reply

In competition moots, the right of reply for counsel for the appellants is usually optional. Save in very exceptional circumstances, however, it is highly desirable that you should avail yourself of this important opportunity to speak. The judges will want to see you show that you have the intellect to be flexible and respond to your opponent's case.

In assessed moots, it is pretty much obligatory to utilise your right of reply. The judges will, of course, be looking to allocate marks for your ability to respond to the other side. If you do not use your right of reply, you will probably miss out on all of these available marks.

11.3.6   Team members

Some mooting competitions allow team members to change during the course of the competition. The normal rule, however, is that the same team members have to be involved at the semi-final and final stages. This is particularly useful if you have more than two good mooters, who are keen to be involved. It is also useful if you have mooters who are very strong in some subjects, but are not confident mooting on other areas of law.

If the moot is assessed, you should be assessed individually. As a result, who your partner is does not really matter, except that you may wish to use a good partner to bounce ideas off and help you to prepare.

Some moots allow teams to consist of mooters from different institutions, such as the UKELA mooting competition.

11.3.7   Judges

The number of judges you will have in your moot can also vary enormously. Some moots may have just one judge, who may be quite well known to you as one of your university tutors. A senior moot in hall at one of the Inns of Court, however, could involve a large panel of very senior judges and practitioners. As noted previously, judges can also vary enormously in terms of the number of questions they ask and the way in which they ask them.

11.3.8   Dress

As noted in chapter **3**, it is best to adopt a form of dress that closely approximates to what you would wear in court as a lawyer. Some moot organisers are stricter on these issues than others. In fact, some stipulate that mooters should also wear gowns. Check this with the organisers, and try to demonstrate your respect for the proceedings by the way that you present yourself in terms of dress.

11.3.9   Host's responsibilities

If you are the home team in a moot that is held at the institution of the home team, you need to check carefully what the organisers expect of you as the host. Normally, there will be somebody at your institution who takes responsibility for matters such as preparing a room and finding a judge etc. However, it is not unknown for students to enter themselves in mooting competitions, without any staff help. If you find yourself in this situation, it is vital that you take full responsibility for all organisational matters.

Chapter 12

International mooting

12.1 Introduction

As noted in chapter **11**, there is a flourishing domestic mooting scene in England, Scotland and Wales. This chapter, however, seeks to give you an introduction to the wonderful community that exists in international mooting. There are numerous prestigious international mooting competitions, which give those fortunate enough to participate the chance to pit their wits against some of the best students and mooters from around the globe. It may be that your place of study is already well established in entering teams in international mooting competitions. If so, you will get the benefit of a degree of expertise that is already in place. If your place of study does not have a tradition of entering teams in international moots, you may need to be more pro-active in persuading the institution to commit resources to this activity. One thing is certain: if an institution makes a genuine commitment to international mooting, it can only have a positive effect on that institution's standing in the legal and academic communities.

12.2 The benefits of international mooting

The benefits of mooting generally were considered in chapter **1**. The benefits mentioned there, such as confidence building and enhancement of employment prospects, certainly apply equally to international mooting. International mooting, however, has it's own added advantages. These include:

a)   International mooting competitions take place in all four corners of the globe. If you are lucky enough to participate, you may get the chance to travel extensively with your team.

b)   Travelling to far-flung places with your team is an excellent way of building character, and developing your ability to work as part of a team. As noted previously, teamwork is often essential if you are to practise successfully as a lawyer. Being involved in an intensive international competition with your teammates, a long way from home, certainly tests you in this respect.

c)   Virtually all the participants in a large international mooting competition will be in the same position. They may be a long way

from home, with a team and in an intellectually and personally challenging, but hopefully enjoyable, set of circumstances. This often
brings the best out of people. There is a certain camaraderie to international mooting. Participants develop stronger relationships with
students from their own institution, and with their tutors who will
accompany them. Additionally, students engage in a very significant
shared experience with students from all around the world.

There is a strong sense of "spirit" in the international mooting
community. This is reflected in the fact that some competitions
award prizes for those students who they feel epitomise the spirit that
they are looking for.

d)   International mooting also gives you the chance to broaden your
horizons, as opposed to merely dealing with domestic law issues.
Aspects of what could very broadly be termed "international law" are
increasingly becoming matters that lawyers are expected to know
about. Merely knowing about your own domestic law has a very lim-
iting effect on your own capacity to operate effectively as a lawyer,
and greatly limits your career prospects.

e)   As with domestic mooting, you will often find that you get to
meet, and pit your wits against, some of the best and brightest students around. It is good for you to mix in this sort of company from
an early stage. Additionally, the judges at such events, as with some
domestic moots, are very senior figures who it is beneficial to have
contact with. It is not unknown for success in the moot court to lead
to other career opportunities.

f)   In dealing with some international mooting problems, you can
deal with some of the highly significant legal, political and moral
issues that are important on the world stage, such as armed conflicts
and international humanitarian issues. It could be argued that issues
of the same importance, or on such a large scale, do not arise as often
in domestic moot problems.

12.3   International and domestic mooting compared

Whilst there are clearly going to be many differences between
domestic and international mooting, it should be pointed out that
there are also many similarities. A detailed description of the rules
and regulations of the various international mooting competitions is
beyond the scope of this book. Such information can be easily found
by going to the websites of any competitions that you are interested

in. The purpose of this section, however, is to give a flavour of the many similarities, as well as some of the differences, between domestic and international mooting:

a) The major differences should be fairly obvious. International mooting competitions are usually set in the International Court of Justice (ICJ), rather than in your own domestic courts. As a result, you have to become accustomed to a different jurisdiction, different types of judge, and a different body of law to that of your own country. Because of this, it is generally preferable to have studied international law before you enter international mooting competitions. If you have not done so, you will have to put a great deal of time and effort into teaching yourself. Whilst this is certainly not impossible, it is a major undertaking that will be daunting for all but the most hard working.

b) Most of the major international mooting competitions mentioned later in this chapter are conducted, at least partially, in English. Some competitions also offer the possibility of interpreters for those wishing to use a language other than English.

c) The oral part of most international moots pretty much mirrors that of most domestic moots, in that each moot will normally have four advocates who speak in the same order as they would in a domestic moot. Rights of reply are also available for the applicant (as you would expect in a domestic moot), but also sometimes for the respondents as well. One obvious exception to this is the Jean Pictet Competition.

One difference, that is often apparent in international moots, is that teams will often comprise of more than just the two advocates. As a result, a team may have five members, two of them advocates, the other three being used as researcher/scribes, or becoming advocates themselves for some rounds, if possible and/or desirable.

d) Most of the international moots require some form of written document or skeleton argument to be submitted by teams prior to the oral moot stages.

e) Most international moots also require both sides to exchange the authorities upon which they intend to rely at some point before the oral stage of proceedings.

f) Finally, the reality is that, wherever you are mooting, the judges will be looking at roughly the same assessment or judging criteria as they would in a domestic moot. The setting or court might be different, but the skills needed to be a good mooter are pretty much universal. For more on the assessment or judging criteria for mooting, see chapters **3** to **8**.

12.4 International mooting opportunities

A simple internet search will demonstrate that there are a large number of international mooting competitions that you could try to enter. It should be noted that, at some universities, competition for entry into some of the more prestigious competitions can be intense. This section gives a brief commentary on some of the more well known international mooting competitions. For those readers wishing to investigate further, the website address of each competition is provided.

Jean Pictet Competition
www.concourspictet.org

This competition is based on international humanitarian law issues and is aimed at undergraduate or above students (not necessarily in law). This is not a "normal", adversarial moot competition, but a series of role plays and simulations set over a one-week period. The aim is to test the knowledge of participants, on both a theoretical and a practical level, on international humanitarian law. As well as being a competition where eventual winners emerge, this is also seen very much as a valuable education and training week for those lucky enough to participate. The situations or problems often grapple with fictitious but realistic and thorny issues, typically to do with armed conflicts.

Oxford Intellectual Property Moot
www.oiprc.ox.ac.uk

This competition consists of a written submission stage, whereby each team is obliged to send in two written submissions on the moot problem, which are then judged/scored by a panel of judges. The next stage of the competition is the oral proceedings weekend, usually held in spring at one of the colleges of Oxford University (in 2009, St Catherine's College). A maximum of 24 teams are permitted for the oral weekend. If more than 24 apply, the scores from the written submissions are used to pick the best 24 teams. Senior figures from the English and Welsh judiciary often act as judges.

Phillip C Jessup International Mooting Competition
www.ilsa.org/jessup

A prestigious and extensive international mooting competition, the Jessup Competition, organised by the International Law Students Association, attracts around 2,000 entrants a year, from around 500 universities worldwide. The moot is a simulation of a problem before the International Court of Justice.

Copious amounts of information about the rules, requirements and history of this competition are available on the competition's website. In order to progress to the international stage of the competition, teams first have to pass through regional or national rounds in January of each year. The international rounds are conducted over one week, and are held in Washington DC in March of each year, where a "world champion" mooting team emerges. This competition involves written and oral stages. High-profile figures are regularly used as judges.

Telders International Mooting Competition
www.telders.leidenuniv.nl/

This competition, dating back to 1977, consists of moot problems involving disputes between nations in the International Court of Justice. The competition consists of a written and an oral stage, and can only be entered by the teams winning their own national version of the competition, as only one team from each country is permitted to enter the main competition. Real judges from the International Court of Justice are used to judge the moots, with the final being held at the International Court of Justice.

Willem C Vis International Commercial Arbitration Moot
www.cisg.law.pace.edu/vis.html

This competition has two stages: the written stage and the oral stage. The written stage is held at the Law Faculty of the University of Vienna, annually around Easter time.

It also has an Eastern sister competition, held each year in Hong Kong (see the website at *www.cisgmoot.org*). This is a completely separate competition to the Vienna competition, although the same moot problem is used each year.

See also:

- European Law Students Association Moot Court Competition (www.elsa.org/emcc/index.asp)

- Manfred Lachs Space Law Moot Court Competition (www.spacemoot.org).

Chapter 13

Further reading and viewing and sources of information and inspiration

13.1 Introduction

When it comes to further reading, there are a vast array of sources that the budding mooter can consult. When you become seriously involved in mooting, it will probably be because you are considering a career as a professional advocate. The skills that you are being introduced to as a new mooter could, therefore, be the skills that you subsequently use for the rest of your professional life. If you are to be successful and happy in this pursuit, it is clearly desirable that you consult sources that are going to be informative and also inspirational. The best advocates are often those who have a sense of vocation, in that they feel that they belong in the courtroom spiritually and intellectually. If you are really interested in life as an advocate, whilst you are still a student who is involved in mooting, you stand at the threshold of what could be a fascinating and stimulating world. Reading around the subjects raised in this book is one way in which the aforementioned sense of belonging can be instilled.

As a result of the huge number of available sources, it is not the purpose of this chapter to provide you with a complete, exhaustive list of all the sources of information available on the various issues and topics raised in this book. Because of this, many worthy sources do not get a mention, or are only mentioned briefly.

Instead, the aim is to provide you with a guide to some of the things to look for when reading around the subject of mooting, as well as instilling a sense of why it is important to read around the subject in the first place. It is hoped that you will derive pleasure from embarking on your own journey of discovery in this rich area and form your own tastes in the process. If you are to take pride in yourself as a mooter, and perhaps as a professional advocate thereafter, you will certainly benefit from extensive consultation of a wide range of sources, and from regular visits to court to see real advocates at work. It is only through seeing real advocates at work that you will be able to exercise a degree of discriminatory power in deciding which fictitious and other sources have any merit.

Not all of the sources that are referred to in this chapter are sources which are necessarily entirely dedicated to advocacy, let alone mooting. The aim of this chapter, however, is to give you a start in reading and searching around the subjects which are relevant to mooting. How wide you wish to cast the net is up to you. In writing this chapter, I have presumed that you may at least be considering a career as an advocate, and that your mooting is by way of preparation for this.

As will probably be obvious, it is not necessary to confine yourself merely to reading textbooks. There is also a wealth of literature, film, theatre, television and radio that is dedicated to subjects that are relevant to you as a mooter.

13.2 The benefits of further reading/consultation of other sources

When it comes to further reading, viewing or listening, there are **two** main aims that you should have in mind.

13.2.1 Information

Finding authoritative sources is the most obvious aim that you will have in mind. If you are going to be involved in mooting, and if you wish to enter the legal profession thereafter, it is important that you have a realistic impression of what is involved. As a result, glossy legal dramas on the television will probably not provide you with much of an insight into the way that you should conduct yourself in a moot, or in a real courtroom.

Generally, lawyers in most jurisdictions do not strut around the courtroom whilst they are speaking, nor do they wear light-coloured designer suits and shout things like "I object!"; nor do they, in my experience, simultaneously have sexual relationships with their clients. Some films and books of this type (many of them, incidentally, are English as well as American) can paint a bizarre and misleading impression of what it is to be a lawyer. As a result, some students can mistakenly form the impression that success in the law is easily achieved by donning a snazzy suit and adopting a cocky manner. Try and avoid being too impressionable when confronted with such sources.

Whilst there may be a place in the learning process for reading and watching such material, it is important that you learn to recognise what really happens in the real courts in your country and in the moot courts that you might appear in. Visiting the various courts that are available in your country is an absolute must for all mooters. This way, you can learn the forms of eloquence that are appropriate to the courtroom setting. To supplement this, there is a wide range of material that you can also consult, from fiction to textbooks, some of which is referred to later in this chapter.

13.2.2 Reading, viewing and listening for pleasure and inspiration

In the section above, it was suggested that watching or reading some sources may not provide you with a particularly good insight into how to moot, or how to be a good advocate. Having made that observation, however, it should be pointed out that there is a huge place in the learning process for reading, viewing and listening for purely pleasurable or inspirational purposes. There is nothing wrong, for example, with watching *Judge John Deed* or *LA Law*. Watching or reading such material often, in some indirect way, fosters enthusiasm for the real business of mooting or being a lawyer. Many perfectly respectable lawyers watch or read such material, and enjoy them in terms of pure entertainment. Some sources will, of course, be more realistic, and thus more informative, than others. As a result, the general rule is the more realistic the better, if you are consulting it for any purpose other than pure entertainment.

Where some students, and some mooters, go wrong, however, is in not appreciating the unrealistic nature of the material they are watching or reading. Most tutors of mooting will have seen inexperienced mooters who seem incredibly disappointed that the real courts, and therefore the moot courts, do not match the somewhat fantastical world that they have been inhabiting through television, film or literature.

As a result, whilst you can draw inspiration and pleasure from a wide range of sources, the core of your inspiration should come from realistic sources if you are to prosper. If all of your enthusiasm for advocacy stems from the fact that you are labouring under a series of misapprehensions, then this does not bode well.

Much of this chapter will, however, be dedicated to sources of reading, viewing and listening that do not, on the face of it, have much direct relevance to the mooter. As long as you understand the limitations or follies of what you are reading, watching or listening to, you should not go too far wrong.

There are many books that I refer to in this chapter that are, unfortunately, out of print. However, if you are interested in becoming slightly bookish, there are many secondhand or antiquarian bookshops that stock books of a type that could interest the mooter. Additionally, online services, such as Amazon, now make it very easy to find even the rarest of out-of-print book.

If you are in London, an excellent place to have a look around for this purpose is Wildy and Sons (www.wildy.com), who have their main premises in Lincoln's Inn, with a smaller shop on Fleet Street. This is a wonderful old shop where you will find many books, old and new, in print and out of print, including biographies of notable lawyers and judges, books on the Inns of Court, mooting and advocacy, the legal profession, works of fiction, legal history etc. The benefit of this type of shop is that you are not restricted in terms of only having in-print, current books to choose from. A look around such a place gives you an idea of just how much material is available for the purposes of reading both for pleasure and for information. Once you have seen shops such as this, it makes online searching for books much easier, as you may have more of an idea what you are looking for.

Unfortunately, in recent years, many secondhand and antiquarian booksellers have closed down or have simply gone online. As a result, the opportunities for old-style browsing have diminished somewhat. However, the burgeoning online market in books now provides a very valuable, if less charming, source to the reader who has more of an idea of what he or she is looking for. You are strongly advised to make use of services such as Amazon to see what is available on mooting-related subjects that are of interest to you. The romantic in me would, however, prefer that you also use some of the excellent bookshops that still exist to this day.

13.3 Sources on the Inns of Court and aspects of legal history which might be of interest to the mooter

As was noted in chapter **1**, mooting still takes place where it began, in the four great Inns of Court: Gray's Inn, Lincoln's Inn, Middle Temple and Inner Temple. Whilst you do not need to know much about the Inns of Court to be a good mooter or advocate, there is a wealth of writing on the Inns of Court and legal London generally that is well worth reading, for the historically minded mooter. The study of legal history is greatly neglected in many English universities, with students often suffering from the lack of context for their law that a good historical background can provide.

Many of the works in this area, not surprisingly, have sections or chapters on mooting in the inns, and chart the way in which mooting was, and still is, used as a tool of legal education. What follows is a list of some of the works in this area which will give you a small taste of what is available:

- JH Baker, *An Introduction to English Legal History* (4th edn, 2004, Oxford University Press).
- JH Baker, *The Common Law Tradition* (1999, Hambledon Continuum).
- N Cawthorne, *The Strange Laws of Old England* (2004, Judy Piatkus Publishing).
- F Cowper, *A Prospect of Gray's Inn* (1985, Graya).
- T Daniel, *The Lawyers – The Inns of Court: Home of the Common Law* (1976, Wildy, Simmonds and Hill Publishing).
- M Herber, *Legal London: A Pictorial History* (2007, Phillimore).
- A Holdsworth, *A Portrait of Lincoln's Inn* (2007, Third Millennium Publishing).
- R Megarry, *Inns Ancient and Modern* (1989, Wildy, Simmonds and Hill Publishing).

In addition to the books listed above, there are countless other books, some out of print, which can be found if you search for them, either in bookshops or online.

Finally, one excellent source of information is the Selden Society (www.selden-society.qmw.ac.uk), which is a society entirely dedicated to English legal history. Membership rates are very reasonable, and the benefits of membership include access to a formidable collection of materials, some of them specifically on mooting.

If you get the chance, have a wander around the Inns of Court, all of which are in a very small area just to the east of central London. The inns are interesting from an historical and architectural perspective, but are also so much more than that. Whilst there is a strong sense of history around the inns, the fact is that they are a living, breathing, working and flourishing place, where history and the modern world converge in a unique way. Having a stroll around the inns can be a great source of inspiration and information for the mooter. It may also give you more of an idea of whether the legal profession really is for you. Pop in to *El Vino* wine bar on Fleet Street whilst you are at it. This was John Mortimer's inspiration for *Pommeroys* wine bar in the *Rumpole* stories and is much frequented by the bar. It is also associated with older, more rotund barristers hanging around, pretending to be Horace Rumpole.

13.4 Books on mooting and advocacy

There are many books on advocacy generally, and a much smaller number dedicated specifically to mooting.

13.4.1 Mooting books

> - D Pope and D Hill, *Mooting and Advocacy Skills* (2007, Sweet and Maxwell).
> - C Kee, *The Art of Argument* (2007, Cambridge University Press).
> - J Snape and G Watt, *How to Moot: a student guide to mooting* (2004, Oxford University Press).
>
> NB *The Art of Argument* is mainly aimed at students taking part in international mooting competitions, but is also of use to students taking part in domestic moots.

13.4.2 Advocacy books

There are far more books on advocacy generally than there are on mooting. It is a good thing to immerse yourself in the art of advocacy generally, as well as simply concerning yourself with the specifics of mooting. You should, however, be aware that advocacy books will cover many matters which are not directly relevant to what you will have to do in a moot, such as cross-examination and examination-in-chief. Whilst there is nothing wrong at all with reading about these things early on, indeed it should be encouraged, you should avoid making the mistake of not distinguishing advocacy from the narrower field of mooting. All moots are, of course, set in the appellate courts. As a result, mooters do not have to master the art of trial advocacy.

Below is a **selection** of the available books on advocacy:

> - J Davis, *The Criminal Advocate's Survival Guide* (2007, Harriman House). This book gets a special mention, as it was written by an old friend of mine, who dealt with many cases with me at various Oxfordshire courts.
> - R Du Cann, *The Art of the Advocate* (1993, Penguin).

- K Evans, *The Language of Advocacy: What to Say and How to Say It in the English-Speaking Courts* (1998, Oxford University Press).
- I Morley, *The Devil's Advocate: A Short Polemic on How to be Seriously Good in Court* (2005, Sweet and Maxwell).
- D Pannick, *I Have to Move My Car: Tales of Unpersuasive Advocates and Injudicious Judges* (2008, Hart Publishing).
- D Ross QC, *Advocacy* (2007, Cambridge University Press).
- A Scalia and B Garner, *Making Your Case: The Art of Persuading Judges* (2008, West Publishing).

In addition to the above, there are advocacy manuals, which come out each year, for those students on the Bar Vocational Course or the Legal Practice Course. These are well worth reading.

13.5 Books on the English legal system

In chapter **2**, it was noted that a sound knowledge of your legal system is essential if you are to become a successful mooter. Without such knowledge, it is very difficult to successfully research and prepare your submissions and to know what is appropriate when you get into the moot court. There are countless textbooks on the English system. What follows is a short list of some of the most well known. Of course, it is highly desirable that you acquire a strong knowledge of basic principles when you study them at the beginning of your course:

- S Bailey, M Gunn, N Taylor and J Ching, *Smith, Bailey and Gunn on the Modern English Legal System* (2007, 5th edn, Sweet and Maxwell).
- P Darbyshire, *Darbyshire on the English Legal System* (2008, 9th edn, Sweet and Maxwell).
- A Gillespie, *The English Legal System* (2nd edn, Due May 2009, Oxford University Press).
- D Keenan, *Smith and Keenan's English Law: Text and Cases* (2007, 15th edn, Pearson).
- G Slapper and D Kelly, *The English Legal System* (2008, 9th edn, Routledge-Cavendish).

- ATH Smith, *Glanville Williams: Learning the Law* (2006, 13th edn, Sweet and Maxwell).
- R Ward and A Akhtar, *Walker and Walker's English Legal System* (2008, 10th edn, Oxford University Press).

13.6 Literature on the law

13.6.1 Legal literature, including film, television and theatre

There is a huge amount of literature dealing with the law and lawyers of wildly varying quality. Finding truly realistic portrayals of courtroom scenes is not easy, as, understandably, most writers are not necessarily that interested in merely accurately reporting court proceedings, but are more concerned with writing entertaining drama or comedy. As a result, it is probably best to use reading/viewing of this sort as a source of pleasure and inspiration, rather than as serious reading for information or educational purposes. In spite of this, it should be pointed out that many books, television, films and plays do have shades of realism or do convey a moral or ethical message that is perhaps more important than mere procedural accuracy.

As noted previously, there is a large volume of material that could be consulted in this area. Not surprisingly, law and lawyers provide a rich source for writers of books, films and television. As a result, your personal tastes will dictate what you will enjoy. What follows is, therefore, no more than a small selection of personal recommendations. There may well be many perfectly good sources that are not referred to. Nevertheless, it is probably best to avoid what might be termed the trashier end of the market, if you really want your reading, viewing and listening to have a positive formative affect on you. As noted previously, if you merely want to be entertained, then you can read, watch or listen to what you like, provided that you appreciate the nature of the source you are consulting. I have deliberately sought to recommend sources that might be a little out of the way for many modern law students. Some of the recommendations may, therefore, be a little old-fashioned for some tastes.

English literature is full of stories about, or references to, the law and the legal profession.

Anthony Trollope is more famous for his portrayals of ecclesiastical or political life, but he also dealt with law and lawyers in some of his works. Part of the reason for this is probably that Trollope's own father was a barrister, with Trollope often spending the school holidays living in his father's chambers in Lincoln's Inn. The novel *Orley Farm* (1862) deals with a dispute over a will, and provides a wonderful evocation of legal London and the legal profession at the time.

Similarly, in *The Warden* (1855), one of the *Barsetshire* novels, Trollope deals with the Warden of a charitable hospital's dealings with the Attorney-General, who is advising him on a disputed will. The scene is once again set in Lincoln's Inn: Trollope did not like the place at all, and portrayed it in rather bleak terms.

In his short story, *The Spotted Dog* (1870), which is not really a story about the law at all but is set in the vicinity of Gray's Inn, Trollope returns to his Inns of Court theme. He describes a walk through London's legal quarter, starting in Gray's Inn and ending up in Fleet Street, after taking in the Temple. Lincoln's Inn once more gets something of a hammering, in particular Old Square, in the line "than which we know no place in London more conducive to suicide".

Bleak House (1852), by Charles Dickens, concerns a long-standing dispute in the Court of Chancery, *Jarndyce v Jarndyce*. From a legal historical point of view, it is of interest because it focuses on the interminable procedures that made it far more difficult to get justice in equity than in the common law courts, before the passing of the Judicature Acts of the 1870s. Dickens spent time, in his early career, working as a clerk in a Gray's Inn chambers. The experience stayed with him, and he often referred to law and the legal profession in his novels. The references were not always the most glowing. The works of writers like Trollope and Dickens provide a fascinating insight into the law and legal London in the Victorian era's atmosphere and humour. They are well worth a try.

If you are looking for some fiction that is slightly more up to date, the works of John Mortimer, who sadly died early in 2009, are warmly recommended, particularly his *Rumpole* stories. Horace Rumpole is an ageing barrister, who never makes it to become a QC, due to not fitting in with the establishment. He takes great pride in himself as an advocate and in the idea of barristers as freelancers, who exercise their calling without fear or favour.

Whilst the most recent *Rumpole* was only written in 2007 (*The anti-social behaviour of Horace Rumpole*), my impression is that his readership is largely confined to a slightly older generation, many of whom are practising lawyers. From contact with modern undergraduates, it seems that the younger generation do not read him much. This is a great shame, as the *Rumpole* stories capture the spirit of advocacy and, also, aspects of the atmosphere of legal London. They are written in a light comic style, and manage to be both funny and poignant.

John Mortimer was himself a high-profile QC, and his legal knowledge is used to good effect in some of the stories. The courtroom scenes are not always intended to be terribly realistic, with the emphasis often being on humour and drama, rather than procedural efficacy. The stories also grapple with many of the difficult legal, moral and ethical issues which often confront the law and lawyers. The effect is a very humane and touching collection of stories.

The *Rumpole* books were also turned into a highly successful ITV television series, with the part of Horace Rumpole played brilliantly by Leo McKern. John Mortimer refused to sanction any more television episodes of *Rumpole* after McKern's death in 2002, on the basis that McKern had become so closely associated with the role that it was hard to imagine any other actor playing it. These are often repeated on various TV channels, and are widely available on DVD. They have a wonderful stage-like atmosphere and are well worth watching. There are also some rather less well known BBC radio broadcasts starring Maurice Denham, which have much to commend them.

As well as the *Rumpole* stories, Mortimer also wrote plays set in a legal context: *The Dock Brief*, first broadcast in 1957, and *Edwin* (1984). Both of these plays still receive regular airings throughout the country.

Have a look also at the works of Henry Cecil, a twentieth-century writer and judge. He wrote many works with a criminal law aspect to them, some of which were turned into films.

In addition to the above, there are also many volumes of legal anecdotes, and great or famous trials, that are available in most decent bookshops, as well as online.

13.6.2   Biographies, autobiographies and memoirs

To read of the life experiences, observations and thoughts of some of the great figures in legal history can provide you with much in the way of interesting and inspirational material. There are many such books available. The list below includes some prominent examples that you may wish to read. As before, it may be that some are no longer in print, and that you have to be a bit more innovative in your searching:

- P Ackroyd, *The Life of Thomas More* (1998, Chatto and Windus).
- J Campbell, *FE Smith, First Earl of Birkenhead* (1983, Jonathan Cape).
- D Carman, *No Ordinary Man: A Life of George Carman* (2001, Hodder and Stoughton).
- P Devlin, *Taken at the Flood* (1996, Taverner Publications).
- E Heward, *Lord Denning, A Biography* (1997, 2nd edn, Barry Rose Law Publishing).
- G Lewis, *Lord Atkin* (1999, Hart Publishing).
- E Marjoribanks and J Mortimer, *The Famous Trials of Marshall Hall* (1989, Penguin).
- E Marjoribanks, *Life of Sir Edward Marshall Hall* (Various publishers, first published 1929).

Edward Marjoribanks, mentioned above, wrote a number of books on great advocates, which you can find if you use services such as Amazon. Another writer you would do well to look up is H Montgomery Hyde.

13.6.3　Film

There are many good films set in a legal context that you could look out for. Below is a small selection to look out for in particular. Apologies for the slight 1950s bias, but this was a good period for British films:

- *Twelve Angry Men*, 1957.
- *Brothers in Law*, 1958.
- *Witness for the Prosecution*, 1957.
- *The Trials of Oscar Wilde*, 1960.

13.7　Conclusion

This chapter could easily have turned into a book in its own right, such is the volume of material to do with law and the legal profession. As a result, a vast number of sources that could have been mentioned have not been, due to the fact that this is primarily a book on mooting, and not a book on literature, theatre and film. Hopefully, however, this chapter will provide you with some leads that you can follow up yourself, if you decide to look further afield when it comes to sources related to mooting.

Part 4

Appendices

The three moot problems and sample skeleton argument used in these appendices belong to the English-Speaking Union (ESU), and were submitted by participating universities for the annual ESU Essex Court Chambers National Mooting Competition. The ESU would like to thank all the universities and individuals that have contributed problems over the years. For more information about the English-Speaking Union, visit www.esu.org.

Appendix 1

Examples of moot problems

In the House of Lords

Shanks v Porter

John Shanks is the sole beneficiary of a trust of which Victor Porter is the sole trustee. Ten years ago Mr Shanks suggested to Victor Porter that he might wish to invest some of the trust fund by purchasing shares in a company, Flush Ltd, owned by Mr Shanks. Mr Shanks assured Mr Porter that the company was run on a sound financial basis and was highly profitable and with good prospects. Mr Porter took Mr Shanks at his word and invested one half of the trust fund in shares in Flush Ltd. Mr Porter did not seek expert advice or make any independent inquiries into the suitability of the investment. Flush Ltd subsequently became insolvent, rendering the shares virtually worthless. Mr Shanks brought the present action claiming compensation for loss arising from Mr Porter's breach of trust in failing to invest according to the general standard of care required of trustees.

Mr Porter relied in his defence upon a clause in the trust instrument purporting to relieve the trustee of all liability for any breach of trust apart from "dishonest" breaches. He also claimed, in the alternative, that if the exemption clause did not relieve him of all liability his liability should be reduced due to the fault of Mr Porter in recommending a risky investment in the first place.

At first instance Fidel J held that the breach of trust had been reckless, but that there had been no dishonesty on the part of Mr Porter, with the result that the exemption clause supplied a complete defence to the breach of trust (applying *Armitage v Nurse* [1998] Ch 241, Court of Appeal). His Lordship held further, that if he was wrong with regard to the exemption clause, he would nevertheless have reduced the trustee's liability by half to reflect the claimant's contributory fault.

The Court of Appeal overturned the decision of Fidel J, holding that an exemption clause can never be relied upon to exempt a trustee from liability for a reckless breach of trust and that the contributory fault of a beneficiary can never be relied upon to reduce a trustee's liability for breach of trust.

Mr Porter now appeals to the House of Lords on the following grounds:

First, that a trustee exemption clause exempting a trustee from liability for all breaches of trust apart from "dishonest" breaches is competent to exempt a trustee from liability in respect of a reckless breach of trust.

Second, that it is permitted to reduce a trustee's liability for breach of trust to take into account the beneficiary's contributory fault.

In the House of Lords

Greenfield v Allen and Miller

John Greenfield was married to Avril Greenfield in 1996. He separated from his wife in late 1997. They reconciled in early 2000, and started living together again. In April 2000, he tested positive for the Human Immunodeficiency Virus (HIV) at a genito-urinary medicine (GUM) clinic. He had attended the clinic after he had been contacted as a result of a partner notification scheme. It transpired that he had been an intravenous drug user at various points in 1998 and 1999, and had contracted HIV as a result of needle-sharing.

He informed the consultant at the GUM clinic (Dr Allen) that he was now living with his wife again, that they were currently engaging in protected sex (that is, using condoms) but that his wife was keen to try for a child in the near future. He was advised that he should disclose his HIV-positive status to his wife in order that she could be appropriately counselled on the risks and treatment options involved, but stated that he did not feel able to disclose to her. He indicated that he could not guarantee that he would not engage in unprotected sexual intercourse with his wife without disclosure. With Mr Greenfield's consent, his HIV-positive status and circumstances were disclosed to his GP (Dr Miller) in June 2000. Dr Miller was also Mrs Greenfield's GP.

Mrs Greenfield discussed the possibility of conceiving at a consultation in July 2000, and gave no indication that she was aware of her husband's HIV-positive status. Dr Miller did not feel able to disclose this fact to her. He had a consultation with Mr Greenfield in July 2000, in which Mr Greenfield indicated that he did not intend to disclose his HIV-positive status to his wife, but intended to engage in unprotected sexual intercourse with a view to conceiving, in line with her request. Dr Miller strongly advised Mr Greenfield to disclose to his wife, but took no further action, and did not in fact have any further consultations with either Mr or Mrs Greenfield before moving to a different practice in late 2000.

Mrs Greenfield subsequently contracted HIV and brought an action for damages against both Drs Allen and Miller. It was not disputed that (a) Mrs Greenfield had contracted HIV subsequent to July 2000 and (b) that this would not have occurred had either Dr Allen or Dr Miller disclosed Mr Greenfield's HIV status to her directly, as she would not have engaged in unprotected sexual intercourse with him in light of that knowledge.

Drayton J held that both Drs Allen and Miller were liable to Mrs Greenfield in negligence, which was upheld by the Court of Appeal. Drs Allen and Miller now appeal against the decision of the Court of Appeal on the following grounds: (i) No duty of care was owed by Dr Allen to Mrs Greenfield. (ii) The duty of care owed by Dr Miller to Mrs Greenfield (and any duty of care owed by Dr Allen, should submission (i) be rejected) had been discharged by the provision of appropriate advice to Mr Greenfield. The duty of care did not require the breach of the doctors' duties of confidentiality owed to Mr Greenfield.

In the House of Lords

R v Devagne

Deborah Devagne, aged 12, had been suffering from an inoperable malignant brain tumour for 6 months. Although she was receiving significant amounts of medication to help with her pain, she was still, in the terminal stages of her life, suffering considerably. All other curative treatments had ceased and she was being nursed at home by her parents.

Following her prolonged illness, Daniel Devagne, Deborah's father, felt that neither he nor his daughter could cope any longer with her pain and suffering, and he suffocated her with a pillow.

Devagne was charged with murder, and at his trial pleaded necessity as a defence to the charge. Jumble J. held that, if necessity was recognised as a defence to murder, which in itself was debatable, the approach to its requirements, as set out in *Re A (Children) (Conjoined Twins: Surgical Separation)* [2000] 4 All ER 961, should be entirely objective. He declined to distinguish *Re A (Children)* and consequently adopt the modified objective test propounded by the Supreme Court of Canada in *R v Latimer* 2001 W.C.B. (2d) 279.

On the question of the *mens rea* for murder, the trial judge concluded that the test of foresight of virtual certainty adopted in *Re A (Children)* was correct, and that a result foreseen as virtually certain is an intended result.

Devagne was found guilty of murder and unsuccessfully appealed to the Court of Appeal, which agreed with the trial judge on both points.

Devagne now appeals to the House of Lords; The questions certified by the Court of Appeal which gave permission to appeal to the House of Lords are:

1. Is the defence of necessity available outside the particular circumstances that arose in *Re A (Children)*, and, if so, do the three requirements for the defence as set out in *Re A (Children)* leave room for the jury to take into account the defendant's reasonable belief, or are they purely objective?

2. Is the test of foresight of virtual certainty as interpreted in *Re A (Children)* consistent with the earlier House of Lords decision in *R v Woollin* [1999] 4 All ER 103, which held that where a consequence is foreseen as 'virtually certain', the jury may (not must) find that the defendant had the necessary intention?

Appendix 2

Example mooting feedback sheets

Example 1

STUDENT NAME: _____

Name of moot: _____

ADVOCATE ROLE: _____

CRITERIA	FEEDBACK
PRESENTATION	
Address the court clearly using language and wearing dress suitable to the forum	
Does not read submission	
Maintains eye contact with judges	
Allows judge time to locate references to law and facts	
Speaks effectively (adequate volume, persuasive language, appropriate pace and mannerisms)	
Completes submission within time allocated	
STRUCTURE	
Correctly addresses the court and judges, introduces self, allows time for name to be noted and indicates which party s/he represents	
Summarises factual and legal background of the action and proceedings (as appropriate)	
States relevant issues and client's position on the issues	
Develops argument on each issue by analysis of relevant legal principles and authorities and applying them to the facts in issue	
RESPONSE	
Deals effectively with points raised by opponents	
Demonstrates flexibility and comprehensiveness in the rebuttal of opponents' arguments	
QUESTIONS	
Responds promptly and effectively to questions	
Maintains composure when questioned	

Example 2 (with weightings for assessment criteria)

NB: The weightings given to each particular assessment criterion could vary, depending on the institution you are mooting with.

1. **Style and presentation of legal argument** (30 marks)

2. **Structure and content of legal argument, including references to authorities** (30 marks)

3. **Dealing with the judges, including answers to judicial questions** (20 marks)

4. **Ability to respond to opponent's submissions** (20 marks)

Appendix 3

Example of a skeleton argument

In the House of Lords

Parrot Quay Limited (Appellant)
-and-
Armoury Football Club Limited (Respondent)

Respondent's Skeleton Argument

Ground 1:

1. The pre-cursor to the operation of promissory estoppel is that a recognised legal relationship exists between the parties.

Thomas Hughes v The Metropolitan Railway Company (1877) 2 App Cas 439 (cited as [1874–1880] All ER 187)

Central London Property Trust Ltd v High Trees House [1947] 1 KB 130

Attorney General of Hong Kong v Humphreys Estates (Queen's Gardens) Ltd [1987] 1 AC 114

Law of Property (Miscellaneous Provisions) Act 1989, s 2

Chitty on Contracts (Vol 1) at 3-083 to 3-096

2. No legal relationship exists between the parties to the present appeal. There is no contract. There is no pre-existing legal relationship. The operation of promissory estoppel provides that a party promises not to enforce their "strict legal rights".

By definition such rights must already be in existence. In the present appeal there are no rights that give rise to a promissory estoppel.

Central London Property Trust Ltd v High Trees House [1947] 1 KB 130

Amalgamated Property Co. v Texas Bank [1982] 1 QB 84

3. In the alternative, if the House of Lords find the requirements of promissory estoppel are satisfied, it is submitted that the Court of Appeal was bound by precedent. English contract law rests upon the indivisible trinity of offer, acceptance and consideration. The nature of promissory estoppel does not require the presence of consideration because it is not a contract. To allow a cause of action to be founded upon a promise unsupported by consideration would be to undermine the doctrine of consideration.

Brikom Investments v Carr [1979] 1 QB 467 at 486

Combe v Combe [1951] 2 KB 215

Ground 2:

1.   It is accepted that accelerated payment of an anticipated contract at the specific request of the other negotiating party can give rise to a quantum meruit. However, in the present case there was no specific request.

William Lacey (Hounslow) Ltd v Davis [1957] 1 WLR 932

British Steel Corp v Cleveland Bridge and Engineering Co Ltd [1984] 1 All ER 504

2.   Where work is done in order to put oneself in a position to obtain and perform a contract, the costs incurred are at one's own risk and do not give rise to any form of liability.

Regalian Properties plc v London Docklands Development Corporation [1995] 1 WLR 212

Marston Construction Co Ltd v Kigass Ltd (1989) 15 Con LR 116

3.   In any event, the services in the present case did not benefit the defendant and, as such, there is no liability under a quantum meruit.

Regalian Properties plc v London Docklands Development Corporation [1995] 1 WLR 212

The Respondent submits that the appeal be dismissed.

Leading Counsel: Junior Counsel:

Index